11-23

BEYOND REAGAN

Beyond Reagan

Alternatives for the '80s

——— Edited by ———
Alan Gartner, Colin Greer
and Frank Riessman

A Social Policy Book

1817

HARPER & ROW, PUBLISHERS, New York
Cambridge, Philadelphia, San Francisco, London
Mexico City, São Paulo, Sydney

FIRST EDITION

Library of Congress Cataloging in Publication Data

Main Entry under title:

Beyond Reagan.

(A Social policy book)

1. Political participation—United States—Addresses, essays, lectures. 2. United States—Politics and government—1981-   —Addresses, essays, lectures. 3. United States—Economic policy—1981-   —Addresses, essays lectures. 4. United States—Social policy—1980-   —Addresses, essays, lectures. 5. United States—National security—Addresses, essays, lectures. I. Gartner, Alan. II. Greer, Colin. III. Riessman, Frank, 1924-   . IV. Series.

JK1764.B49   1984   361.6′1′0973   83-48347

ISBN 0-06-015254-0

ISBN 0-06-091100-X (pbk.)

84 85 86 87 88 10 9 8 7 6 5 4 3 2 1
84 85 86 87 88 10 9 8 7 6 5 4 3 2 1

Contents

Acknowledgments

In preparing this book we have been greatly helped by many people. Some have contributed essays; others in the wide *Social Policy* and *New World Foundation* networks of scholars, activists and policy planners have provided important idea and people connections that made these essays possible. We would like to thank especially Marilyn Clement, Norman Fruchter, Larry Goldberg and Robert Stein for spoken and written remarks that helped in developing some of the introductory notes that thread through the book.

We would also like to give special thanks to Audrey Gartner and Geraldine Harrison—the former for her editorial assistance and careful work with authors and the latter for typing the entire manuscript and for smoothing a very difficult book-production process.

Preface

The People Yes
—Carl Sandburg

All of the essays that follow emphasize in one way or another the theme of participation. For some, participation means the achievement of full inclusion in the society for previously excluded groups. For others, participation means citizens playing new roles in the economy as well as the polity. For still others, participation means the inclusion of previously excluded issues in public discourse and public policy. And for yet others, the participatory thrust means citizens involved in the decision-making that produces the outcomes sought in the previous three. In all, participation is the wellspring of democratic energy.

In reviewing Walter Lippmann's seminal *Public Opinion* in 1922, John Dewey considered Lippmann's critique of contemporary democracy in the United States and questioned his route to solution. To Dewey's mind—or his "feeling," as he put it—Lippmann was right that special interests built on wealth and prestige dominated decisions and the formation of public opinion. The solution was not, Dewey believed, the better training of neutral experts to bring social-science rigor to policy development; rather, Dewey saw the health for democracy to lie in the "direct enlightenment of popular opinion" through the press and through the schools:

> Democracy demands a more thoroughgoing education than the education of officials, administrators and directors of industry. Because this fundamental general education is at once so necessary and so difficult of achievement, the enterprise of democracy is so challenging. To sidetrack it to the task of enlightenment of administrators and executives is to miss something of its range and its challenge.

xi

This book is a collection of essays by authors who, while differing on many issues, share with Dewey the imperative to remake society free of the barriers of prejudice, privilege and distorted commitments to defense, prestige and morality. Also shared with Dewey is these authors' conviction that it is not the organization of intelligence that must finally be relied on to achieve political democracy, equitable economic distribution and social justice; expert opinion and professional management of the political economy alone are insufficient instruments for doing public business.

"Political" in this perspective is broader than party political matters and deeply dependent on the informed participation of the public in decisions affecting their lives. Thus, "broadened participation" refers both to the roles of individuals and groups as well as to the scope of issues to which they attend. By that broader participation alone can the needs and interests of various segments of the public be part of the consideration in decision-making that will have impact on them. The view expressed in these essays is that the problems of society can be solved only when the choices and decisions to be made are made with the participation of those to be affected.

In our system, it has often seemed that the ordinary citizen's participation must consist almost entirely of choosing representatives. We are, however, pointing to a range of elements in the environment that require local and national action as the terrain in which a good deal of participation is feasible for ordinary citizens. Indeed, the absence of it has in many of these areas made even well-intentioned national policy ineffective at times and even counterproductive at others.

After reviewing worker participation in the European workplace, Carol Pateman found support for G. D. H. Cole's argument of a half-century ago that the best preparation for participation is participation. Ordinary citizens are then able to see the connection between the public and private spheres. While the ordinary citizen might still be more interested in things nearer home, in a participatory society they would be better prepared to assess the performance of representatives at the national level, better equipped to make decisions of national scope when necessary, and better able to weigh the impact on their lives and immediate circumstances of decisions taken by national representatives. The citizen in such a context is at once a private individual and an educated, public citizen, not, as in recent decades, an apathetic voter waiting to receive services.

The essays in this collection are designed to confirm participation both as at the heart of the means to identify and address social problems and as an essential characteristic of ends to be won. After Watergate, Abscam, and tax protectors for privilege have led to the delegitimation of authority in the institutional life of this nation, the people must and are beginning to recognize themselves as the source of authority. Public policy must support that thrust.

PART I

ECONOMIC VISIONS

Editors' Introduction

Discussions of the economy generally focus on developments in Wall Street or Washington or matters of high technology or smokestack industries. Yet few topical issues captured the crisis in the American economy and the potential for change as did two local stories, side by side, in the *New York Times,* on October 4, 1983. The one reported on the apparent suicide of a dispossessed Minnesota farmer, who had days earlier apparently murdered two bankers who he felt were denying him the opportunity to try once again to earn a living as a farmer. The other reported on a march in Hill City, Kansas, organized by the American Agriculture Movement to protest the sale of the farm of a black couple whose family had owned the land for six generations. The white organizer of the march said, "This is not a farm issue. We are losing control of our lives and our institutions."

The same theme—both as to the breadth of concerns and the potential for alliances—was echoed a week later at another march, protesting yet another farm foreclosure, when the head of the Illinois Farm Coalition said, "We've seen a lot of ebb and flow historically in farm movements. But this one is different. It goes way beyond the farm."

While headlines in the fall of 1983 hailed the rise in stock-market prices and the declining rate of unemployment—nonetheless representing more than 10 million people out of work—the Farmers Home Administration reported holding twice as many pieces of foreclosed property as a year earlier and five times as many as the year before, and the number of borrowers behind in payments had reached three in ten.

Whatever the length of the current upturn—and few are confident as to length or breadth—the U.S. economy faces a condition of long-term stagnation. The problems, as a recent report prepared for the Levinson Foundation notes, go deep into the structures and institutions of the economy.

New realities in the international economy, major shifts in the composition of jobs and the structure of production domestically, and many years of policies that have failed to address those changes have contributed to severe economic dislocation and stagnation. Even a stronger than expected short-term recovery will not be able to sustain itself unless these new world, technological and institutional realities are addressed. On the most general level, the current structure of public and private economic decision-making, and the incentives built into that decision-making, are inadequate to generate the kind of coordinated and mobilized effort necessary to solve our economic problems. In many particular areas, policies and institutions are based on outmoded arrangements that must undergo a long-term process of restructuring in order to serve the needs of the American people for economic security, prosperity and stability.

These problems can only be addressed by an economic program that departs significantly from the free-market ideology that has provided a cover for allocation policies toward large corporations and the wealthy, and from liberal and neoliberal attempts to make limited adjustments without challenging the structure of economic decision-making. Without the affirmation of humane and equitable principles of economic organization, and without public-sector interventions more direct, powerful and effective than our current economic structure allows, it will be very difficult to restore the economy to a path of economic progress.

The promise of the dramatic technological changes taking place in the production process, in communications and information, and in the nature of work is enormous. We stand on the verge of an era in which more people can be engaged in more creative and fulfilling activity than ever before; in which the process of production of the necessities and pleasures of material life can be less taxing of people's labor than ever before; in which the ability to communicate with others, to have access to education and entertainment, and to participate in the society is greater than ever before; and in which the distribution of wealth-generating productive activity throughout the globe can be broader than ever before. To achieve this potential, the institutions of the society must be capable of harnessing those changes and making them work for the people in the society.

As Friedman and Miller point out in the first of our essays, just as the problems are systemic, so, too, must be the solutions. Critical are matters of planning—that is, the decisions as to the allocation of resources, particularly investment decisions.

The first step toward democratic planning is the recognition that a form of national economic planning already exists, in implicit form and often dominated by narrow interests for their own benefit. Such "backdoor" planning takes place in the multibillion-dollar purchasing decisions of federal and state governments; in the manipulation of tax credits by various private interests; in the extensive sectoral interventions in such areas as housing, medical care and agriculture; in labor-market and employment programs; and, of course, in the worldwide planning decisions of multinational corporations and banks, often undertaken in conjunction with government commitments, subsidies or expenditures. In the most general terms, the implementation of national economic planning will initially involve making public choices clear and explicit, and allowing participation in and national debate over previously implicit planning decisions.

But national economic planning must also embrace and integrate a much more aggressive and effective set of regional policies, sectoral policies, and labor and employment policies. Current regional policy consists of a politicized "market" in which localities fight for grants and give public-sector concessions for industrial location, leaving location decisions entirely in the hands of corporate leaders with the power to make or break communities or regions. Sectoral policies are based on whether particular interests or industries can obtain protection, subsidy, tax breaks, or contracts for services, not on what long-term strategic policies should be followed. Labor-market and employment policies consist of a hodgepodge of training and development programs, along with bureaucratic and ineffective labor laws, which provide for neither the needs of workers nor the skill requirements of a changing job market. Planning must integrate these general areas of policy and develop mechanisms to make them work.

Planning policy will have to generate explicit choices about how to promote economic growth and employment security. In particular, the challenges of the world market require industrial policies that are an alternative to the negative choices of protectionism on the one hand and employment losses on the other. Planning policy will have to answer a number of questions, such as: Which sectors of the economy are growing and which are declining, and what should public policy be, if any, toward those sectors? How can the time horizons of industrial decisions be lengthened to make necessary investments that an orientation toward short-term profit-making avoids? How can we control capital outflows and direct new investment toward those areas of the country that are experiencing economic distress? What kinds of new productivity policies can be promoted and encouraged in order to increase the international competitiveness of certain sectors? What consistent sets of labor-market policies can encourage productivity increases and increased real incomes? How can we promote broader participation in the decisions about who benefits and who sacrifices in the economy? Which national policies are in conflict because of budgetary constraints or competition for the same scarce resources? What concerted national efforts should be undertaken to break through bottlenecks in energy or for highly technical humanpower? Clearly, an effective industrial and sectoral planning policy must have mechanisms that not only can answer the continually changing sets of questions about the economy but have the ability to implement policy in a direct, efficient and meaningful manner. Rosen looks to these topics in the second of our essays.

The key feature of effective planning policies is the ability of the public sector to get a real response from the private sector in exchange for the dollars granted or policy enacted. The mechanisms for getting that response include *quid pro quos,* in which the public sector enacts specific, legally binding concessions or terms in exchange for agreed-upon policies; direct targeting of credit, in which the public sector directly loans money, or guarantees loans, for particular programs or strategies; public participation, in the form of worker, community or government representation in the direction of particular projects or companies; equity or royalty shares in a project held by the public sector, with a sharing of both risks and rewards; and direct public ownership, either in the form of full ownership or joint ventures with private industry. All of these types of programs have been undertaken in different circumstances, frequently at the local and state levels. But all too often the public sector gives the subsidy, protection, guaranty or tax break without any explicit guaranties of response or direct control over policy.

The question is not whether we should have a set of policies oriented toward different industries—we already have them, in a variety of forms—but whether they should be made the subject of explicit national goal-setting in the context of public debate, and whether we will use the effective tools, mentioned above, for implementation. If the goal was to modernize the steel industry, for example, then explicit modernization programs should have been established, with clear public controls and participation, as a condition for the protections and subsidies that were granted. What we got with regard to steel was the worst of both worlds—protection and no modernization, but capital flight and diversification without investment by steel companies instead.

In no area is the question of the public's interest stronger than in that concerning the endemic poverty (discussed in the last essay of this section) of minority youths and their older siblings, women, and the farmers mentioned at the beginning of this introduction.

Gold addresses the ways of democratic investment and planning decisions, while Stanback focuses on the endemic poverty which is both the shame of and challenge to our system.

1

The Reconstruction of Finance:
Implications of Industrial Policy

Susan Friedman
S. M. Miller

Full employment as a policy goal is an endangered idea. New approaches to achieving it are needed. *Industrial policy* is the catchphrase for many versions of a new approach. One version seeks only to improve the transportation infrastructure and expand corporate expenditures on research and development and training by providing tax subsidies. Another version concentrates on tax breaks to promote "cutting edge," high-tech, "sunrise" industries, the purported export leaders of the future. A third version, more oriented to employment than the others, seeks to rebuild the "mature," "smokestack," "sunset," "basic" industries through government loans. Limited understanding and great uncertainty prevail.

Guiding investment is central to most industrial-policy proposals. But what is missing—disturbingly, crucially absent—in almost all versions are proposals for reshaping capital markets so that they result in useful investments. This essay aims at bringing attention to the problems that have been created by the malfunctioning of capital markets—a system failure—and to ways of restructuring them to encourage useful investments.

Industrial policy is about planning—which sectors of economic activity are to be promoted. Planning is about investment. Investment is about the use of capital funds. When it comes down to this basic step of the deployment of capital, which undergirds investment and planning, imagination and courage stop. The AFL-CIO and investment banker Felix Rohatyn recommend types of new development banks, a revival of the Reconstruction Finance Corporation (RFC) of

Susan Friedman is research director of the Massachusetts Governor's Commission on the Future of Mature Industries. *S. M. Miller* is professor of sociology and economics at Boston University.

the 1930s. But such additions to the banking system do not change the basic structure of capital markets. It is our contention that the failure of investment and capital markets lies not in a shortage of investable funds nor in the absence of a particular lending facility. Its source is the powerful distortions produced by the day-to-day functioning of the main capital-market systems. Proposals that only tinker with the tax system or add another agency to direct some investment capital will have very limited impact. Investment will not move to secure tracks for long-term development and full employment until capital markets change in fundamental ways. Effective changes will require governmental action.

In Japan and much of Western Europe, shaping the allocation of capital funds is accepted as basic to the operation of a successful economy and as constantly occurring through the activities of government whether designated as capital allocation or not. The United States is just beginning to address industrial policy issues. Already the view of what is needed is terribly foreshortened. Both the theory and practice of industrial policy require restructuring capital markets. Since many people suffer from the distortions of current capital-market practices and demands, there may be many allies in a search for better functioning of the markets that allocate pivotable investable funds.

WHICH INDUSTRIAL POLICY?

The call for industrial policy recognizes that the United States is different from most capitalist countries and many developing nations. The range of policy instruments used to influence the course of the U.S. economy has historically been very limited. The main levers pushed and pulled have been macroeconomic ones such as monetary (supply of money, interest rates) and fiscal (government spending, tax structure) policies.

However, as Barry Bluestone has argued, a much more extensive and industry-specific "de facto industrial policy" has long existed here.[1] These activities, whether they take the form of defense outlays or health and welfare programs, affect the situation of particular industries, regions of the country and occupational groups. In fact, despite the attention paid to improving the overall or macro growth rate, governmental activities differentially stimulate specific industrial sectors.

But the explicit macro and the implicit de facto industrial policy of the United States will not work in the Eighties and Nineties. The strategy of limited direct involvement in the economy will fail because the economic world of the future will differ from the world we have experienced until now. Four interrelated economic factors are transforming the world: new technological advancements leading to new products and production processes; the rise of Third World markets as both users and suppliers of manufactured goods in the growing international economy; the expansion of international competition between developed countries; and the international flow of capital that is making all this possible. These are the economic facts of the Eighties. The trends they represent must be addressed.

The task is to find ways to attain full employment at sustainably high wages in a relatively inflation-free economy. If the U.S. does nothing, the future is clear: The country will continue to lose jobs to low-wage nations, automation and competition from developed countries. While the U.S. will no doubt gain jobs in new industries and some forward-thinking traditional businesses, it is likely that it will be a net loser. In addition, as the participation rates of women and older workers continue to climb, unemployment rates are likely to increase over the business cycle.

The Content of GNP

Industrial policy forces the question of what kinds of goods and services should comprise the economy; monetary and fiscal policy do so less directly. This focus inevitably leads to issues of how and where goods are produced, how they are priced, and how to shift from the present situation.

The content of GNP is the issue, not a percentage increase in some abstracted, concocted—yet revered—measure known as the gross national product.[2] GNP is a poor indicator of what is happening within the economy and what satisfactions emerge from it, because it does not reflect what is produced and how it is distributed. An act of production is an act of distribution.

This vital understanding has been lost in the fixation with rates of growth in overall production levels. Two GNPs of the same dollar value can yield quite different results in terms of how much and what kinds of employment result, who gets income and who does not, which regions grow and which decline. The goal then becomes learning how to influence economic processes so that a desirable GNP is achieved in terms of employment and quality of life.

INVESTMENT AND CAPITAL

Everyone agrees that investment is the central economic process to be encouraged, and it is capital that makes investment possible. The importance of influencing the pattern of investment in the economy is one of the major tenets of industrial policy. There may be differences of opinion on whether "sunset" industries are worthy of investment and whether "sunrise" industries need any more investment capital than the market already provides, but industrial-policy proponents do agree on one issue: Capital funds are currently not well directed.

Surprisingly, supporters of industrial policy seldom draw the inevitable conclusion that changing the pattern of investment requires changing the system of financing investments so that the appropriate ones get made. The proposals they do put forward do not sufficiently address the problem. For example, the Reconstruction Finance Corporation proposed by Felix Rohatyn is not enough. Such an institution could only marginally affect investment patterns. It is unreasonable to expect that any one financial institution could make the necessary difference in the patterns of investment in this country. No one agency could have the scope or knowledge necessary to do this.

The solution lies not with a new financing source—a new player—but with *a new set of rules* that will redefine the game for all the participants in the serious activity of determining the investment patterns in the U.S. economy. Not an RFC, but a reconstruction of finance is necessary.

Minor Problems?

Many argue that there is nothing wrong with the capital markets as they exist. By changing traditional macroeconomic variables, most difficulties could be eliminated, according to this school of thought. If interest rates were lowered and a sufficient supply of low-cost capital assured to industry, U.S. economic problems would be over, so they say.

This elixir however, is not likely to provide the needed cure. Because of the size of projected government deficits and continuing fears of inflation, it is unlikely that real interest rates will fall sufficiently to generate the massive levels of investment that are necessary. In addition, if rates were seriously lowered relative to those of other countries, capital would leave the U.S. for higher foreign returns, leading again to higher U.S. rates. Nor do lower interest rates in themselves guarantee that capital will go to projects that can generate long-term full employment. New approaches to influence the pattern of investment are needed in this period of intense international competition with countries that are more able to guide their economies.

In general, industrial-policy advocates diagnose the cause of misdirected investment as corporate focusing on short-term profitability rather than on long-term market position. The explanations for this are variously given as faulty business-school training; greedy managers who want to maximize the value of their stock options sooner as opposed to later; the inability of American companies to adapt to new "flexible" production systems; the ease of creating paper profits through financial machinations that do not improve existing businesses; and sundry characteristics of an unproductive, unmotivated work force and corporate bureaucracy.

All of these, and more, are no doubt true. This malfunctioning could not happen, however, unless the controllers of capital in this economy—bankers and other financial intermediaries and equity shareholders—allowed it to occur. Because the financial system acts as if the long-term were just a string of short-term episodes, business is acting as the capital markets demand: maximizing short-term profitability.

The Nature of Capital Markets

By *capital markets,* we mean the combination of sources of investment funds, equity ownership patterns, the range of debt instruments,
stock and commodity exchanges, internal corporate investment decision-making processes and classes of financial intermediaries. They all
interact to determine the pattern of investments made in an economy.
Changing this pattern requires changing some part of this interactive
system.

Capital markets are usually thought of as simply comprising savers
(investors) and borrowers. A quick review of some of the most important characteristics of these two classes of market participants will
help set the stage for a later discussion.

Savers have changed. Gone are the legendary "poor widows and
orphans of Boston" who were portrayed as the mainstay of the stock
market. They were seen as conservative, seeking a steady return, not
short-term gains. Uninformed about competing opportunities, they
were reluctant to sell their blue-chip stocks to buy new ones.

Few, if any, of this kind of saver remain. In the stock market, the
institutional investor—e.g., pension funds and insurance companies
—has become the prototypal equity or shareholder. Those individuals who continue to save through savings banks have become savvy
owners of money-market accounts and competitively priced CDs.
Such savings, in addition to individuals' pension-fund entitlements,
are invested for them by the institutional investors who now hold
sway.

We who are savers often think of ourselves as investors—that is, we
"invest" in various financial instruments such as stocks, bonds, or any
of the wide range of pieces of paper that reflect ownership of a financial asset. The true investors in an economy are the corporations who
make the nitty-gritty decisions on how to allocate financial resources
to real assets such as new plant and equipment, investment in R & D,
a new marketing program, or increased levels of inventory and receiv-
ables to improve customer service. In recent years, however, corporations increasingly have been acting like financial institutions. They
have found that more money can be made quickly by mergers and
acquisitions, by buying the debt of other companies and even by

speculating on the value of the stock of other corporations. They are behaving less and less like Buddenbrooks who husband their capital to reinvest in their long-established businesses. They are free agents in a vast empire of financial possibilities.

What Is the Problem?

Capital is often misused and thus often unavailable for productive investments. The problem is therefore twofold: Money is wasted on nonproductive investments such as mergers and acquisitions, and potentially productive investments are not getting made.

The stock market provides an apt example of how the current system acts to stymie long-term investments that can lead to sustainable employment through building strong, competitive businesses. As described above, companies once faced a stock market composed of individuals who provided a steady, if somewhat cyclical, supply of investment capital. In recent years, institutional investors have provided the majority of the action in the stock market. They trade in large blocks of stock and move in and out of the market very rapidly. Small changes in interest rates or the threat of revolutions in Central America can influence the buying behavior of a relatively small number of large institutional hitters.

Attractiveness to institutional investors therefore is important but difficult for a company. These investors must be coddled through constant contact, and many leading companies manipulate their financial numbers in ways they think will perk institutional investors' interest. But steady earnings growth is not easy to achieve in the competitive, technologically turbulent times we face. It is therefore not surprising that companies look to creative financial reporting and (more seriously) short-term deployment of their investable funds to try to give the market what it wants. This short-sighted approach may include

- buying existing firms, which can affect financial variables such as current earnings and price/earnings ratios, but does nothing to upgrade the company's base business;
- trying to improve profitability during downturns by reducing expenditures in R & D and new-market development, thereby hurting future performance;

- generating "other income" by using available cash to buy financial instruments like Treasury bills that maintain the government's debt burden but do not improve the economy's capital stock.

Corporations correctly understand that capital markets desire consistent growth in earnings; that growth is believed to lead to appreciating stock prices and increasing dividends. This growth in profits is about all a company can do (along with a lot of good PR) to improve its stock price. The problem is that the stock markets cannot by their nature consistently provide the stable or rising share prices that companies want. Large swings in stock prices are inevitable, given the structure of buyers and sellers into a relatively small number of large institutional hitters. These hitters cannot afford to strike out, because they are designated hitters, swinging with someone else's money. Institutional investors are responsible for directing small investors' pooled equity investments in the form of equity funds, retirement nest eggs in the form of pension funds and IRAs, and, yes, the income and wealth of the proverbial widows and orphans through bank trust departments.

Institutional investors have a fiduciary responsibility for the moneys they invest. They try to preserve the value of the capital they control. They will try to sell fast when a stock is losing favor in the market, and buy only those stocks they feel the market will continue to bid up.*

Although this sounds like appropriate behavior for an individual institutional investor, it does not work out so well for a market made up of many of them. A few of these large institutions can cause a stock price to gyrate because their orders are so large relative to the market in general. Their size guarantees the stock-churning and stock-price fluctuations that are exactly what they and the companies they invest in want to avoid. In such a situation, companies act rationally when they try to manage short-term earnings at the expense of long-term investments.

Present-day capital markets are not capable of assuring that the

---

* Herein lies the problem of using pension funds as a source of investment capital for long-term, risky investments, a suggestion offered by many progressives. There is a serious question as to the level of risk to which these moneys should be subjected. If such investments turn out to be unsuccessful, as some undoubtedly will, or to yield a low return, pensions will be jeopardized.

"right" investments will be made in terms of employment and long-term growth and development. The most socially desirable investments are not necessarily those with the highest level of short-term financial returns. But changing the investment pattern of the country is a serious undertaking. We must be very sure of what needs to be done differently. A starting point is understanding what types of investment currently are not being made and why. They can be loosely grouped into the following categories:

- *Investments in new production equipment in a stable industry.* Such investments would reduce operating costs and make the business more cost-competitive, but are not getting made because (a) the company has been unprofitable and cannot borrow at a reasonable interest rate, or (b) there is no need for additional capacity and corporate management feels it is too risky to invest in cost-saving equipment.
- *Investments in low-return businesses.* Such businesses cannot attract money because they cannot sustain high interest rates and expected stockholder-return levels. Because of scale factors or local market size, they will never become large or generate significant returns, but they could supply decent jobs and products if they could minimize the level of financial return they had to make.
- *Investments that are high-risk because the potential returns are not known or are many years away.* Companies will shy away from these types of investments because they are usually able to find less risky uses for their money. Risk in and of itself is not necessarily something one should seek out. At this time of technical and market change, however, risks must be taken now to guarantee future success.

When risky projects have the characteristics of relying primarily on the skills of a small number of people and can be isolated from any large business infrastructure, then it is possible for the project to be spun into a new company with access to venture-capital funds. However, when these investment opportunities are not separable from the larger corporation, the internal corporate process of choosing among many investment opportunities is biased against high-risk projects whenever there are surer ways to make money or when there are investments with shorter-term paybacks. It is important to emphasize that the problem here is not the unavailability of investment funds but the unwillingness of the corporation to allocate money to these types of investments.

- *Investments that are high-risk because of the magnitude of the investment required.* In such cases, two types of risk exist: One risk is inherent in the uncertainties of the project itself; the second risk is that the company might fail because of a weakened financial structure due to the strain of added high interest payments. Even where the company's financial position is strong, the project may be too large for the company to undertake alone, and antitrust and/or competitive reasons may forestall a potential joint venture.

There are, of course, many types of useful investments that America's capital markets are designed to encourage. In general, working capital, venture capital, consumer credit and, until recently, cheap home mortgages are provided in great abundance by this country's capital-market system. These are all socially useful ways in which to allocate scarce investment capital. The capital markets, however, are not providing for other important uses, which are becoming critical at a time of immense change in the American economy.

The challenge is to find ways of reorienting investment patterns to include more projects that provide decent jobs without pushing up prices, and projects that will lay the foundation of the economy for the coming decades. The task is to identify the broad types of investments that the U.S. capital-market system should encourage and to design the best means possible to assure their occurrence.

No one solution will provide for or stimulate all the types of useful investments. Important changes in governmental policies are needed: a coordinated package of changes in the tax code; new regulations for financial activities; possibly some new financing roles for government at the national and local levels. At the "macro" level, money supply and interest rates, exchange rates and the federal deficit all must be directed to strengthening productive capital markets and investments.

Within the context of nudging the business sector toward changing its investment strategies, a businesslike approach is necessary. This means recognizing that businesses have to remain profitable. At the same time, it means that we should demand quid pro quos for any incentive used to motivate the business sector. For example, a trade policy utilizing import quotas should be initiated only with the assurance that businesses will make the investments needed to regain international competitiveness.

RESTRUCTURING CAPITAL MARKETS AND REORIENTING INVESTMENT

Capital markets are the creations of humans, not nature. As such, they can be shaped in many different ways. Nations have unique capital-allocation systems, most of which have evolved over hundreds of years. Different systems encourage different types of investments.

The Japanese system, for example, allows for large amounts of capital to be invested in ventures where the payback is likely to be many years in the future. This is because equity in Japan is held mainly by the banking sector, which is also the provider of business debt. As a result, bankers are less concerned about short-term profitability than they are with the ability of companies over the long term to pay back their loans and remain viable well into the future. Concentrated equity ownership gives them the ability to influence corporate strategy.

Capital costs in Japan have recently been estimated at roughly 50 percent less than in the U.S.[3] This is partly because the required return on equity holdings is lower than in this country and because Japanese firms have a much higher reliance on debt (which is cheaper than equity in part because it is a tax-deductible expense) than U.S. firms.

The U.S. cannot and should not try to mimic Japan in trying to redesign its capital-market system. It must recognize, however, that finance is an arena of international rivalry, and not just in terms of the competing export-financing schemes of the U.S. and other countries. Finance affects all companies. Solutions must be uniquely American, because the financial infrastructure of this country is unique.

We do not offer detailed proposals; rather, we indicate general approaches to consider. Our hope is to stimulate examination of the possibilities of restructuring capital markets so that they promote employment and social returns, not just short-term financial profits.

Providing Capital to Small and Medium-Size Firms for Upgrading Production Technology

Commercial banks are a major source of financing for these firms. Their financing responsibilities could be increased. They currently use the Small Business Administration (SBA) program in which the federal government guarantees risky small-business loans. This concept of government-as-guarantor could be greatly expanded so that firms could have greater access to commercial bank capital at low-interest rates.

The industrial-revenue-bond (IRB) program, currently a way for companies to receive low-cost funds through the issuance of tax-exempt bonds, needs to be made available to smaller firms. The concept of "umbrella" bonds, which allows smaller firms to pool their needs so that large issues can be floated with governmental support, is an idea whose time has come. Whether or not the IRB program is continued beyond its 1986 current phase-out, some program like it for smaller companies should be instituted.

Government regulations requiring some proportion of financial institutions' portfolios to include these kinds of loans would create a market for such borrowers. Local bankers would then be on the lookout for companies that could benefit from this kind of investment with the assurance that (in the case of an expanded SBA program) the government would guarantee the loan. In the case of an IRB-type program, companies would still have to meet some kind of credit review by the banks or the agency approving a company's participation in the program.

Providing Capital for Businesses that Cannot Meet Financial-Return Requirements of the Market

Many businesses are starved for capital. They cannot compete for funds against governments and major corporations. Interest rates are driven up, partly because nonproductive investments such as real-estate speculation and mergers allow corporations to generate high returns without creating an increase in real wealth. The social returns on investments in capital-starved businesses can be great, especially at a local level, when they result in maintaining jobs. Local governments should take this into account in their calculus. They can provide financial assistance to local businesses.

Governmental assistance could take many forms: local-government lending programs at reduced interest rates; equipment-leasing programs subsidized by local governments; or promotion of local worker ownership with equity participation by local government. Such policies are not meant to ensure the continuance of basically noncompetitive firms, but rather to recognize that businesses should not necessarily have to meet the full financial returns demanded by capital markets in order to contribute substantially to local economies.

Promoting Longer-Term, Higher-Risk Investment

As mentioned earlier, companies shy away from high-risk investments when safer ones provide acceptable return levels. This is philosophically a sensible policy, but pragmatically it has led to avoiding investments that must be made now to ensure future competitiveness. Companies must be prodded into making more of these types of investments.

One way to do this is to increase worker and community involvement on corporate boards of directors through Securities and Exchange Commission (SEC) regulations. The inclusion, through collective bargaining, of Douglas Fraser on Chrysler's board of directors is a first step in the representation of union interests in a corporation. Companies have always included outsiders on their boards, but their purpose has been to protect the stockholders or to provide token representation for minority stockholder interests.

In this area, the U.S. is far behind other developed nations, where unions, the banking sector and in many cases the government are typically included on corporate boards. A leading example is the Vredeling rule of the European Common Market, which specifies labor representation on corporate boards of directors. The purpose of the inclusion of these various groups is to add spokespersons for long-term projects aimed at assuring the long-term viability of the corporation and workers' jobs, in contrast to projects aimed at maximizing short-term returns to stockholders. Over the long term, stockholders should benefit as well from the introduction of this broader view. SEC policy should require that a board of directors include representation of workers and the community affected by a corporation. It is not a novel step in the evolution of corporate structure.

Another way to encourage long-term investments is to utilize companies' concern with maintaining their profit levels. The government could require, as in Sweden, that companies allocate a percentage of their before-tax income to a fund that can be used only at particular times for long-term investments. At the designated times (usually periods of recession), they could pull out the withheld profits (plus interest) and add them to their bottom line. In effect, there would be a profit penalty for not making these types of investments.

Still another idea would work from the market side. Stockholders could be severely penalized by high tax rates for holding securities for less than some significant period of time, say three years. Investments in equity should reflect an evaluation of the long-term prospects of a company's performance. Today this is so only to a limited extent. Equity trading should not be a means by which an individual can "play the market" and realize gains through a sophisticated pyramiding scheme by which stock prices are influenced by bets on whether others will bid up the price tomorrow just because it rose today.

This proposal is meant to take the pressure off companies to generate short-term profitability (because of market reaction) at the expense of long-term viability.

Increasing the Absolute Levels of Capital Available to a Company

Because many businesses must upgrade their production processes to remain competitive at this time of great technological advancement, and because many new business opportunities need to be created from scratch, large amounts of capital relative to a company's size are required. To some extent, the venture-capital market is answering the latter need, but more-established firms are still in need.

One way to provide additional capital is to increase the ratio of debt to equity that a company can access. These ratios are the result of the capital markets' determination of the safe levels of debt that can be extended to a corporation. Japanese and Western European countries have financial-market structures that allow for much higher proportions of debt to be lent to companies than does the U.S. It is not clear at this time how such a change can be achieved in this country through any means other than expanded use of government guaranties or lending programs, but it is an area worth investigating.

Even this approach may not be enough, however, for certain large-scale efforts in new technological areas. In such situations, it may be appropriate for the federal government to become a direct partner in the venture by making loans or buying equity. The Defense and Energy Departments have followed such lines. It should be done through a Department of Technology. This would promote a separation of commercial and military programs and allow for a more appropriate focus on commercially viable areas that demand national attention.

These proposals would reorient the roles of existing financial institutions, challenge the investment decision-making process of businesses, and widen and deepen the involvement of government in the investment process. More ideas are needed. They must be the outgrowth of a clear picture of how the U.S. economy should evolve over the coming decades—toward full employment, less inequality, and a balanced economy.

THE ROAD TO WHERE?

The arguments supporting an industrial policy based on higher productivity and export-led growth often cite the deterioration in the quality of living in the United States as indicating the need for this approach. But how does becoming more internationally competitive guarantee improvements in the living standards of any but a small group of people?

Recapturing the former American share of the automobile market does not necessarily correlate with a longer life expectancy or reduced infant mortality. No "invisible hand" ensures that all or most will benefit from increasing support to industry. What is good for General Motors may not do much for the rest of the country. It might not even do much for GM workers if productivity advances reduce the number of employees while give-backs to enhance international competitiveness contract living standards.

This is a worst-case scenario. It should not lead to automatic rejection of export-led growth but, minimally, to an insistence on clarifying the multiple goals of economic growth and on specifying the "trickle-down" processes that are assumed to result in widespread benefit. Not enough is being demanded by liberals and progressives. Temporary employment programs of the sort on which Democrats often rely are important palliatives, but they do not change basic economic functioning and bring about a sustained full employment level. The political process today is not facing these issues. Conservative economic thinking has won the day, and it will continue to maintain its hold on policy and philosophy unless new thinking and demands become attractive. Politicians will not move to more far-reaching solutions just because things are terrible, but only when people demand new approaches.

An enormous task remains. People must see that the economy can do better than aim for a 6- or 7-percent unemployment rate as a "full employment" objective. The politics of the business cycle must be moved back to a full-employment goal, not only aimed at curtailing inflation. To do that, people must feel this employment objective is realistic. This change will require demystification of and feasible proposals for structural changes in the American economy, in the nature of GNP, investment processes—and capital markets.

Notes

1. Barry Bluestone, Testimony before the Joint Economic Committee of Congress, 18 May 1982.
2. See S. M. Miller and Donald Tomaskovic-Devey, *Recapitalizing America* (Boston: Routledge & Kegan Paul, 1983), 134–139.
3. See Dr. George N. Hatsopoulos, *High Cost of Capital: Handicap of American Industry* (Waltham, Mass.: American Business Conference and the Thermo Electron Corporation, 1983).

2

Economics for People

Sumner M. Rosen

Failure to solve the problem of effectively managing the economy is a bipartisan affair stretching over more than a decade. The central issue is more than a choice between monetarist or fiscal remedies for halting inflation, or between Keynesian or "supply side" measures to raise the rate of economic growth and productivity; though these are not trivial issues, they omit a central question on which their efficacy depends. When Keynes wrote the General Theory and his successors and disciples developed the arsenal of macromanagement measures associated with his name, they could assume—or thought they could —that if things could be properly managed at the macro level, the micro level would take care of itself; with a correct level of adequate demand in place, sustained by a judicious mix of fiscal and monetary measures, market forces would assure a proper allocation of resources, and employers and workers would clear labor markets, leaving only a relatively small number unemployed.*

Macromanagement has failed to operate satisfactorily not because its analysis was wrong but because the assumption proved increas-

---

Sumner M. Rosen is professor of social work at Columbia University.

* Keynes's views are worth recalling; these words appear on page 379 of *The General Theory of Employment, Interest, and Money,* by John Maynard Keynes (New York: Harper & Row, 1936):

To put the point concretely, I see no reason to suppose that the existing system seriously misemploys the factors of production which are in use. There are, of course, errors of foresight; but these would not be avoided by centralising decisions. When 9,000,000 men are employed out of 10,000,000 willing and able to work, there is no evidence that the labour of these 9,000,000 men is misdirected. The complaint against the present system is not that these 9,000,000 men ought to be employed on different tasks, but that tasks should be available for the remaining 1,000,000 men. It is in determining the volume, not the direction, of actual employment that the existing system has broken down.

ingly flawed; defects in the economic structure required correction in order to assure that macromanagement would operate well, but the political will to address these defects has been absent. The problems requiring attention have exerted an increasingly severe and debilitating effect, amounting to an institutional paralysis and rigidity that were dramatized by the spectacle of a level of unemployment unmatched since the 1930s; an increase in the number of people officially classified as poor, which was higher in 1982 than in any year since 1965; stagnation of family and individual income in constant dollars; dramatic slowing of the rate of increase in economic growth and productivity; and inflationary forces that proved strong enough to frustrate all but the most draconian measures. Nor were these problems confined to the United States.

As the election of 1980 exerted its influence on politicians and policy analysts alike, the search for solutions took on new urgency. Conservatives, liberals, progressives and others agree that some simple restoration of things as they once were is neither practical nor plausible. Because of the appeal of their arguments, as well as the status of their proponents, those who project what we can call a "corporatist-liberal direction"—people like Felix Rohatyn, Robert Reich and Lester Thurow—have dominated the discussion of alternatives to Reaganist policies. They argue that the central governing mechanisms of the economy, private and public, will continue to malfunction unless and until they are subjected to firm rational control.

Internationally, they would apply the same principle, coordinating policies to finance international trade and transfers of capital, linking loans for economic development to domestic policies that control wages and consumption, counter monetary inflation, and ensure a favorable climate for foreign capital investment and repatriation of profits. The crisis of unpaid interest and principal, with the threat of default by such major debtors as Brazil ($90 billion), Argentina ($37 billion) or Poland ($25 billion), is worrisome and may prove dangerous, but it does not represent a long-term problem if the conditions and controls indicated can be imposed and managed, either by a consortium of central banks or by the International Monetary Fund.

Domestically, they are highly critical of competitive struggles between states and regions, which threaten to wipe out much of the older industrial base, and they share the viewpoint of liberals and

progressives that pursuit of profit at the expense of both social stability and preservation of the economic base has proved too destructive and threatens to polarize haves and have-nots to a politically
dangerous degree. They argue that a more rational pursuit of
growth and profit, more responsive to the need to take account of
the condition of the working class and the middle class, represents
our best hope of restoring economic health. They repudiate the
know-nothing and unconditional solicitude for business welfare of
the Reagan program; in its place they would make choices, impose
conditions, manage and direct the process to assure a smooth and
less painful transition, leading us from the old industrial base into
the new economy, which they see being built on the basis of the
transformation of information and the technologically advanced
methods coming into use that promise to restore productivity to
high rates of growth.

They favor and foster programs that substitute cooperation between management and workers—unionized or not—for the adversary system that has developed through collective bargaining and
unionization in the past half-century. They would work hard to preserve the core of the industrial work force, what one author once
called the "hard-core employed," against the possibility of wholesale
layoffs and loss of any prospect of work, both of which have occurred
under Reagan policies in many areas. At the same time, they believe
that wage and benefit levels in many industries have become too high
to restore needed levels of profits, and they applaud, and would extend, management actions that have successfully imposed wage reductions, benefit cuts or postponements, and relaxation of "restrictive"
work rules, which could be accepted in an era of affluence but have
no place in an economy struggling to recapture its lost hegemony.

The logic of this approach requires that capital intensity be raised
and that for an indefinite period, never specified, direct wages as well
as the "social wage" of protection against old age, illness, unemployment and disability be controlled or reduced, all in the name of
sacrifice for the common good. They are prepared to support better
access to jobs and income for women, blacks and others, but they
resist proposals to expand total jobs to meet the needs of the unemployed as well as the millions of potential workers who remain out of
the labor force because they see no opportunity to find jobs. They
share with the Reagan administration the view that restoring growth

requires higher levels of savings and investment, and they support the existing pattern of inequality in the distribution of wealth and income. But they would coordinate investment decisions in order to reduce wasteful commitments of scarce capital and to prevent further erosion of the social and economic infrastructure of the older industrial areas. They favor reducing military spending because they see the need for greater expenditures on the economic infrastructure in order to facilitate and promote the operations of the corporate economy. But they might favor raising some of the funds by reducing taxes on income and wealth, and raising taxes on consumption, as via a national sales or value-added tax.

While it might work, this program is both regressive and elitist. Any success it would have would come at a high economic, social and political cost; its plausibility arises from the prestige of its proponents, from the fact that these costs would be both lower and less vindictive and heartless than those already imposed by the Reagan programs, and from the reality that no other serious alternatives are being widely discussed. In such circumstances, painfully aware of the fact that Reagan policies have inflicted great harm and achieved nothing of substance, people tend to look favorably on this corporatist program. Its supporters are people of proven ability and seriousness who are willing to criticize those in power without appearing reckless or doctrinaire. More fundamentally, they provide assurance that the basic institutions of our economic system, which people believe has served this country well for a hundred years or more, need no fundamental overhaul or replacement but only better, stronger, more sensitive management and direction in order to become once again effective instruments of economic progress and stability. These arguments are hard to resist.

CRITIQUE OF CORPORATISM

There are two sets of problems with this approach. The first is political: These proposals involve a high degree of centralized planning and control, which replaces the uncontrolled power of private, concentrated capital with an even more centrally managed system of governance. However wise and humane it may be, it vests power in a governing elite and excludes or severely limits the ability of people to share in the democratic process of deciding what our economic goals and priorities should be, and how economic activity ought to be organized and carried out.

The economic objections to this approach derive from the argument that it leaves in place the central mechanisms and structural characteristics that have produced the economic crisis of our era. If these structures remain substantially intact, neither a full-employment commitment nor an adequate and decent system of social protection can be ensured. Market forces would remain marginal to the allocation of resources and the process by which individual businessmen and small enterprises develop new products, production processes, and access to the pool of savings. Instead, small firms would remain dependent on the economic fortunes and managerial decisions of the large firms that dominate economic life. Dominance by large firms in the control of investment decisions that shape the lives of workers, communities and regions and which determine what the economy will produce and provide will remain intact, though subject to more rational and socially responsive direction and control than is now the case. And though the 500 largest firms directly employ only 19 percent of the labor force, their impact on the employment choices open to the bulk of the labor force, which is significant today, would remain.

CORPORATIONS AND THE ECONOMY

How large corporations behave and conduct their economic affairs needs explication in order to connect structure with policy choices. The transition over much of the twentieth century from a competitive to a concentrated industrial economy carries with it profound consequences. The depression of the 1930s helped to dramatize some of the consequences of this transition, and the Roosevelt administration, having developed responses to the emergency conditions in the early years of the New Deal, began to look in some depth at the nature and impact of concentration through the Temporary National Economic Committee. But by the time the TNEC, appointed in 1938, was ready to propose its remedies, the acute phase of the depression had ended, the nation had begun to focus on the issue of war or peace, and the moment had passed for any serious effort to deal with concentrated economic power. Since then, the degree of economic concentration has grown and the scope of concentrated corporate power has expanded to global dimensions through the multinational corporation, the growth of U.S. investment outside of the U.S., and other instruments. Mergers and buyouts lead to indirect influence and reduced competition; conglomerates centralize decision-making across previously separated markets. The top 200 U.S. corporations owned 48 percent of corporate assets in 1950, 56 percent in 1960, 60 percent in 1970 and 1980. The heritage of the Sherman Antitrust Act of 1890, while still part of the value system, has lost most of its energy in practice and policy.

Large firms may achieve dominance through the economic and productive superiority of their methods of production and distribution—what economists call "economies of scale"—but they can sustain their power by other means when the productive edge ends, as it often does. These means include their ability to erect and sustain barriers to the entry of new firms, often through joint action with other firms like themselves. The motive for joint action is joint survival and prosperity. Firms sharing a market have a joint interest in preventing new firms from entering, and in preserving price and production levels that protect their profit-making ability. Overall stability is prized, and serious departures from shared product characteristics and methods of production are limited by concern that the impact, if it is unpredictable, may prove injurious not only to the firm but to the industry of which it is a part. These aspects of what economists call "oligopoly"—competition among the few—distort economic processes and lead to built-in deviations from the theoretical ideal of a competitive allocation of scarce economic resources. The concentrated sector—what Galbraith called the "planning sector"—competes at the periphery rather than through innovative products or methods, or serious price competition.

The role that large firms play in generating and allocating investment resources requires special attention. One source of their predominant influence is the degree to which large firms are able to raise their own investment resources from their cash flow: depreciation allowances plus retained earnings. They use their power in the marketplace to set price and volume levels intended not only to yield a satisfactory rate of return to owners and managers but also to generate funds for expansion, modernization or diversification. Funds from this source are preferable to funds from sale of securities because they conserve and enhance, rather than dilute, the value of existing shares. The funds are used to improve corporate profitability. If this also promoted economic efficiency and productivity, one could have no quarrel with the method, but there is no reason why it should if corporations can utilize their market power, their persuasiveness through advertising, and their ability to bar or limit market access to newer or smaller firms to sustain or increase the rate of return on their new as well as their older bases of capital.

One result of this is a tendency in many industries to overcapacity; in turn, this exerts upward pressure on prices as corporations seek to generate a level of revenues that will meet their targeted rate of return on a capital base that is now greater than before. A second result is a misallocation of investment away from industries where firms are smaller, more numerous, more competitive and, in many cases, more efficient and innovative but which lack the power to raise capital this way. Large firms also enjoy preferred access to the credit markets because of close links between them and major banks on which they rely. When a bank like Chase Manhattan owns or votes as trustee major blocks of shares in several airlines, its influence in ensuring stability as well as its ability to help meet credit needs follow inevitably. Similar links connect large firms to other sources of investment capital, such as pension funds managed by major banks. Taken together, the pattern that emerges is of a coordinated investment process whose first priority is the well-being and continued dominance of the large corporations at its center.

This power can be used not only to distort the shape of the economy, through its control over the future, but also to damage existing firms and the workers and communities that depend on them. In an analysis by Bluestone and Harrison,[1] we see in detail how firms that acquire others develop a policy first of denying funds for maintenance and modernization and then, as the plant begins to lose in competitive ability, of cutting back or closing down hitherto productive and profitable operations in order to shift funds to areas where the rate of profit is higher. In the process, enormous damage is done to the work force, the community and the region, but no mechanism exists for compensating the victims, much less for preventing the damage in the first place. By 1981, to cite one example, 65 percent of the business of the

United States Steel Corporation was in activities other than steel, while steel employment had plummeted.

THE MILITARY ECONOMY

Concentration as well as capital allocation is an important though neglected aspect of the way the military economy operates in the United States. Most military production is done by private contractors. This production is highly concentrated among firms like General Dynamics, McDonnell-Douglas, Lockheed and United Aircraft, all of them large. The top 100 military contractors regularly receive over 70 percent of total military contracts. They in turn subcontract with many smaller as well as other large firms. The capital investment and skilled labor used in the military industry are not available in civilian production, particularly in the technologically advanced areas in which major industrial countries compete. A large military sector preempts scarce capital investment and contributes its share to the trend of declining productivity and stagnant rates of growth. It is no coincidence that industrial countries showing the highest rates of growth spend far less in proportion to their GNP on military goods than do either the United States or the Soviet Union. Programs to cure our economic difficulties cannot rely on a military component; proposals to shift the regional focus of the military budget as a solution to economic problems are futile.

LABOR MARKETS AND EMPLOYMENT POLICY

Employers are the ones who hire and pay workers. How well these labor markets work becomes a key to any proposals to cure our economic ills and reconstitute economic structures and processes. Recent events dramatized the vulnerability of the economy to large-scale and sustained unemployment, but the problems of unemployment and underemployment cannot be dealt with effectively by simple reflation and stimulus of aggregate demand, because of important structural distortions that have become more serious over time.

Eli Ginzberg, in an important survey,[2] found that over the 1950–76 period, while the total number of jobs had kept rough pace with the growth of the labor force, the proportion of total jobs that can be called "poor" had risen—jobs paying low wages with few or no benefits, high susceptibility to termination or layoff, a limited use of skills —what are often called "secondary" jobs[3]—while the share of good jobs had fallen. In 1980, 116.8 million people worked part-time or full-time, but there were only 65 million full-time workers. Good jobs are found almost exclusively in the full-time category; more are filled by men than women, and by whites than blacks or Hispanics. While 44 percent of full-time workers earned $15,000 or more, 90 percent of part-time workers earned less than $15,000, and 12.8 million full-time and 42.7 million part-time workers earned less than $10,000, many of them women and blacks. Women are 42 percent of the work force but only 35 percent of the full-time group, and even in that group their earnings averaged $13,112 as compared with $22,196 for men. Thirty percent of men are in the highest-paid categories of professional, managerial and technical occupations as compared with 24 percent of women and 20 percent of blacks who work; at the other extreme, 26 percent of blacks and only 17 percent of whites hold jobs as operatives and laborers. In 1982, average measured unemployment was 9.7 percent, the highest since the depression, while the (July) rate for blacks was 18.5 percent, for black teen-agers 49.7 percent, for men aged 20–24 12.9 percent, for women heads of households 12.0 percent, and for Hispanic workers 13.9 percent.

Clearly, high levels of overall unemployment impose very substantial burdens on groups disadvantaged in the jobs they hold or the skills they bring to the labor market. Others, like government or managerial and professional workers, have substantially greater protection against the risk of layoff even in times like 1982.

These are some of the symptoms of structural disarray that require attention, and cannot be dealt with by the simple-minded tool kit that has passed for a labor-market policy in the period since 1962; the expenditure of $62 billion on so-called manpower programs has failed utterly to address the underlying issues. They are of two kinds. The first can be schematized under the rubric of "human capital"—its development, and its ability to earn a "rate of return" through gainful employment. The second deals with the workplace itself—its safety, relation to both physical and mental health, and the scope it provides for both individual fulfillment and democratic influence or control over one's destiny as a worker. For economic policy, only the first of these is germane, but the connections between the two areas are often close. For example, while occupational hazards exact a high toll of illness, disability and premature death, our costly health-care system, highly dependent on public funds, has little interest or capability in addressing and dealing with work-related hazards.

The business system has engaged in a steady reorganization of work, which involves, as it always has, significant changes in the mix of occupations, standards of employability or advancement, the use of new technologies—first the computer, now the robot—and other developments. All affect the level of the demand for labor, levels of compensation, the terms of access to jobs, and other aspects of what might be called the "opportunity system." Rates of skill obsolescence are rapid, in addition to the problems posed by the geographic shifts that business creates in its ceaseless search for cheaper labor, lower taxes, less governmental regulation and better access to markets and materials. For example, the ratio of nonproduction workers (managers, technicians, supervisors, inspectors, etc.) to production workers in American industry rose from 13.1 per 100 production workers in 1947 to 23.1 in 1978. This is one reason why total unit costs rose and measured rates of productivity fell, even though direct unit labor costs in the U.S. rose less over the 1970–80 decade than in Japan, West Germany or Sweden.

It also emphasizes the historical division of labor between workers and management, a hierarchical and directive approach to management that requires us to be skeptical of widely touted concern with worker participation and job enrichment. The dominant trend in industry is toward more control over the work process and the worker through mechanization and computer control, sophisticated methods of deskilling of jobs, particularly in clerical work, and the rollback of limits on managerial discretion imposed by negotiated work rules. The latter became a major management objective during the 1981–83 recession, when unions were confronted with the choice of "givebacks" in wages, benefits and work rules or seeing plants closed. As a result, even a full recovery of demand and production in many recession-hurt sectors will leave the work force far smaller than it was, and will impose higher demands on those who remain at work. In the nonunionized sectors, which are a majority of the economy, the process proceeded with little resistance, though largely unnoticed by the media or by observers. The result is an added number of superfluous hard-to-employ workers, many unable to realize the expectations they had of reaching pensionable age.

WHY FULL EMPLOYMENT MATTERS

This scenario makes clear how distant and difficult to realize is the once-conventional view that full employment is both achievable and important for policy-makers. Yet without full employment, most of the goals articulated by labor-market policy cannot be met. Without high levels of employment, employers need not lower or alter their hiring criteria to admit the less skilled or the disadvantaged, however assiduously training and placement agencies work to help. Only when labor is in short supply does the queue shorten enough to make jobs available; as long as "qualified" candidates are in ample supply, conventional criteria of age, sex, race, education and prior experience remain effective. If employment is not increasing, affirmative-action programs can improve the employment outcome for their client groups only by displacing members of the majority, and this, as we have seen, raises major political problems as well as issues of equity and fairness not easily resolved. The result is that attributes based on group, race or class remain decisive in the sorting process, and the burden of proof remains on the candidates rather than on those who bar their access or limit their choices. It will not be easy to alter the reality that women constitute 63 percent of computer operators, 57 percent of insurance adjusters, and the vast majority of nurses, teachers, secretaries, clerks, bank tellers, sewers and stitchers, bookkeepers and telephone operators; and that blacks are disproportionately employed as garbage collectors, nurses' aides, postal clerks, hospital orderlies, cooks, file clerks, bus drivers and social workers.

Except for a few, work is what determines income. Flaws in labor markets artificially increase the earnings of the relatively privileged and depress those of the disadvantaged. Shifts in the location of jobs reduce the earnings and shorten the work lives of those displaced. An increase in the share of jobs represented by professionals, managers, technicians and other white-collar groups increases the relevance of formal education and credentials as tickets to good jobs; and despite the expansion of higher education in recent decades, the bulk of those who get the good jobs and whose job status improves over their working lives are from the upper tiers of the income distribution. Unless the terms of access are improved, existing patterns of inequality in income based on differential access to the different job categories will persist.

Yet full employment maintains its hold over the minds of liberals and remains the key to change in the job-income nexus; as someone once said, "A tight labor market is a worker's best friend." The last serious effort to restore a full-employment mandate and priority in national policy-making was the effort organized by Congressman Augustus F. Hawkins (D-California) which culminated in passage of the Full Employment and Balanced Growth Act of 1978, better known as "Humphrey-Hawkins." Its goal of restoring the concept of full employment that was dropped from the 1946 Employment Act was important, but the compromises exacted prior to its passage have rendered it virtually without meaning, with no discernible effect on economic policy. Skeptics and opponents argue that the goal itself cannot be attained; others attack the principle, saying that government ought to leave economic life to the marketplace and the benign if slow effect of a freer hand to the private sector. Given the combined power of these arguments, it is no surprise that recent years saw unemployment rise, workers' incomes stagnate and fall, and enforcement of affirmative-action programs and health and safety legislation virtually cease.

GOVERNMENT AND THE ECONOMY

No complex economy can operate unless government plays its role. Aside from its direct effect on economic life, government must see to those needs that the economy cannot itself meet, or that are created by the workings of the economy—unemployment, income for the retired, education and training of young people, regulation of union-employer relations, etc. A major thrust of recent conservative governments has been to limit or abandon these roles in the name of the marketplace, identifying government as the problem rather than as the solution to problems. In addition to lifting or relaxing regulatory controls and sharply reducing the burden of taxes on corporate profits, a major thrust of the Reagan administration has been to reduce social-welfare expenditures and to challenge the very concept of social-welfare entitlements as a valid principle of governmental policy.

Corporatist-liberal spokesmen have expressed their sharp dissent from this view; like the Marxists, they understand that a modern welfare state is indispensable to the stability of the social order as well as the economy. The Right suffered a defeat when they sought to roll back benefits and alter the eligibility of future beneficiaries of old-age and survivors insurance (OASI) under Social Security. But the attack on less coherent and more exposed groups such as food-stamp beneficiaries, children receiving school lunches, women and infants requiring nutritional support, single women with dependent children (AFDC clients), and Medicaid eligibles was more successful and has continued; further efforts will be made to reduce the scope and costs of Medicare, disability insurance and other programs.

The fervor of the attack on these aspects of the modern welfare state bears witness to the power of Darwinian views among the key members of the Reagan administration and their followers. It matches perfectly their view of the Soviet Union as the center of evil in the world. Just as they seek to dominate and humiliate the Soviets, they wish to extirpate from our society any remnant of doctrine that can be attributed to collectivist ideologies; social-welfare programs and those who defend them are candidates for anathema, dupes at best, like their nuclear-freeze and peaceful-coexistence counterparts in public and intellectual life.

The fact is that ours is a threadbare welfare state in comparison to those of other advanced countries and that our tax burden is relatively low, as illustrated by the accompanying table. We protect 58 percent of our work force through unemployment insurance, compared to 90 percent in Sweden, 81 percent in Japan and 75 percent in West Germany. Benefit levels are about half of average wages, compared to 77 percent for France, 63 percent for West Germany and 62 percent for Japan and Britain. Like South Africa, we still lack a national health-care program. Our antipoverty and welfare programs are stigmatizing and mean-spirited. More than 10 million workers and their families lost their job-related health coverage when they lost their jobs in the 1981–83 recession.

	Taxes as Percent of GNP	Social Spending as Percent of GNP
Sweden	43.5	31.6
France	36.9	29.7
West Germany	37.3	26.3
Canada	33.9	20.9
United Kingdom	32.8	19.6
United States	28.0	18.0
Japan	22.6	14.4

Source: Institute for Labor Education and Research, "We Are Not the Problem," 12–13.

THE BACKWARD STATE OF THE AMERICAN WELFARE STATE

Two reasons can be advanced for the backward and vulnerable state of the social-welfare system. One is a simplistic view that the traditional reliance on private sources of support is best. Family ties, ethnic links, community-based services and voluntarism were the principal sources of help and protection for many decades until the shock and magnitude of the depression forced national action and legislation, notably the Social Security Act of 1935 and other New Deal laws. Traditions of self-reliance and reluctance to acknowledge dependence on the state die hard, particularly in the wake of long-term affluence and economic growth.

We also suffer from an intellectual failure to establish the rationale for social welfare in modern industrial and postindustrial American society. Such a rationale would begin with the principle that forces external to the lives of individuals and communities are decisive in determining outcomes and in posing the risks from which none are exempt; this is the fundamental principle, painfully won, on which the advanced welfare states of the social democratic systems have been built and to which most of their citizens subscribe.

The second component of the conceptual base is the recognition that preventive measures are superior to curative measures in dealing with social problems arising from the forces of economic life. In virtually the entire scope of social programs, aside from education, we respond after problems have hit rather than before they arise.

The third element is acceptance of the fact that only the state has the resources as well as the mission to deal effectively with problems whose scope is national and whose resolution cannot be left to private benevolence, though private programs have an important role to play.

Finally, the rationale for a welfare state would recognize that it is social outcomes, in the lives of people, that must constitute the acid test of any economy's structure or performance. How well a society meets peoples' needs for health care, housing, education, culture and enjoyment of life is more important in the last analysis than growth or profit rates. The state thus is directly involved in shaping economic forces and mitigating their impact, beyond its obligation to heal the wounds inflicted by economic processes or helping enterprises to employ qualified workers or find better markets.

THE STATE AND THE ECONOMY

The state's role in the economy itself has largely been limited to macromanagement, regulation of business behavior when it affects the public interest, funding of the military subeconomy, and management of international economic relationships. Social as well as economic well-being would clearly and significantly be advanced if we developed and put into effect planned programs to restore and improve the infrastructure on which much of economic life depends—roads, bridges, public and rail transport. In these and other areas where capital expenditure and maintenance are large enough to require state involvement and support—schools and universities, national parks and recreational areas, public housing—the process as well as the level of support are poor. The case for planned programs in these areas rests on solid economic grounds.

First, if we had the equivalent of a national capital budget, we would recognize the need, and allocate the resources to improve, extend and modernize these facilities in orderly fashion instead of depending on the vagaries of the appropriation process and the pressure of other budget needs to determine the level of spending. Precedents exist in the highway trust fund among others, and they appear to have operated reasonably well on the whole. This is not surprising given the American love affair with automobiles, but the imbalance in other areas needs to be corrected. We would also pay for these capital improvements over time, as we should since the return they provide takes place over long periods of time. A well-planned program of public works has the added merit of serving as an effective countercyclical instrument, which is badly needed.

HUMAN CAPITAL AND LABOR-MARKET POLICIES

If we need programs to develop and deepen our stock of physical capital, we need even more programs to remedy deficiencies in what we have called the stock of "human capital"—the education and training that people rely on in the central event of their lives, the work they do. Schools and universities, training programs and employer in-service programs constitute major ways in which people acquire the stock of skills and education that they then bring to the labor market. How well that market works in matching jobs to people determines the degree to which the economy will properly reward them for the qualifications they possess. Both require serious attention and improvement in view of the dismal record so far. Indeed, the quality of the work force today and in the future constitutes the economy's most important asset. If we do poorly here, we cannot succeed, however brilliant the other economic policies we put into place. In this we have much to learn from others, and not just the Japanese.

In some of the Social Democratic countries, and also in those with strong labor movements out of power, active labor-market measures have proved their worth in both economic and human terms. Access to retraining throughout one's working life is one example of a measure that pays high returns while ensuring against skill obsolescence as the economy changes. Advance notice of layoffs or plant closings are required in many countries, though only two states and two cities in the U.S. have such laws. This makes it possible for government agencies to develop alternative reemployment paths well ahead of the time of separation, and the record—in Canada, Sweden and elsewhere —is impressive in terms of placement rates and maintenance of earnings levels.

Methods that improve the channels from small to larger enterprises for workers who face job loss, or who want the broader range of job opportunities more frequently found in large firms, merit testing and development. In-service upgrading and career advancement represent unutilized tools with a high potential return, but U.S. programs have never provided sufficient incentives or technical know-how to make them operative in the large private and public systems of employment, which employ many with unrealized potential and desire for advancement.* The government as employer for those who need and cannot find work is a widely used instrument of countercyclical policy, pioneered and then rejected in the United States. The schools, dams, roads, post offices and bridges built; the books and plays written; the concerts performed under the WPA were important contributions to social well-being in addition to providing jobs for those who needed them, and today's agenda of unmet public needs is long enough to justify such programs over many business cycles of the future.

The conclusion of this line of reasoning must be that our public sector is too small, not too big. Meeting our social, capital and work-force needs of the future requires not only that the military share of public spending be drastically cut but that the resulting "peace dividend" be earmarked for the establishment of a public and social sector able to meet the needs we have outlined. Nor should we be discouraged from this by the mythology of government as wasteful and incompetent, and by the notion that government involvement in this area is a diversion from the "real" tasks of the economy, etc. When we have taken government seriously, we have been able to put into place competent, accountable, productive and highly useful programs. It is because the mythology rules that these self-fulfilling prophecies often come true, but our own past as well as examples from many countries demonstrate the potential of government to organize and act effectively.

WHAT A WISE GOVERNMENT CAN—
AND CANNOT—DO

Corporatist-liberal advocates will agree with much that has been proposed here, and argue that they offer concrete steps to put propos-

---

* Attention should be called to the program developed by the Service Employees International Union (SEIU) for implementation in health services and other areas. Called Lifetime Education and Career Development (LEAD), it serves as a model and prototype of what can be done.

als like these into effect. To the degree that power at the top needs to be exercised competently and humanely, they are probably right; macromanagement, restoration and expansion of the infrastructure, support for innovative labor-market programs, and establishment of a decent and comprehensive set of social-welfare protections are tasks that the central government must undertake, and which cry for attention. But their competence and their interest do not lead them to engage some of the structural problems that we have identified as keys to the reconstruction of the economy along democratic as well as productive lines. For progress on these fronts, we need programs that go well beyond what this school of thought would undertake.*

In an economy where the commitment to full employment had been restored and needed programs put into place, and where the power of the federal government in economic decisions was clearly utilized to ensure responsible exercise of corporate power, peace in industrial relations, support for small firms, subsidies for basic as well as usable research, and effective management of trade and currency relationships with the world, we would still need to address the issues of power and democracy that are the heart of the matter.

TOWARD DEMOCRATIC CONTROL OF ECONOMIC LIFE

Democratic control of investment decisions is at the head of the list because of the harm that has been and can be inflicted when such decisions are not controlled, and because these decisions are decisive in determining how the economy will operate over long periods of time. Such control is needed, too, in order to assure that they do good, not harm; that they increase the economic well-being of workers and consumers; that they are respectful of accumulated social investments and commitments; and that they are made with the informed consent of those whose lives, as workers or consumers, will be affected. Social control is not socialization of capital but its management to ensure that it does not injure those whom it affects. Social Democratic countries have demonstrated for decades that such management of capital is consistent with private ownership and op-

---

* The material that follows derives in part from Samuel Bowles, David M. Gordon and Thomas E. Weisskopf, *Beyond the Wasteland: A Democratic Alternative Program to Economic Decline* (Garden City, N.Y.: Anchor Press/Doubleday, 1983).

eration of business, and even with the accumulation of wealth.

One direct approach to decentralizing corporate investment control is both simple and effective but, because of its effects, remains unimplemented even on a trial basis. It would involve both the repeal of the corporate income tax—largely accomplished de facto by recent legislation—and a tax on undistributed earnings approaching 100 percent. The effect would be to force corporations to distribute most profits to shareholders. Thereafter, corporations wishing to expand would have to bid for this pool of savings against the field—competitors, new or innovative firms, and other uses of savings, including social investment. The usefulness and profitability corporate investment plans would be weighed on the scale with other uses, rather than being carried out just because top management decides to do so. The impact of their plans on the industry, communities and workers they affect, and on consumers, would become subject to public scrutiny. Making corporate planning visible is a step toward making it accountable. And owners would pay their fair share of income taxes rather than having their added wealth hidden as corporate net worth. This has the look of a drastic measure, but it fits the formulas of a competitive society and a viable capital market far better than the process we now must live with and appear powerless to affect.

Some areas of economic life, however, should be directly owned and controlled by the state. Two stand out: energy, because of its great power and frequently irresponsible exercise; and health care, because it is central to everyone's life and because our system falls so far short in terms of access, disease prevention and health maintenance, and cost. Like education, food and housing, health care is properly seen as a public right best provided through direct public management. There are other economic rights to be established. Workers are entitled to safe and healthy work settings, and to access to improvement of their skills and earning capacity through lifetime educational entitlement. Consumers are entitled to products that work, that last and are safe, and to a range of choices best provided by many alternative sources of supply. People are entitled to choices in how they spend their leisure time (e.g., many television channels and also live performances, subsidized to make them accessible). Good local and intercity transportation belongs on this list.

Central government has a role to play in legitimating and supporting these and other rights, but central government has no role to play in deciding the content of these rights. Within the national and international economy that constitutes the framework, there are many subeconomies, widely varied in almost every respect: size, specialization, stage of development, composition of the work force, tastes and interests, etc. Democratization of the economy means maximizing the degree of control and choice that communities and regions have about the shape and content of their economy. In the past, such choices have largely been thrust upon them, but in some cases localities have been able to influence their own future. New York City provides some insight on this matter. A precipitous economic and financial decline between 1969 and 1977 brought together government, labor, financial, political and other interest groups in a collective and successful effort to reverse the decline and develop new directions for the economic development of the city. New York City's experience, even though costly to many people, demonstrated a capacity for broad coalitions and responsible participation on the part of key constituencies. Many of Felix Rohatyn's proposals derive directly from this experience. A recent study[4] demonstrates how conscious economic planning would work in this and similar economic settings, provided that the political system was effectively deployed to promote and manage the process.

As the economy moves increasingly into a nonindustrial phase— what some call "postindustrial"—many of the assumptions about the superior productive capability of large enterprises are proving to be superseded; in an increasing number of cases, the small firm has proven or will prove equal or superior to the large in flexibility and adaptability to changing conditions; the services sector and some of the newer technological sectors have already demonstrated impressive potential for smaller, decentralized units of production or other activity. In northern Italy, small firms have developed world markets in special areas of high and intermediate technology, yielding high value added and strong potential for growth. As these trends develop, the decentralized aspects of the economy, and a further democratization of entrepreneurship, will strengthen the prospects for democratization of economic life.

Direct ownership by workers is a related and important aspect of democratic control. Transfer of basket-case firms to workers gives the concept a bad name, but there have been exceptions and more will develop as the feasibility of economic survival without reliance on giant corporate auspices increases. Such efforts need access to investment and working capital, help in managing the transition, and short-run subsidy or market preferences as they begin, and such resources can be pooled and managed at the local or regional level on a democratic basis.

What is proposed here is to combine the strength of a responsible and responsive central administration with a range of policies and entitlements that bring concentrated power under control while encouraging and supporting the democratization of much of economic life. No single element in what has been proposed has not been utilized effectively somewhere; what is lacking so far is the integration of these programs and approaches in an economy as large, complex and important as ours. The other missing component is the political process that will validate and bring to life ideas so far confined to paper and to the minds of those who share them. Our motto now should be, Let us begin.

Notes

1. Barry Bluestone and Bennett Harrison, *The Deindustrialization of America* (New York: Basic Books, 1982).
2. Eli Ginzberg, "The Job Problem," *Scientific American,* Nov. 1977
3. Peter B. Doeringer and Michael J. Piore, *Internal Labor Markets and Manpower Analysis* (Lexington, Mass.: Health, 1971).
4. Sumner M. Rosen, *Building a Program for Full Employment in New York* (New York: Community Service Society, 1983).

3

Democratizing Investment

David Gold

Reinforcing private control over investment has been central to the politics of the Reagan administration. Supply-side economics—or "Reaganomics," as it has become popularly known—was billed as an attempt to reinvigorate the private mechanisms for accumulating capital and, in the process, establish a firm basis for long-term economic growth.

As economics, Reaganomics was seriously flawed with a weak theory and almost no supporting evidence. More important, it has failed if one looks at the outcome. The initial result of supply-side policies was not the immediate burst of creative energy forecast by the president, but the worst recession since World War II. The 1981–82 recession and the following recovery fit traditional business-cycle patterns far better than they fit any model of supply-side economics.

An extremely tight monetary policy pushed the economy into recession, and an easing of monetary policy, rising consumer spending, and stimulus from federal budget deficits have led the recovery. The monetarist prescription of putting the economy through a wringer yielded predictable results: high unemployment; an attack on wages and unions; bankruptcies and cutbacks among weaker businesses; and a lowering of the rate of inflation.

The recovery will do little for employment. Basic industries trimmed their labor forces and expect to hire back far fewer workers than they laid off. High-tech industries will not be major generators of new jobs. Even if the recovery is stronger than the average postwar recovery, the unemployment rate will drop slowly and remain high. The continuation of high budget deficits and high interest rates threatens to undermine the recovery by reducing new investment. With

David Gold is director of the Institute on the Military and the Economy.

savings remaining low and business investment lagging behind, it is hard to find signs of the long-term boom in investment that supply-siders are still predicting.

By its own political criteria, Reaganomics has been a success. The wealthy have more income, and probably even greater control than previously over how the nation's wealth is used. The tax and regulatory burden on business has been eased. Labor has suffered some serious setbacks, and the Democratic party has yet to devise a serious alternative to the president's policies.

The supply-side "solution" emerged from the failure of Keynesian policy during the stagflation of the 1970s. Early in that decade, conservatives began arguing that the root cause of the combined problem of slow growth and inflation was a capital shortage. The twin burdens of heavy taxation and government regulation had reduced incentives to save and were making investment in productivity-enhancing capital equipment less profitable. High wages and the decline of labor discipline were also pointed to, but the main conservative critique was aimed at Keynesian policy, with its emphasis on high levels of government spending and taxing, and at the welfare state, with its swollen social budgets and its attempts to manage the workplace via a growing regulatory apparatus.

Most discussions of the conservative attack on Keynesian policies focused on the budget deficit, inflation and related issues. Two points tended to get lost. First, the conservative attack was not just against a bloated state apparatus that was hampering accumulation but was also aimed at attempts to widen access to the state and distribute more evenly the benefits of state actions.

The New Deal had come to power by forging a political coalition that included greater representation from labor, minorities and urban populations, and contained much greater awareness of the problems of the poor, the unemployed and the elderly. Many New Deal programs and policies had a distinctly redistributive and democratic character: Social Security, support for unions, and the Tennessee Valley Authority, for example.

The New Frontier and Great Society were modeled, at least rhetorically, on the New Deal, and did lead to some measures embodying both redistributive and democratic initiatives: Medicare, for example, and the War on Poverty with its attempts at community involvement.

While the New Deal and 1960s measures ended up being less democratic and egalitarian than initially projected, often being dominated by some of the forces they were supposed to be controlling, conservatives feared the potential openings these programs represented. When the economy declined in the late 1960s and early 1970s, the welfare state came under increasing attack.

A second point was that the Keynesian policy that developed in the United States had been heavily influenced by a business-dominated coalition seeking to retain control over investment. The initial Keynesian policy proposals included an emphasis on expansionary policies embodying a substantial amount of direct intervention. In some early versions of Keynesian economics, planning mechanisms were discussed. Keynesian economics was seen by many as a marriage of stimulative macroeconomics with a continuation of New Deal social-welfare policies. The marriage was to yield full employment.

Following the Eisenhower years, liberals saw the election of Kennedy as a signal for the revival of New Deal initiatives, including expansionary macroeconomic policies. By then, however, a centrist coalition had been formed that dominated economic policy-making. Keynesians learned quickly that the road to expansionary fiscal policy was blocked by business's demand for continued control over investment. The first measures passed by the first Keynesian administration were the investment tax credit and accelerated depreciation allowances, in 1962, before the large personal tax cut. Both had a distinct "supply-side" flavor.

Thus, the initial core of Keynesian thinking—that government would lead the private economy in seeking expansion, including, in Keynes's words, the "socialization of investment"—was turned on its head. Only when business was assured continual control over investment was the rest of the expansionary Keynesian apparatus put into place.

The failure of Keynesian economic policy to control inflation led to its downfall. But earlier compromises had stripped Keynesian policy of the tools that might have prevented inflation, or made it easier to control. These were, specifically, direct intervention to control inflation, and more control over the size and direction of new investment. Without such tools, Keynesian policy had no choice but to follow the lead of business investment.

By leaving control over investment in private hands, economic and social development remain subject to the whims of the market on the one hand and the decision-making power of corporations and financial institutions on the other. This system is being pushed to its limits under Reagan, and while it may achieve some positive results in the short term, there is very little chance of long-term growth.

One alternative is to build on the demands for participation and equity that underlay political movements in the past, aimed explicitly at control over capital and new investment. The objective of such control would be to have investment reflect social priorities and to achieve more stable, and higher levels of, economic growth.

Progressive ideas and politics, at least since the Populist movement, have emphasized control over production, finance and new investment. Schemes have included producers cooperatives and labor banks; government regulation of railroads and power companies; public-works programs including public power; and many others. State governments have owned banks, as in North Dakota, and insurance companies, in Wisconsin. Workers have assumed ownership of businesses, a movement that has grown in recent years. There are community planning boards, even in a city as large as New York, and there is a periodic revival of interest in economic planning.

A motivation behind democratizing investment is to use expanded participation in decision-making as a means of improving economic performance. While traditionally this has emphasized social objectives, such as housing, income maintenances, etc., there has also been an emphasis on economic growth. Infrastructure investment has been a high priority, as has investment in the skills of the work force. One objective of worker management is to improve productivity through participation.

Public control over investment can also make inroads into developing a more effective macroeconomic policy. Such a policy could emphasize high employment and high consumption, with efficient mobilization of savings and a targeting of new investment into areas that are both socially and economically productive.

TWO EXAMPLES

Capital is formed when the savings of the economy as a whole are transformed into new investment. Savings represent the excess of what is produced over what is used for current consumption. The transformation of savings into new investments—factories, machines, farm implements, research laboratories, residential and commercial buildings, etc.—generates jobs and income in the short term, and larger output, new processes and, hopefully, less costly products over time.

Converting today's savings into higher standards of living in the future involves a number of institutions. Savings go into banks, insurance companies, savings and loan associations, money-market funds, etc. The institutions then lend the funds to others making the actual investments. Savings are used to buy corporate stocks and bonds, giving companies funds for investment, and, especially for corporations and also occasionally with individuals, used directly to purchase investment goods. Savings are also used to finance government, through the purchase of government securities or via taxation. The number and range of financial institutions involved in the savings-investment process have grown enormously in the last decade and a half. This growth began with one of the first pieces of deregulatory legislation, the Bank Holding Company Act of 1969, which removed many of the restrictions imposed upon banks during the 1930s. Fueled later by inflation and the rapid growth in money and finance of the 1970s, financial intermediation has become a boom industry. One result has been a wave of large mergers, with such giants as Shearson/American Express, Prudential/Bache, and Sears Roebuck seeking to become financial supermarkets of the 1980s.

The conversion of savings into investment is influenced by the policies of the institutions who gather the funds and make the loans, and by market conditions, including interest rates, costs of investment equipment, profitability of new investment, etc., which provide the incentives that influence investment decisions. Reaganomics emphasizes incentives—so did Keynesian economics, but that wasn't apparent at the time—and the traditional free-market approach has long argued that it is expected rates of return and costs that dominate investment decisions.

Any attempt to influence savings and investment decisions needs to confront both the way in which those decisions are made and how the incentive system operates. Two examples of the use of savings to fund investment are the activities of pension funds and of government. Both are large and present possibilities for change.

Pension Funds

Private-sector and government-employee pension funds have grown tremendously over the last few decades, and today represent a massive conglomeration of wealth. Pension funds are fed by regular contributions from employees and employers. Both forms of contribution represent personal savings; employer contributions are mostly in lieu of wages, as greater pension contributions and higher wages have usually been taken as alternatives in collective bargaining. The contributions are invested in various financial and real assets by fund managers, and they accumulate over time. The ultimate objective of a fund's investment strategy is to be able to generate enough cash to meet the fund's obligations to workers as they retire.

While contributions to a pension fund represent savings by wage and salary earners, rarely do the workers who contribute have a say in managing the assets. Except in industries with large numbers of small employers—such as construction or trucking, where unions frequently manage the funds—private pension funds are managed by the company or by a third-party trustee, usually a bank trust department or an insurance company. Government-employee funds are usually managed by an agency established for that purpose. The investment practices of pension funds have tended to be very traditional ones, with much of their money being invested in government bonds and the stocks and bonds of large corporations.

The structure and policies of pension funds illustrate why democratization is needed. Those who contribute their savings do not have a say in how those savings are to be used. They receive the benefits of their use, in the form of income after retirement, but the ability to use that wealth to achieve other economic and political objectives has been taken out of their hands.

In a significant number of instances, the situation isn't even this favorable. There have been numerous problems of workers losing pension rights when companies fail or disappear through merger and acquisition, or workers losing rights because they change companies or industries, or have spells of unemployment interspersed among many years of productive labor. The federal government addressed some of these abuses with reform legislation in 1974, but many problems persist.

Not only have workers little control over the use of their accumulated pension wealth, but all too often the companies and trustees who manage the funds have used that wealth in ways inimicable to the interests of the workers. Funds, for example, will purchase the stock of a company irrespective of whether that company is unionized or not. Fund managers will consistently vote their stockholdings in support of management, thereby reaffirming the basic power structure of corporate America. And there have been instances where pension funds have been invested in housing, office construction and other real-estate projects where the ultimate users are the wealthy or the upper middle class, rather than union members or government workers.

The justification for such practices is that the primary responsibility of pension managers is to generate sufficient returns to meet the fund's obligation to pay out pensions, and the way to accomplish this is to seek a portfolio in which high returns and minimum risk are the guiding motives. While this may be a laudable objective, even here there have been many instances of investment policies being geared to the needs of the company, not the fund. For example, many funds emphasize stock-market investments in the hope that rising stock prices will generate capital gains, which, when realized, will take the place of cash contributions from the company. Company-managed funds have also been known to buy company stock to fight off hostile take-over attempts.

Changing the practices of pension funds requires, first of all, a change in how funds are managed. Elected union representatives should have decision-making authority, and these representatives should come from throughout the union, not just the international headquarters. The criteria for pension-fund investments, and the institutions eligible to be fund managers, could both be broadened. Another objective would be to end internal abuses.

The primary purpose of the pension fund is to ensure that those who contribute have income after retirement. In the absence of a broad and effective Social Security system, this must remain the primary objective. But while respecting the need for pension funds to earn income for their recipients, it is still possible to have the funds managed in such a way as to have a more positive effect on economic development.

One approach is to follow the lead of investors who have adopted social performance criteria in choosing which corporate securities to purchase. A portfolio that rates companies not just on their profitability and risk but also on their performance on social criteria—such as whether they are unionized, their record on pollution and hiring of minorities, whether they do business in South Africa, etc.—will perform as well as portfolios chosen solely on the basis of expected return. The state of California has begun using social investment criteria in managing its employee pension funds.

There is some scope for moving even further from the traditional definitions of return, which tie any pension-fund strategy to corporate profits, however indirect. It might be desirable to invest pension assets in health, education, housing or other socially needed projects where those who are contributing to the fund and those already retired can share directly in the benefits from the investment. Investing in condominiums for the wealthy, which some pension funds have done, gives a monetary return to the fund. Investing in housing for the middle and lower income groups may provide a lower direct return; but if the housing is then available to fund contributors at less than market rates, there is a second flow of returns, not captured by the portfolio but still very relevant.

Funds that are geographically based, or at least have a substantial presence in an area, can target investments to aid in the economic development of the area. Following this principle, the New York City Police Pension Fund is loaning money for housing rehabilitation in poor and moderate-income neighborhoods. The loans will be insured by state and federal agencies, suggesting a formula for cooperation that can be applied in a wider variety of situations.

Another area of cooperation is that pension funds can work with other democratically managed agencies, such as community planning boards, or appropriate government agencies in coordinating investment strategies to meet social and economic objectives of both the union and a larger community.

Government and Investment

The government is already very active in managing capital and carrying out investment products, but such activity is rarely called "investment" and is usually hidden amid a confusing set of budget categories.

Governments in the United States have built roads, airports and harbors; carried out research leading to new products and processes; built factories; constructed educational facilities, etc. All of this would be considered investment by any reasonable definition of that term.

One of the major problems in assessing government's role in the savings-investment process is definitional. Government budgets typically do not distinguish between outlays for current expenses and expenditures for capital projects. Public-finance economists have long argued for separating the two types of expenditure, on the grounds that they are different in their economic effects and can and should be financed differently. For example, current expenditures could be financed out of tax revenues, while investment expenditures could be financed out of borrowings on the grounds that these expenditures will improve the prospects for higher income and tax revenues in the future. Whatever the justification, a serious attempt at constructing a capital budget for the United States government would show how government activity contributes to investment, and be a useful tool for future planning.

Any redefinition should also tackle the notion of return. Typically, private investment is evaluated in terms of expected returns, or profits. But it is widely accepted that focusing on private returns is insufficient. Some of the costs of investment, such as air and water pollution, are not borne by the company undertaking the investment, so that the economic returns to society as a whole are less than the returns to the company. And in some cases, the potential economic benefits for the entire society are much greater than those that can be realized by a single company. This is likely to be the case for such traditional public-works expenditures as highways and harbors. It is also now recognized to be the case for education and worker health and safety, items not traditionally considered as investment. Because companies cannot or will not undertake such investment, it is clear that even in a largely private-enterprise society, there is substantial scope for improving economic performance via public-sector investment.

The acceptance of a narrow definition of return has hampered many of the efforts of governmental and quasi-governmental bodies. The Port of New York Authority, a bistate governmental agency responsible for much of the transportation resources of the metropolitan New York area, has adopted extremely conservative investment policies. The Tennessee Valley Authority, while continuing to maintain a low price for its power, has nonetheless acted like a private company in its attitude toward environmental issues. In both cases, concern for the bottom line has become a dominant motive.

With agencies such as the Port Authority and the TVA, redefining return is only a surface issue. These agencies act like private firms because of the constraints imposed on their behavior over many years of political give-and-take. Government departments and agencies have been largely prevented from engaging in activities that directly compete with the private sector, or which follow principles that contradict those of the private sector. Thus, government was brought in to reorganize the railroads in the Northeast when they were in trouble, but now that Conrail is ready to make a profit, the administration wants to sell it to private capital. The TVA is another case in point. Its success in spurring development in the Tennessee Valley and in keeping power costs low led to private power interests redoubling their efforts to prevent other regional authorities from being established. These examples suggest that it takes good politics as well as good ideas to change investment practices.

Politics impedes progress in other ways. Government, with its immense taxing and borrowing powers, has access to tremendous amounts of potential capital. A substantial portion of existing efforts to turn this potential into reality is undermined by political pressures that have little to do with long-term investment strategies.

Half of all federal government research and development expenditures are for the military, and little of that has any explicit role in economic development. The government owns a substantial chunk of the plant and equipment used by military contractors. These facilities are leased to the companies, frequently at attractive rates. There are also military production facilities that are both owned and operated by the government.

The economic costs of a large military budget have been extensively documented. With the military budget a major contributor to the federal deficit, and with military contractors using the scarce labor and other inputs needed for civilian capital expansion, the rising military budget may be one of the biggest barriers to achieving long-term economic growth.

There is an alternative, which is to reduce military spending to levels needed for true national security and convert substantial portions of the defense sector to meeting civilian economic objectives.

Conversion planning has been debated in the recent past, but it has never achieved widespread support. There are many reasons for this: Success of right-wing hysteria around the "Russian threat" undercuts moves for defense-budget cuts; political links among defense contractors and members of Congress help keep the money flowing; the availability of defense jobs in a weak economy ties communities to defense interests; the lack of extensive planning mechanisms makes conversion seem unrealistic—to mention the most obvious.

Past difficulties in bringing progressive economic ideas to policy fruition are legion. But knowledge of these difficulties can lead to positive change in the future. An agenda should include the following items.

Those institutions that control investment should be democratically managed, or have their activities subject to supervision by democratically chosen government or private bodies. Election of pension-fund managers is one suggestion, but this can be extended to apply to banks, insurance companies, corporations, etc. The apprioriate governing bodies of these institutions could be opened to include representatives of labor, their customers, regions and communities most affected by their activities, etc.

A related goal is to have institutions that control investment funds follow criteria designed to achieve both social and economic growth objectives. Democratizing the institutions will help achieve this goal, but greater awareness and pressure from others, imaginative schemes for accomplishing such objectives, government aid in the form of tax breaks, subsidies, etc., would also be needed.

Each institution has its own needs, and does not exist solely to meet broader community or national economic or social goals. Pension funds need to provide income for retirement; some military production would be needed for national defense irrespective of its economic consequences. If individual practices are more successful in achieving economic growth and meeting social objectives, then it will be less necessary to emphasize the individual goals. But they will always exist.

Democratic investment policies will not succeed if they are not coordinated with each other, and if they do not exist in the context of a national economic-growth policy. Thus, an overall strategy aimed at economic growth would be needed, including more direct intervention to control inflation rather than relying on the traditional mechanism of high unemployment and a deep recession, combined with greater coordination of local and regional investment strategies. This does not imply highly centralized planning; much could be coordinated at local and regional levels. The positive fruits of such examples as the Tennessee Valley Authority can be built upon. But without a national, and effective, commitment to expansionary policies, each institution will have to fall back upon protecting its own interests as its primary objective.

None of this is new and none of it is particularly difficult, at the conceptual level. What is difficult is putting together the political coalition to bring it about. Without such an effective coalition, the best progressive ideas will, as has happened so often in the past, turn into conservative programs, providing some of the benefits hoped for but also reinforcing the very power they were designed to replace.

4

Attacking Poverty
with Economic Policy

Howard Stanback

By the early 1960s, liberalism achieved its political pinnacle with the election of John Kennedy as president. The election not only returned Democrats to power but brought out in the open the principles of Keynesian economics to guide federal policy on practically every issue. In regard to the issue of poverty, there emerged the fairly new assertion that poverty could indeed be eliminated through a combination of direct economic subsidies to the poor, programs to break the so-called culture of poverty, and, most important, fiscally inspired economic growth. In fact such subsidized consumption by the poor (and those working in poverty programs) was considered an integral element of economic-growth policy. The elimination of poverty was both an expected outcome of growth and a vehicle through which growth could be created.

The very idea that poverty could be eliminated or even should be eliminated was rather novel—at least until the Great Depression, at which point the Keynesian variant of economic liberalism entered the national debate on economic growth. Traditional wisdom to that time held that poverty, as reflected in the unequal distribution of wealth and income, was an essential element of the economy. Inequality allegedly inspired competition and productivity. Those at the bottom were inspired to work, and to work harder, by the relative affluence of those at the top. Those at the top, through their savings and investment, provided "trickle-down" resources for those at the bottom. Those in the middle were so fearful of winding up on the bottom, they worked harder not to get there. People who did not work had made the "voluntary" decision not to work. To the extent that poverty

Howard Stanback is assistant professor of economics at the New School for Social Research.

was seen as solvable, it was viewed as a product of personality flaws as opposed to a product of systematic processes.

The rise of the right and Reaganism seems to have returned in part to the old wisdom on poverty while offering some new and interesting claims. While not stating outright that poverty is essential, it should be abundantly clear by now that the direct subsidization of the poor is no longer an acceptable economic-growth strategy. Reagan's tax cut and budgetary policies are designed to benefit the upper end of the wealth and income scale—a return to the concept of trickle-down economic growth. Such a growth strategy implicitly accepts and even advocates inequality because there must be those who will save and invest, and only the rich can do that—so the theory goes.*

It is apparent in the design of current federal policy that the elimination of poverty is no longer a goal, nor is it even on the list of desirable or possible accomplishments for the U.S. The current dilemmas of the U.S. and world economic crisis have shifted any discussions of the elimination of poverty to the issue of economic recovery.

The economic crisis has not only increased the incidence of poverty among high-risk groups—minorities, female heads of households, children and the elderly—it has also brought white male industrial workers into, or to the brink of, poverty. Yet poverty persists and intensifies. A brief review of the data suggests that there are at least two sides to the poverty in the United States. The first side is not very new—it consists primarily of minorities and women, usually female heads of households and their children. Based on the official (1982) federal poverty standard of $8,380 for a parent and three dependent children, the poverty rate for blacks declined significantly between 1959 and 1970 from 54.9 percent to 32.2 percent. However, by 1980 the proportion of blacks in poverty had remained virtually unchanged. In 1975, 30.1 percent of blacks were in poverty, and in 1980 the proportion rose to 31.1 percent.[1] This represented an increase of over 600,000 black people in poverty between 1975 and 1980. The proportion of whites in poverty fell from 16.5 percent in 1959 to 8.1 percent in 1970, but rose to 8.6 percent in 1980. The proportion of the U.S. population in poverty fell from 22.0 percent in 1959 to 12.6 percent in 1970, but has risen from 11.4 percent in 1975 to 16.4 percent in 1981. This trend will be examined below.

* George Gilder and David Stockman are the most glaring representatives of this perspective.

Many social scientists and advocates for the poor have long been calling for use of the U.S. Bureau of Labor Statistics "lower-than-moderate" budget standard as a measure of poverty. Even this level is quite austere, allowing adults only two beers a week and five movies a year. Using this standard—$12,585 for a family of four in 1979—the proportion of black families in poverty was 54.0 percent. The proportion of white families in poverty was 26 percent.[2] Over one-half of all black families and over one-fourth of all white families were in poverty at the beginning of the 1980s based on this standard. The decline in the economy strongly suggests that these numbers have grown since 1979.

An examination of the impoverishment of women presents an equally if not more dramatic picture. According to the National Advisory Commission on Economic Opportunity: "All other things being equal, if the proportion of the poor in female households [i.e., female-headed families] were to continue to increase at the same rate as it did from 1967 to 1978, the poverty population would be composed solely of women and their children before the year 2000."[3]

The feminization of poverty is the rather recent process whereby women make up a rapidly increasing share of the poverty population in the U.S. While there is a mixture of male- and female-headed households entering poverty status, the probability that a female-headed household with children will be impoverished is significantly greater than the same probability for a male-headed household with children. For blacks in families headed by women, the odds are three times that of black families headed by men—64.8 percent to 20.3 percent in 1980. For whites the comparable odds are 4.5 to 1, 41.6 percent to 9.0 percent in 1980. The proportion of impoverished blacks in female-headed families has declined only slightly since 1970—67.7 percent to 64.8 percent in 1980—but the population has increased absolutely by almost 500,000 people.[4] The population of impoverished whites in female-headed households has increased by almost 600,000 people.[5]

While the feminization of poverty is rather contemporary, its roots are at least as old and deep as the racist process of black impoverishment. The growth in female-headed households in poverty, especially among whites, is most immediately a product of the growth in the number of female single parents. As women, for whatever reason, were "forced" from the patriarchal securities of marriage, they had to confront the sexist character of unequal pay and discriminatory hiring in the labor market. Sexist domination, which was experienced primarily in the household, moved thoroughly into the labor market. The impoverishment of minorities and women is a product of deeply rooted racism and sexism as well as faulty economic policy.

Between 1970 and 1980, the proportion of impoverished whites in male-headed households with children grew from 7.3 percent to 9.0 percent—an increase of over 100,000 people.[6] While black and female poverty is rooted in the long-term entrenchment of racism and patriarchy in the U.S. economy, this new wave of poverty appears to be directly associated with the crisis character of the economy as evidenced in the past fifteen years. This does not suggest that the trend is temporary; given the severity of the structural economic shifts that have emerged, such workers may find themselves and their children permanently out of work. The point here is that the processes that created the "usually poor"—minorities and women—are rather distinct from those that have forced white male workers out of employment in mining, automobiles, steel and other depressed U.S. industries.

The problem with much of the economic-recovery debate is that it fails to address those factors that reproduce the usually poor. "Putting America back to work" typically excludes policies that address those elements of the U.S. economy that foster extreme inequality between minorities and whites and between women and men. It is generally assumed that economic growth will benefit some minorities and some women in poverty, but the extent of its impact is highly questionable.[7] One gets the impression from the economic-policy debate that such inequalities either do not exist or will be automatically removed if such policies are implemented. The remainder of this essay will consider both the characteristics of the U.S. economy that create and re-create poverty and economic-policy proposals in light of such characteristics.

THE CREATION OF POVERTY

There are at least three broad arenas endemic to the U.S. version of capitalism that make poverty a systematic product of our society.

First is the entrenchment of racist and patriarchal relations that establish unequal economic (and political) status. Second is the structure of labor markets that divides good jobs from bad jobs. And third is the organization of production in such a manner that decisions about production are made by those whose primary if not only goal is profit. While there are certainly other features of U.S. society, such as our education system, that influence the reproduction of poverty, it is in these three arenas that the principal shaping of an impoverished population emerges.

Since the beginnings of our society, race and sex have been major determinants of the division of labor and of the distribution of the fruits of labor. Numerous studies have documented the allocation of the worst jobs—lowest-paying jobs—by race and sex: Blacks, Hispanics and women have consistently found themselves in the lowest-paying jobs. Moreover, race and sex have been fairly constant criteria in allocating the burden of the periodic recessions and crises that characterize the economy. Minority unemployment, especially, runs consistently higher than white unemployment. It seems logical that the combination of excessive unemployment and excessive concentration in the worst jobs would generate excessive poverty. While this is borne out statistically, few of the proposals for economic recovery speak to this endemic feature of the U.S. economy.

Economic policy, if it is to address this poverty-producing feature, must be of the type that closes the income, unemployment and occupational gaps between racial minorities and whites and between women and men. This requires policies that generally equalize incomes across occupations. Specifically, in regard to race and sex inequalities, comprehensive and stringent enforcement of affirmative-action laws are necessary. Moreover, the timing of such policy must make equalization a priority. Economic growth as a priority is inadequate to address these traditional forces of impoverishment. Even as stagnation persists, many minorities and women are working or looking for work. To postpone such policies is to accept one of the most endemic features of American poverty.

It is worth recalling that the U.S. economy is structured in such a way as to divide labor-market competition into rather distinct segments.[8] There are labor markets associated with a primary or core sector made up of giant corporations. The jobs in this sector tend to be higher-paying and more secure than jobs not in this sector. While there are trend variations in the security and pay of jobs within the primary sector, such jobs are quite distinguishable from jobs in the secondary sector. Firms in the secondary sector tend to be small or marginal and in highly competitive industries. Jobs in this sector are less secure and lower-paying. They include the jobs held by the working poor. They are also, not coincidentally, the jobs held disproportionately by minorities and women. Over one-third of all jobs are in the secondary sector.[9] Policies of income equalization, publicly planned subsidization, and publicly planned generation of good jobs —nonpoverty jobs—will be necessary if poverty is to be ameliorated. This ultimately requires addressing the ways in which the organization of production systematically generates poverty.

The first aspect is the control of investment solely by owners of capital. The second is the allocation of capital on the criterion of profitability. The private control of capital is accepted as an absolutely necessary condition for economic prosperity. The private pursuit of profits is heralded as the driving force behind economic development. To stray from these dictums is to invite something just short of death and destruction, not to mention charges of heresy. However, evidence from the current economic crisis, along with comparisons with other capitalist nations, suggests strongly that the lack of public authority over investment has helped foster economic hard times.[10] Moreover, the criterion of profitability has led to massive disinvestment in the U.S. and the subsequent deterioration of communities and the impoverishment of its citizens.[11]

TOWARD AN ALTERNATIVE

The current economic-policy debate in the U.S. involves essentially three perspectives. Only two are dominant, but neither holds promise for the problem of poverty. The third perspective, while not yet politically strong, represents significant promise with certain qualifications.

The clearly dominant perspective is Reaganomics. This perspective has been adequately critiqued and reviewed elsewhere,[12] and thus requires little to assert that it holds forth no positive promise for the poor—new or old. It should be noted, however, that the principal economic development of Reaganomics directed toward the poor is the Urban Enterprise Zone proposal—a job-creation strategy based on the principle of dramatic cost reductions for enterprises who locate in poor urban communities. Such cost reductions would come from tax breaks and—most important for this discussion—from the elimination or reduction of the minimum wage. While this may (doubtfully) succeed in creating jobs, the jobs would be of the worst type in terms of wages and overall working conditions. Such enterprises and their jobs would be in the secondary sector and would be a new series of jobs for the working poor. Needless to say, this fails to address the second criterion cited above.

Reagan's affirmative-action strategy also obviously falls far short of what is essential, as does the policy of leaving the economic decisions in the hands of capital.

The second popularly discussed set of economic policies, which are currently not on the political agenda, are those of the industrial-policy proponents. Often referred to as "corporatist," most noted industrial-policy advocates[13] call for rational government intervention in the economy in order to "guide" investment in such a way as to generate economic growth. Such guiding would come from a central but politically insulated economic planning body that would base its decisions on criteria of profitability. The body would represent labor, business and government and would operate on the principle that a unified consensual approach is necessary given the history of adversary relations among these three. Industrial policy would join with monetary and fiscal policy to generate government-"induced" economic growth. The implicit assumption is that such growth would reduce if not eliminate poverty.

While many advocates of industrial policies in the Democratic party and in the corporate world recommend the expansion of safety-net provisions for the poor, there is little or nothing in the dominant industrial-policy proposals that speaks to the elimination of the most traditional forms of U.S. poverty. First of all, such proposals are essentially designed to either reindustrialize certain depressed industries, such as steel and automobiles, or expand new and promising industries, such as high tech and some services. If this aspect of the industrial-policy scheme were successful, it would reach into the ranks of only the recently poor—the recently laid-off industrial worker. Moreover, the new jobs to be created in high tech and services are overwhelmingly lower in pay. To a large extent they expand the pool of working-poor jobs. One study reports that 70 percent of all new private-sector jobs created between 1973 and 1980 were low-paid, mostly women's jobs, in retail and services sectors. The so-called sunrise industries do not shed much light on the relief of poverty.[14]

Without special features, industrial-policy proposals rely on profit-led growth, which has historically failed to address the endemic character of poverty for minorities and women. In fact, some of the proposals would reproduce such inequalities on an even wider scale by relying on the profitability criterion. If high profitability is present for industries that provide low-paying jobs, the number of working poor in this country could in fact grow along with the economy.

A third set of policy proposals is progressively aimed at "taming" the unstable and poverty-reproducing character of capitalism.[15] Traditional progressive wisdom asserts that nothing short of a socialist transformation could bring about the stability essential for eliminating poverty and inequality. But the new set of progressive economic-policy proposals would attempt to reform capitalism by democratizing economic decision-making, reducing income inequalities through public policy as opposed to market activity; public subsidy of home child care as well as child-care facilities; public guaranties of decent jobs; the development of community enterprise; and generally empowering workers to democratically participate in economic decision-making. The axis of these developments is the call for democratically planned economic growth through consumer subsidization, and the reduction of waste rooted in a profit-led system.

Certain elements of this set of proposals at least begin to address the poverty complex described earlier. The explicit call for wage/income equalization through solidarity wages, affirmative action, and direct and substantial subsidies of child care for single-parent families clearly addresses the inequality problem of race and sex. The right to and development of decent jobs speaks to the problems created by a secondary labor market. The most questionable element is whether the democratic planning dimension of the proposals can overcome the inherent instabilities of the economy that help reproduce the first two problems—race and sex discrimination and segmented labor markets. The principle in these proposals is to elevate objectives other than profits to the top. With such social criteria as clean air and water, equality and security, the belief is that instabilities can be minimized if not eliminated.

Theorists, planners and community activists agree that neither giant corporations nor the federal government will ever speak completely to the issue, which few other proposals from the Left or Right really address. One particular aspect of such proposals stands out for more discussion. The call for the development of nonprofit, community-based enterprises speaks to a problem that confronts other proposals and also confronts historically poor people. There is an implicit recognition by the "democratic alternatives" camp that neither Reaganomics nor the standard industrial-policy proposals address the fact that the economic growth that has traditionally characterized this economy confronts poverty only in the last instance, if at all. That is, economic growth, as we have witnessed it, fails to completely (or permanently) eliminate poverty—to reach into the usually poor population and significantly transform it.

This requires a bottom-up approach to economic policy. It requires policies that facilitate the struggles of local communities to develop community-owned and -controlled enterprises that reflect both the indigenous character and the democratically determined needs of those communities.

The question must be raised as to why a nonprofit, community-based economic-development strategy is critical to the resolution of endemic poverty. There are at least three reasons that justify this component of economic policy.

First, macroeconomic and industrial-policy schemes are primarily schemes of national planning. While in principle there is no reason why such schemes cannot reach the endemic poor, the history of U.S. economic planning suggests strongly that they will not reach the endemic poor. This is largely a result of the functional nature of racism and sexism in the reproduction of poverty. For economic growth to reach deeply into the ranks of the usually poor would be to destroy that function. Additionally, most industrial-policy proposals, as indicated earlier, fail to address the systematic nature of poverty in the U.S. or other capitalist nations. The examples of other developed capitalist nations also offer little evidence that the national economic planning of the industrial-policy type will lift either minorities or women out of their traditional position of impoverishment. Consequently, localized development activity is essential, if only to fill the "natural" voids of national planning.

Second, not only is poverty endemic to the normal macro processes of U.S. capitalism, it is also endemic regionally within the U.S. Such poverty may be rooted in the uneven development of the economy, but what such uneven development leaves are different levels and types of skills, different levels of infrastructural development, different levels of dependencies on resources outside the region, and different levels of public resources between cities, counties and states. To be eliminated, the particular character of poverty by region must be integrally considered. No macro scheme of developing high-tech, targeting sunrise or sunset industries, or free-market mechanisms will take these particulars into account.

Third, economic development is as much a political process as it is an economic process. Such development reflects the efforts of individuals and groups to obtain the power necessary to control the social, economic and political relations that determine the overall quality of life. It is especially true for minorities that their degree of control of political and economic resources in this country is a critical determinant of their quality of life. Given the history of racism in the U.S., the only way that minorities can ensure that their interests are even reasonably represented is to establish control of critical political and economic institutions that shape their lives. The power to do this currently exists primarily at the city and county levels, with some expanding influence at the state level.

But it is not enough to control the institutions—they must be controlled in such a manner as to bring the most broad-based benefits, hence community (democratic) control. One cannot rely on the individual entrepreneur, white or black, to act in the interest of the entire community. Additionally, as stated earlier, such a structure of control of enterprises is a poverty-reproducing factor.

What about profit? The two important aspects of profits in any enterprise are, first, that the existence of profits (of a minimal size) attracts further investment to the enterprise and, second, that profits provide income, hopefully growing for the entrepreneur(s)/investor(s). If the primary interest, however, is to improve the overall economic well-being of a community, then our concern is not with profits in the form of income to the entrepreneur; our concern is with providing adequate revenues to pay decent wages, to provide quality services, and to grow and expand if socially desirable. Without the requirement of providing income to entrepreneurs/investors, the ability to do all three of the above increases. That portion of excess revenues over costs can be channeled toward wages, quality products and expansion. It is even logical that the elimination of the entrepreneurs' income will improve price competitiveness.

What about competition? The record of community-owned enterprises is both negative and positive in terms of competing and lasting. The principal vehicle through which such enterprises have developed has been community development corporations (CDCs), although cooperatives, worker-owned enterprises and publicly owned enterprises are included in the category of community enterprises. While there exist no recent comprehensive data on the success or failure of CDC enterprises, a random sample taken in 1972 indicated that as few as one in fifteen survived the first five years.[16] This is twice the rate of average business failures. This study took place only a few years after federal funds were made available and as CDCs were learning the ropes of enterprise development. With the massive withdrawal of federal funds under Reagan and the intensification of the economic crisis in the 1970s, it is doubtful that any dramatic change has emerged in the success rate.

It is reasonable to suggest, however, that the excessive failures of CDC enterprises are due to the following technical reasons that can be readily overcome through the provision of adequate resources: (1) undercapitalization; (2) poor market analysis; and (3) lack of various technical skills related to the type of business developed. None of these reasons represents a theoretical obstacle to the effective competition of CDC enterprises. Adequate capitalization must be available to provide the time and other resources necessary to compete. These resources include training, research and technology. The adequate provisions of all of these does not ensure success, but in the context of community control, the fate of the employees and other social criteria are central determinants in deciding whether an enterprise will remain open or not.

Some CDCs/Coops have in fact proven to be quite notable successes—the Federation of Southern Rural Cooperatives in Alabama, the Delta Foundation in Mississippi, and the East Los Angeles Community Union, for example. While each has suffered tremendous setbacks with the withdrawal of federal funds, all had established strong local political and economic foundations to sustain them through the current period.

Given the obvious need for strong capitalization, a key question emerges: From where will the capital for such ventures come? It should be fairly obvious that the only source of significant potential is the public sector—the local, state and federal governments. While some community enterprises have and will receive corporate and foundation support, the bulk of support must be drawn from government units.

Why should local and state governments be interested? There are two answers. First, state and local governments are caught in the game of "who can provide the best business climate" to create jobs. Tax cuts to corporations, relaxation of minimum-wage proposals, and antiunion policies are basic public-policy tools used today to generate local economic growth. In addition to the damage done to public coffers as a result of such competition, reliance on tax measures has done little if anything to attract business to any U.S. location or keep it there. Moreover, these approaches tend to put the citizens of cities and states at the complete mercy of corporations in regard to affirmative action, public education policy, commercial developments, environmental quality, housing stock, and the concentration of infrastructural development. Such control, as stated earlier, serves only to reproduce poverty.

Cities and states do have an option: They can begin to direct their resources toward the development of community enterprises of the types discussed here. This option not only places more control of economic development in democratic processes, it also permits the kind of economic planning that speaks to the indigenous poverty of a region. It allows the shaping of enterprises to meet local employment needs as opposed to simply bringing in a new source of tax revenue—which has been abated for ten or more years.

The second reason for city and local interest is connected to the political action essential to making any proposed economic policy a reality. Very simply, political activism will have to make elected officials intersted in an alternative to the traditional vehicles of economic development. It is obvious that without the necessary political activism that advocates supportive officials and policies, few government units will consider them.

What can federal, state and local economic policy do to facilitate this kind of development? At the federal level, at minimum, a restoration of the over $40 million allocated by the mid-1970s to community economic-development corporations. However, much more is necessary. The allocations should be very long-term if not permanent, and should cover not only capital costs but also training and policies that favor such enterprises to facilitate competition. These could include priorities in government contracting as well as special protections if international trade is involved.

But to expect much from the federal level at this point implies that there will soon be elected supporters of such policies. This appears to be more likely at the state and local levels. Cities and states can do the following to support the development of community enterprises:

1. Set aside a substantial amount of public revenues to capitalize community efforts to create or purchase enterprises that meet the social needs of the community. This may come through worker-owned or community-owned enterprises.

2. Utilize powers of eminent domain to take over the facilities of enterprises that attempt to leave without fair compensation to employees or without providing a reasonable opportunity for the employees or the government to purchase them. Such enterprises can be then run by either the government, the community, the workers, or some combination.

3. Utilize powers over bank loans, pension funds and other sources of investment to direct them to community enterprises.

4. Provide special considerations to such enterprises in the contracting of government services.

5. Provide centralized support in research and development and training to reduce the costs to the enterprises.

6. Generally encourage and facilitate the formation of community and/or worker organizations whose goal is to develop such enterprises.

While there have indeed been failures, the successes of community enterprises—profit and nonprofit—are most notable given these times of economic crisis and federal cuts. Two cases are cited for consideration.

In 1979 five former employees of the bankrupt Bertie Industries, a textile firm in Windsor, North Carolina, organized the Workers Owned Sewing Company in response to the shutdown. By the end of 1983, there were forty worker/owners with firm funding commitments that will allow an expansion to sixty-five or seventy worker/

owners. One hundred jobs were lost when Bertie shut down. Although most of the workers in the firm are new, many are former Bertie employees. An employee becomes a member after the contribution of $100. This gives workers voting rights in the policy formation of the firm. While workers initially paid themselves slightly less than Bertie Industries paid, they have since made up these losses through wage increases.

The Workers Owned Sewing Company broke even in 1982. In the 1984 fiscal year, they expect to receive a *500-percent* return on the membership investment. The success in large part is due to two factors: (1) production contracts with K-Mart, Sears and other smaller firms; and (2) low-interest investment loans from churches and foundations. Only after the company broke even did they receive a $300,000 federal Community Development grant for modernization and expansion. Bank support has been negligible, although they are now in a position to afford bank rates.

This example only hints at the possibilities. The Workers Owned Sewing Company managed growth during an economic crisis and within an industry in extremely difficult times in this country. With creative financing, sound marketing and a democratically controlled management structure, they are a success. With an expansion of state and federal aid, there can be many other such firms.

The Federation of Southern Cooperatives began in 1969 and has long been recognized as the critical rural economic-development center in the South. The federation has organized and provided technical assistance to agricultural and manufacturing cooperatives and credit unions throughout the Deep South. Since 1969 over 10,000 small independent farmers, mostly black, have participated in cooperative marketing, purchasing and business management. It is reasonable to suggest, given land-loss trends in small farms, that without the federation's assistance many of these individuals would have lost their land by now. The twenty-five credit unions currently include 13,000 members with $3 million on deposit. Over the years the credit unions have provided approximately $18 million in loans, one-fourth of which were to individual and cooperative enterprises of the profit and non-profit type—leading to the creation of over 1,000 jobs. The manufacturing cooperatives include handicrafts, commercial sewing, fishing, and housing construction. They, too, have created over 1,000 jobs. At the height of federal funding, the Federation employed an additional

465 trainers, organizers, field staff, etc., through VISTA and CETA.

The overwhelming bulk of Federation funds were raised for the independent cooperatives. The Federation, the organizing and technical-assistance unit, relied heavily on public-sector support. Contrary to rightist skeptics, the program has worked. With the Reagan cuts and an expensive court battle against charges of fraud* (from which the federation has been cleared), it has suffered tremendous damage to its core operations. Rather than weaken the foundation of its member cooperatives, the Federation has assumed an extremely austere posture with twenty staff members. The Federation's future is unclear, but the need for it remains strong. They have only begun to scratch the depths of the long-impoverished communities of the Deep South. They have, however, a clear track record that establishes the viability of this approach.

As indicated earlier, the formation of successful community enterprises requires as intense a political struggle as it does an economic struggle. The rationale is clear: Without the political struggle of the indigenous poor to control the economic course of their lives, their poverty will be continuously reproduced. The struggle is to direct resources toward community institutions whose interest truly rests with the interests of the poor. Economic policy that successfully resolves the problem of endemic poverty must include this community-based, community-controlled approach or else poverty will persist.

Moreover, the accomplishment of an economic policy that takes such needs into serious account will come only from the struggle of the poor—the usually poor, the newly poor, the near-poor and their allies—to take control of the formation of economic policy. This struggle is currently emerging at the community level. Workers and communities, facing plant closings, are attempting to find ways of holding on to jobs. City and state governments, facing deteriorating infrastructures and revenues, are looking for alternative vehicles for economic development. Minorities and women, facing intensified discrimination and impoverishment, are attempting to construct and control institutions that address the economic, political and social quality of their lives. It is in the context of these struggles that the core

---

* The fraud charges were instigated by the local white power structure when it was apparent that the Federation was creating a situation in which the poor black residents of the area would no longer be dependent on plantation-like employment or on the local public-assistance structure, which guaranteed whites political power.

of alternative economic policy can emerge. While many of these indigenous struggles are disconnected, they do reflect a growing desire of people in this country to gain collective and democratic control of economic processes.

Prudent policy-makers seriously interested in resolving endemic poverty will take this grass-roots movement into full account. Any economic policy that attempts to address the endemic character of poverty must facilitate the formation of indigenous strategies that reflect the concern and sensitivities of communities to their impoverished or potentially impoverished conditions. While this aspect of economic policy is not enough, it is essential. Only when people can actively participate in economic decision-making beyond their "market votes" can endemic poverty become something to be addressed and eliminated.

Notes

1. U.S. Bureau of the Census, Current Population Reports, *Money Income of Households, Families, and Persons in the United States: 1980,* table 26.
2. National Urban League, *The State of Black America, 1981* (Washington, D.C.: NUL Research Department, 1981), 65.
3. National Advisory Commission on Economic Opportunity, *Eleventh Report* (Washington, D.C.: NACED, June 1979).
4. U.S. Bureau of the Census, Current Population Reports, *Money Income of Households, Families, and Persons in the United States: 1980,* table 26.
5. Ibid.
6. Ibid.
7. Bernard Gifford, unpublished paper.
8. For a thorough review of labor-market segmentation theory, see Richard Edwards, *Contested Terrain: The Transformation of the Workplace in the Twentieth Century* (New York: Basic Books, 1979); Michael Reich and David Gordon, eds., *Labor Market Segmentation* (Lexington, Mass.: D.C. Heath, 1975); and *Segmented Work, Divided Workers: The Historical Transformation of Labor in the United States* (New York: Cambridge University Press, 1982).
9. David M. Gordon, *The Working Poor: Towards a State Agenda,* from *Studies in State Development Policies,* vol. 4 (Washington, D.C.: Council of State Planning Commissions, 1980), 6.
10. Samuel Bowles, David M. Gordon, and Thomas E. Weisskopf, *Beyond the Wasteland: A Democratic Alternative to Economic Decline* (Garden City, N.Y.: Anchor Press/Doubleday, 1983), 37–47.
11. Barry Bluestone and Bennett Harrison, the *Deindustrialization of America* (New York: Basic Books, 1982), chs. 1 and 2.
12. Frank Riessman, Colin Greer, and Alan Gartner, *What Reagan Is Doing to Us* (New York: Harper & Row, 1982).

13. Y. Robert Reich, "Why the U.S. Needs an Industrial Policy," *Harvard Business Review,* Jan.–Feb. 1982, 74–81; and Ira Magaziner, *Minding America's Business* (New York: Harcourt Brace Jovanovich, 1982); Felix G. Rohatyn, "Alternatives to Reaganomics," *Journal Inquirer* (Manchester, Conn.); Lester C. Thurow, *Zero-Sum Society* (New York: Basic Books, 1980).

14. Emma Rothschild, "Reagan and the Real America," *New York Review of Books,* 5 Feb. 1981.

15. For information on various such projects around the country, the following organizations can be contacted: Southerners for Economic Justice, Durham, N.C.; Conference on Alternative State and Local Public Policies, Washington, D.C.; The California Project, San Francisco, Calif.; California Plant Closing Project, Los Angeles, Calif.; Industrial Cooperative Association, Somerville, Mass.

16. James Hefner and Gil Serota, *Community Development Corporations: Hope for Blacks in American Ghettos* (Atlanta: Southern Center for Studies in Public Policy, Clark College, 1972).

PART II

THE FUTURE
OF HUMAN SERVICES

Editors' Introduction

It was to education that Dewey directed us in the essay quoted at the beginning of this book. And it is education, or at least schooling, that has captured national attention with a rash of commissions, studies and recommendations. As with Dewey, the American people see education as both hope and battleground for the future. And Diane Ravitch's *Troubled Crusade* (Basic Books, 1983) reminds us of how much the defenders of the status quo teach us lessons from history in order to shape the future.

Once a decade, since the end of World War II, we have had an educational "crisis." In the late 1950s, the success of the Soviet Union's space program triggered concern about the nation's science and mathematics education. In the 1960s, the tide of the civil-rights movement swept into the schools and left programs for desegregation, remedial education for the disadvantaged, bilingual education, and career opportunities in the schools and other human-services agencies. In the 1970s, the focus was on the role of schooling in encouraging children's growth and development.

While several of the 1983 reports focused on segments of schooling —two reports on the high school, one on science and mathematics, and another on school life—three took a more global view: Secretary Bell's National Commission on Excellence in Education, the Education Commission of the States Task Force on Education for Economic Growth, and the Twentieth Century Fund's Task Force on Federal Elementary and Secondary Education Policy. The underlying concern of these three reports focuses on national survival, defined as our economy's ability to compete successfully in the international marketplace. The reports insist that the failures of our education system threaten "our once unchallenged preeminence in commerce, industry, science and technological innovation. . . . America's position in the world may once have been reasonably secure with only a few exceptionally well-trained men and women [but] . . . no longer" (Commission on Excellence). The intensity of international competition, combined with the increasing inadequacy of our schooling, leads to "a conviction that a real emergency is upon us" (Economic Growth Task Force). "The skills that were once possessed by only a few must now be held by the many if the United States is to remain competitive in an advancing technological world" (Federal Policy Task Force).

All three reports define an effective education system as critical to the continuation of our international economic position, and see the deterioration of our current education system making us "a nation at risk" in the global marketplace. Throughout, educational productivity is assumed to be the critical element in economic productivity. Our nation is termed "at risk" because our schools are failing to produce the highly trained, highly skilled men and women our economy needs to compete successfully in international markets. The press for more science and math teachers, for higher standards and advanced courses is designed to increase our schools' capacities to produce more of the trained labor we need to stave off technological competition from other industrialized nations. In this linkage, education plays a supply-side function; economic productivity is assumed to be dependent on the quality of educated labor produced by our schools. Economic decline is defined as a failure of schooling, rather than as a failure of capital investment or worker productivity or management skill.

But suppose our current economic decline is primarily caused by a capital strike—investment in mergers, real estate, other property speculation, and industrial production in low-wage, less-developed countries—against investment in our own domestic industry. Suppose it is not our "high-tech" industries that are thirsting for more adequately trained labor, but our traditional heavy industries that are dying because of the failure of investment in research and development, retooling and expansion. Evidence of intensive capital flight from domestic industry is widespread; where is the evidence that our schools are not producing the trained labor our "high-tech" industries need to assure our continued global dominance? It might just be that for many young people, especially poor and minority youths, those who are the subject of Peter Edelman's essay, the only jobs available are dead-end jobs for which no schooling is adequate preparation. It is easy to demonstrate that such secondary labor-market jobs (characterized by low wages, few benefits or protections, minimal career opportunities) are expanding, while primary-sector jobs (characterized by good pay, benefits and seniority) are contracting. It is much harder to demonstrate why youths facing a lifetime of such secondary-sector employment should invest in education.

These reports attack the wrong problems because they reverse the direction of causality; the economy affects education far more than education affects the economy. To blame schooling for national economic decline is an entertaining but finally trivial diversion from the knotty structural problems plaguing our schools. It is to assume the situation as it seemed a few years ago when Daniel Bell told us that "the proportion of factory workers in the labor force may be as small as the proportion of farmers today." The observation was part of a general belief in the expansive character of the service society and the corollary significance of education in preparing people for careers in that sector. Less well recognized was Harry Braverman's warning that the service sector would begin to produce more menial jobs than careers and that the transfer of workers from factories to white-collar employment was not going to upgrade the mass of the work force.

The school, at the heart of the early promise of service-sector growth, is now stymied by the same disappointments typical of that sector as a whole—namely, a recent history of very limited service efficacy, over professionalized control of policy and delivery, and the least quality services for poor and minority Americans. While the fiscal cutbacks of the Reagan administration will have to be remedied if equality and access to services is ever to be won, the struggle for decent services, like the struggle for decent schooling, only begins there.

The faults of the school mirror those of the other human-services institutions. Just as too often schools fail to satisfy teachers and students, so, too, social-services agencies fail to satisfy workers and clients. The arrogance of the managers of health institutions is captured in the recent comment of the director of a hospital where four cancer patients died due to malfunctioning of its air-conditioning, who said, "We didn't announce it to the public because the public isn't our constituency."

While focusing on new approaches to funding social-welfare programs, Tom Joe, in the first of this section's essays, points out that one must start by rejecting conventional beliefs as to the causes and conditions of poverty. Frank Riessman, in the next essay, shows how a restructured service system must involve the consumer, not in a replay of the 1960s call for governance but in the very fabric of the service itself. Sizer picks up this same theme when he critiques the formulation of schooling being "delivered" to students and the failure to see them as essential participants in their own education, and Yzaguirre and Orum help us to understand the larger significance of bilingual education.

In the struggle to win access to human services, citizens raised critical questions about their rights, personal needs, social values. Groups of citizens—minorities, women, youth—have been vanguard forces for changes. But having won access to expanded services, these same citizens very often become dissatisfied clients, often unable to get a hearing from professionals and the bureaucratic system. Very soon the same forces that urged expanded service began also to demand a more active consumer role in defining and providing them. The thrust of that citizens' demand remains a vital one. It is through that force once again that the recent drive to blame victims for the conditions produced by mean-spirited and narrowly interested public policy can be resisted and reversed.

5

The Case for Income Support

Tom Joe

Over the past three years, the Reagan administration has orchestrated devastating reductions in the major social-welfare programs that were developed over the past twenty years to combat poverty. Through the Omnibus Budget Reconciliation Act of 1981 and the Tax Equity and Fiscal Responsibility Act of fiscal year 1982, needs-tested programs targeted on low-income persons have borne the brunt of the budget ax:

- Aid to Families with Dependent Children (AFDC), the central "welfare" program, which provides cash benefits to over 10.3 million low-income persons, was reduced by approximately 15 percent.
- Food stamps were cut by nearly 20 percent.
- Medicaid, which provides health coverage to low-income persons, was cut by $4 billion through 1985.
- Child nutrition programs, serving low-income children, were cut approximately 30 percent.

The impact of these federal budget cuts on the lives of low-income citizens has been both severe and immediate. One million low-income persons lost their food stamps entirely; the remaining 20 million suffered benefit reductions. The number of children participating in the school lunch program dropped by 3 million. Across the country, hundreds of maternal and child health clinics, which provide prenatal care, closed. The AFDC benefits of hundreds of thousands of families were terminated, despite the fact that most had incomes well below the poverty threshold. When they lost their welfare grants, a majority of these families also lost their Medicaid coverage.

Tom Joe is director of The Center for the Study of Social Policy.

The cumulative effect of these cuts has been to reduce, on all fronts, the resources available to the needy. The income supports that for years have helped the poor provide their families with the basic necessities of life have now been reduced, and in many cases entirely withdrawn. The erosion of the nation's income-support system comes at a time when almost 11 million people are out of work, many of whom are facing poverty for the first time in their lives.

The Census Bureau notes that federal budget cuts may have contributed to the increase in poverty in 1982, when more than 34 million Americans, or 15 percent of the total population, had incomes below the official poverty standard—the highest level in seventeen years.

This alarming growth in the number of poor people, coupled with the substantial federal budget cuts in human service programs, poses a dilemma of sorts for social welfare professionals. One's initial reaction to this crisis is to patch up, to restore the budgets. Yet at the same time, one understands that social policy structures are desparately in need of a complete overhaul. The Reagan approach, while costly and painful, reflects a justified frustration with current welfare programs. In fact, part of the blame for the Reagan administration's easy victories at the expense of the poor lies in the inability of social welfare professionals to defend programs that were already inequitable and badly in need of reform. Social welfare professionals, then, face a choice: Provide stopgap repairs for a failing system or create wholly new approaches to social policy.

When the human costs of diminishing social programs are as great as they are today, it is difficult to think of anything but immediate and often defensive responses. Yet, such myopia may only perpetuate existing flaws in social policy. What many professionals fail to realize is that the coincidence of the dismantling of our national welfare programs and a growing concern about the rising number of poor people creates a prime environment for the development of alternative approaches to social welfare policy. Instead of defending and fine-tuning past programs, the challenge we now face is to create new alternatives that more effectively meet the needs of the poor. These needs have grown ever greater and more complex during the past two decades.

One of the fundamental problems with our current welfare system is that over the years it has assumed the burden of trying to remedy a wide array of social ills. For example, AFDC is supposed to not only provide income support but also train parents for work and collect child-support payments from absent fathers. Welfare programs have been forced to take on these functions because of the inadequacies of other social systems. It is these systems—such as the manpower system, education, health services, and vocational rehabilitation—rather than welfare, that should be our first lines of defense against poverty and dependence.

The overextension of welfare policy into a sort of social panacea is the root of its failure in terms of efficiency and equity, as well as the source of its political vulnerability. The more a single program is touted to do, the more shortcomings it will be found to have. New approaches to social welfare policy, despite the best of intentions, must be wary of seeking to do too much through a single policy.

This essay briefly poses some illustrative alternative approaches to income support policy. It does so not to provide definitive solutions but to draw attention to the important, yet often overlooked, task of formulating and rethinking the basic questions about fulfilling the public responsibility for dependent populations. We need to devise imaginative new strategies, which, to be effective, should meet several criteria.

First, new alternatives must be grounded in an understanding of the needs of persons in poverty. Nothing less is needed than an entirely new conceptualization of the problems of poverty and dependence. Our current definitions of who needs help and why are bound by mythical stereotypes that, increasingly, bear little relation to the multiple causes and conditions of poverty. Current economic conditions have shown us all too painfully that poverty in the U.S. is a multifaceted condition, not restricted to yet another myth, the unmotivated recipient living on the public largesse.

People are poor for many reasons. The welfare population includes both the young and the old; fathers who are incapacitated, and fathers who are unemployed; mothers who have lost husbands, and mothers who never had husbands; the able-bodied and the disabled; people who work and people who don't work but who, according to various interpretations, should work. People end up in poverty because of poor education; poor health; inability to find work; inability to support a family; illness; injury; old age and isolation; unwanted pregnancy; divorce; desertion; and/or physical or mental handicaps. Yet, despite these facts, which are readily apparent from even a superficial look at the public assistance caseloads or press reports on the plight of the poor, our public programs are predicated on the belief that the poor are a monolithic group. Consequently, we have tried to solve all of the ills of all poor people through a single system, rather than pursue multiple solutions targeted at different needs.

Second, any new welfare alternative must be made comprehensible to the recipient as well as the general public. The social welfare community's recent defensive position stems largely from the fact that it has failed to adequately articulate the composition of what has come to be called the "social safety net." For example, many people oppose the notion of welfare, yet few would deny help to poor children. Similarly, Medicaid, when viewed as a welfare program, is an attractive target for budget-cutters, yet it becomes less vulnerable with the realization that over 42 percent of its funds are used to support long-term care services for low-income elderly and disabled persons. To be successful, new approaches must be better articulated so the public understands them and so more powerful constituencies may emerge to support them.

Third, new policies and programs should begin with those existing mechanisms that are already effectively meeting human needs. This is not to suggest that all new approaches must be confined to existing systems of support, for some may involve entirely new strategies. But we should clearly minimize developing whole new bureaucracies when existing structures can be remolded to achieve the same end. Any new approach must be viable when implemented and must be capable of being easily administered. Existing mechanisms that have already proved themselves may be the best starting point for such implementation.

Examples of existing structures that could be modified to target benefits to the poor are universal insurance programs, such as Social Security and Unemployment Compensation, and the universal tax system. Because programs designed solely to help the poor are exceptionally vulnerable to budget reductions and political attacks, expanded universal programs with targeted benefits for the poor may be more likely to survive future budget squeezes. Thus, any new approaches should ideally begin with existing universal programs, with traditional welfare programs reduced to their original supplementary and supportive function.

It is useful to illustrate the kinds of alternative approaches to income support that meet the criteria discussed above. Consider the following approaches targeted to three groups: (1) low-income children, (2) the working poor, and (3) unemployed adults. While the strategies identified below for each of these groups could be pursued singly or simultaneously, they are examples of approaches to cumulatively achieve long-range comprehensive reform of programs offering assistance to poor families and working-age adults. The following does not represent a blueprint for action; it suggests, instead, a conceptual redirection and is offered for purposes of illustrating new ideas that merit consideration.

AN INCOME-SUPPORT STRATEGY FOR LOW-INCOME CHILDREN

In 1982, 16.5 percent of all white children and 47.3 percent of all black children—in all, 13.5 million children—lived below the official poverty standard. That more than one-fifth of a modern generation lives in poverty testifies not only to the urgent need for an income-support policy for children but also to the failure of past and current programs to adequately protect children from poverty.

One alternative would be to institute a new national minimum benefit financed by the federal government and provided to all low-income children. This would, in conjunction with other elements, replace the AFDC program and would ensure an adequate living standard for *all* children.

The AFDC program, which has historically been the primary line of defense against poverty for children, is no longer a viable mechanism to ensure that children are provided life's basic necessities. The program has been reduced in scope to the extent that it now serves only a portion of children in low-income families. Most of the attention in the welfare debate of the past three years has been focused on the work effort of the AFDC parents, while little attention has been paid to the basic income-support needs of the large numbers of children growing up in poverty. In their zest to recast AFDC as a program for only nonworking families, policy-makers have lost sight of the fundamental goal of protecting needy children.

The focus of a new national minimum benefit would be on the child rather than family composition or employment status. The current AFDC program has dozens of family- and employment-related stipulations and, if a parent fails to follow them, the result can be a child's loss of benefits. For example, if a parent goes on strike, or fails to seek work, or even decides to marry, a child can have his or her AFDC benefits terminated.

The panacea approach to welfare policy, which integrated the goals of income support for children and work incentives for parents, inevitably penalized the most innocent of poor Americans—children. The most basic human needs of low-income children should be secured irrespective of the condition of the labor market or the employment behavior or marital status of their parents. Work incentives for employable adults constitute a significant social challenge, but must not be achieved at the expense of children. By penalizing children for the problems of their parents, we live every economic downturn twice—once today and again in the deficiencies we cause for the next generation of adults.

Under this proposal, the federal government would set a uniform benefit amount to apply to all children. The state would then assume the responsibility, as it now does, to ensure that the benefit is used for the child's welfare, making protective payments on behalf of the child in cases where the parent is not doing so. The federal government would thus maintain responsibility for providing a minimum cash benefit to all poor children, and state and local units of government would retain responsibility for safeguarding these benefits on a case-by-case basis.

INCOME SUPPLEMENTS FOR
THE WORKING POOR

The number of adults who work and yet have incomes below the poverty line is amazingly high. In 1980 over 3 million families were made up of parents who worked at least some part of that year. These low-wage earners are continuing to lose ground today as inflation erodes their buying power and they remain on the fringes of the labor market. Moreover, recent tax policies have widened the gap between the disposable incomes of low-wage earners and middle- and upper-income workers by bestowing larger tax cuts on the higher incomes.

A small number of these working poor—about one-half million people—also receive partial AFDC benefits that used to supplement their low wages. These people have been the most penalized by the recent changes in the AFDC program. The AFDC budget cuts enacted for fiscal years 1981 and 1982 raised the "marginal benefit reduction rate" for these working poor so that for every additional dollar they earn, they now lose a minimum of 99 cents in welfare benefits. Many lose more than a dollar for every extra dollar they earn —clearly a disincentive to increase their work effort. The working poor need supplemental income and work incentives to close the gap between their income levels and those of middle- and upper-income earners. Rather than force low-wage earners to enter the stigmatized welfare system, their incomes should be supplemented through both an expansion of the earned-income credit (EIC) and a revised refundable child-care tax credit.

The EIC is a refundable tax credit for all families earning less than $10,000 per year. It is available to any qualifying family that submits a claim to the Internal Revenue Service. Families can receive a maximum of $500 if their annual income is between $5,000 and $6,000. Because the credit is refundable, families do not have to pay taxes to claim it; the IRS will send them a check for the amount they are due even if they do not owe taxes. The EIC was introduced into the tax system in 1975. It was viewed as a way to reward people for taking, and keeping, low-paying jobs. That principle should now be expanded by widening the level of income eligibility and raising the amount of the credit.

The child-care tax credit is an existing universal mechanism that provides a tax credit to families for child-care costs up to $2,400 per child. However, the credit is out of reach of many low-income earners because it is not refundable and is therefore unavailable to many low-income families who do not earn enough to file taxes. Making this credit refundable would help many low-wage earners, thereby offering another positive incentive to work.

Both of these mechanisms—an expanded EIC and a refundable child-care tax credit—would be federally financed through the tax system and therefore would be relatively simple to administer. These two approaches build on an existing structure and are applicable to others as well as to the traditional welfare population.

AN UNEMPLOYMENT/MANPOWER SYSTEM

Providing work incentives to the working poor is a necessary but insufficient response to the employment needs of many citizens today. While jobs are generally recognized as the first line of defense against poverty, the number of poeple out of work today—and therefore particularly vulnerable to poverty—reveals a national crisis. Yet there is no positive policy to help prevent unemployment. Our current system of unemployment compensation passively allows people to lose their jobs before any action is taken; and when they do lose their jobs, people are provided only with temporary cash benefits. We need to develop more useful means of helping to prevent unemployment. The current high unemployment rates are not likely to yield to small incremental approaches such as tax credits or reinstatement of past employment programs. Today's structural unemployment demands a major new federal commitment to providing jobs and training if we are to reduce poverty among working-age adults in sectors of the population (e.g., minorities and women) for whom poverty and unemployment have been intensified in this administration (though by no means created by it).

The need for job-creation and job-training strategies is no longer argued ideologically—both liberals and conservatives agree that a major public initiative in this area is urgently needed. The only debatable point seems to be how best to pursue this goal. Some type of public works program is generally regarded as essential if it provides services that are productive and useful to society and if such jobs do not detract from the private sector. Clearly there are numerous examples of needed services, and the private sector's expertise and resources should contribute to any such endeavor. But the federal government must make a major financial and intellectual commitment if a comprehensive national job-creation and job-training program is to enhance the productive capacity of our society in a fashion that includes those long in the ranks of the poor. Such a program should have three components:

1. creating jobs in both the public and private sectors;
2. training presently unemployed and unskilled workers for those jobs; and
3. restructuring the institutions that help people find employment.

One aspect of this program should focus on establishing a unified and restructured unemployment compensation/manpower system responsible for providing assistance to all persons who can be expected to work outside their homes and maintain jobs. We should not establish separate work and training programs for welfare recipients; rather, we should build on the more universally accepted unemployment insurance system in a comprehensive design for a new national manpower strategy.

Temporary stipends could be provided through the unemployment insurance system for unemployed persons in training, until they became employed. Rather than a cash extension, the stipend could be used only for job training and job search and thus would be a more positive approach to reemployment than the current system of extended cash unemployment benefits. The stipends would be part of the unemployment insurance program for people whose unemployment benefits expire before finding employment.

A new national manpower strategy would have to realign current programs to provide an integrated system of training, job-placement services and public service employment opportunities to assist those who can, want to and should be helped to find work. For example, existing local unemployment offices or Private Industry Councils (PICs) could be used to distribute stipend benefits. The ultimate goal of this new strategy would be to reduce welfare utilization and poverty in the long term.

In conclusion, the agenda for change discussed here represents an attempt to dismantle the current income maintenance system and reconstruct new approaches that avoid the trap of superimposing multiple objectives on a single program. We must redefine our objectives by targeting assistance on specific needs within the diverse poverty population, and we must utilize a wide variety of mechanisms that are appropriate to specific needs.

The examples presented above—a tax system to expand work incentives for the working poor, an unemployment compensation system including new manpower strategies, and a national minimum benefit for low-income children—are three interrelated alternatives that seek to fundamentally restructure our income maintenance system. Questions of funding levels can be entertained only when we have defined substantive program goals and designed operational parameters.

From both a human and budgetary perspective, we can no longer afford to sit back and watch further growth in poverty statistics. For future generations of children, we need to start now to rebuild viable support structures.

6

The Consumer as a Hidden Resource

Frank Riessman

We want more services than we want to pay for.
Alice M. Rivlin, Director,
Congressional Budget Office.
New York Times, September 4, 1983.

Today's demand for human services, particularly health, education and psychosocial services, continues to outstrip what the nation is able or willing to provide.* When it comes to health care alone, the system as presently organized is incapable of serving all those in need, e.g., the 22 million people with arthritis, 10 million alcoholics, 5 million diabetics, 18 million with hypertension, over 25 million who have emotional problems—on and on goes the list. Moreover, the press constantly dramatizes new needs in vivid fashion, while simultaneously noting the limitations of the services as they are currently delivered.[1]

For some time now, a trenchant critique of professionally controlled human services has accompanied equally valuable efforts to finance basic services for millions of Americans. But even in times of more public moneys available to human services, professional control was perceived by many as inhumane, distant, inefficient and dependency-producing.

Clearly, while the need to finance adequate services is more critical than ever in the face of Mr. Reagan's barbarous hatchet, the task of making them more productive and cost-effective and bringing them closer to the consumer remains as well. For the coming decade, we

---

Frank Riessman is director of the National Self-Help Clearinghouse, Graduate School and University Center, City University of New York.

* For the most part, the focus of this essay is on health and the psychosocial services. What is said here, however, is a perspective generally applicable to human-service policy.

need a resource-building strategy that geometrically expands the help-giving potential of the society and also changes it qualitatively. The most ready resource is the enormous amount of nonprofessional help-giving that is taking place, often unrecognized—an existing reserve that needs to be integrated efficiently with the professional system.

This essay maps some of the existing areas of lay help and describes some new directions for integration with the formal help-giving system. The types of help that we will describe *are not substitutive for professional services* but rather are complementary. This is important to recognize lest the use of new forms of help serve as an argument for service cutbacks.

INFORMAL HELPERS

A study by Donald Warren based on personal interviews with over 2,500 families, describes an elaborate, informal, natural helping network that crisscrosses every community. Its members don't usually know each other. They work without pay. Their "case load" is larger than that of all the professional agencies combined by a factor of eight to one. Nationwide, in a single month, this invisible "organization" provides over 70 million helping transactions, including 176 million different types of help.

Warren states: "We began to trace how people use very close friends and other intimates instead of going to professionals for help with stress. . . . For a range of frequently encountered problems, people put together their own combinations of helpers."

The helping networks work something like this. You are feeling worried about what retirement will be like, or how it will be to return to school, or whether you should change jobs. So you first talk to a neighbor about it. The neighbor mentions a friend on the other side of town who really has some good ideas—perhaps about how to save money on a retirement home. You call that person, who then directs you to another friend who has already done this.

Warren concludes that "our research shows that an optimal number of helpers and types of help significantly reduces the stress of problem coping. Formal agencies and professional helpers need to understand and work with the informal networks of a community."[2]

Emory L. Cowen studied the informal help given by four groups of people. He reports that "moderate" to "serious" personal problems were brought to all four groups, but more to hairdressers and divorce lawyers than to industrial supervisors or bartenders. He observes that only a small fraction of people's psychological problems reach the formal mental-health establishment. The problems brought to informal helpers, however, were similar to the ones seen by mental-health professionals. All the helpers used a variety of helping strategies— some like, others unlike those used by mental-health professionals. Most felt good about providing interpersonal help and believed that they did so moderately well.

These informal helpers dealt with a wide range of problems: depression, anxiety, difficulties with children, marital problems, jobs, sex, drugs, anger, loneliness, feelings of worthlessness and so on. The helpers offered support and sympathy, presented alternatives, shared personal experiences, asked questions, gave advice and listened. In most cases they enjoyed the help-giving role and felt comfortable in it. In some instances they stated that the help-giving was an important aspect of their jobs. One hairdresser said, "To be perfectly truthful I regard myself a B— hairdresser. But my business is booming. Mostly that's because I listen to people, care about their personal concerns, and try to be helpful. The guy down the street is really an A+ hairdresser—one of the best in town. But he's going to go out of business because he can't stand people and is incapable of listening sympathetically to anyone's problems."[3]

Collins and Pancoast observe that natural neighbors and informal caregivers may be the *prime sources of help available to poor people experiencing personal distress.*[4]

SELF-CARE

Self-care in health refers to those activities that individuals undertake to promote their own health, prevent their own disease, limit their own illness and restore their own health. These activities are undertaken without professional assistance, although individuals may be informed by technical knowledge and skills derived from the pool of both professional and lay experience.

Lowell S. Levin estimates that 65 to 80 percent of all health and medical care is provided by individuals to themselves, or by families, friendship networks and other nonprofessional sources.[5]

J.M. Last researched the extent of morbidity in England and Wales as documented by professionals. His study makes clear that for virtually every category of disease, what the medical practitioner saw was only "the tip of the iceberg."[6] This conclusion agrees with an earlier study by Horder and Horder.[7] Here it was found that less than one-third of illnesses experienced by a London population were cared for by health professionals. In an international study of medical-care utilization, White et al. found a similar distribution of symptoms involving lay and professional care. It was found that an average of 82.7 percent of all conditions causing "great discomfort" over a two-week period did not involve consultation with physicians.[8]

The current public emphasis on gaining more self-care skills has been accelerated by changing patterns of disease from acute to chronic; the women's health movement; a rise in public sophistication about health (over 5,000 lay-oriented health texts available); the availability of medical technology designed for lay use (home pregnancy tests, blood-pressure cuffs, etc.); recognition of the realistic limits of professional care; and the limits (including costs) of professional resources.

There is a burgeoning research literature that demonstrates how health costs may be reduced significantly by involving patients in their own care.[9] One study reports a great savings in health services at a university when students are trained to manage their own upper respiratory infections.[10] Another study demonstrates far lower physician utilization when mothers learn to take throat cultures from their children.[11] Still another investigation shows how the use of over-the-counter preparations, such as steroid preparations for skin irritations, leads to decreased reliance on medical personnel.[12]

In the field of hypertension, doctors are now recommending that patients purchase blood-pressure cuffs in order to take their own blood pressure. The readings obtained in this way turn out to be more valid because the patient is under less stress!

Among the medical instruments, supplies and kits that have recently become available for home use are the following:

- A doctor's "black bag," containing a blood-pressure cuff, stethoscope, otoscope (for examining ear and nose canals), digital thermometer, tongue depressor and medical guide.

- A dental emergency kit that covers more than fifteen dental emergencies, including temporary fillings. It contains adhesives, toothache drops, dental tools and instructions.
- An electronic unit that provides an accurate reading of blood-sugar levels for home use by diabetics.
- Several pregnancy-testing kits, which are reported to be 97-percent accurate for a positive test and 85-percent accurate for a negative one.
- Chemically treated sticks that change color to indicate a urinary-tract infection.
- A poison-safeguard kit containing syrup of ipecac to induce vomiting, activated charcoal to administer as an antidote, and educational information.
- A highway-accident and burn-trauma kit containing sprays, ointments, bandages and a shock-treatment blanket—a spin-off from the space program.

Most of these items are available at well-supplied drugstores and hospital-equipment stores or can be ordered directly from the manufacturer.[13]

The relevance of self-care approaches is highlighted when one considers that most of the health problems of our times relate to chronic conditions: heart disease, stroke, cancer, emphysema, arthritis, diabetes, hypertension and mental illness. Over 75 percent of doctor visits are for these conditions, most of which require only a small, selective amount of physician time. What they require most of all is care that can be provided by the individuals themselves or collectively in mutual-support self-help groups.

Anselm Straus describes the abilities necessary to enable those with chronic illnesses to cope with them and with the concomitant crises.[14]

- The ability to read signs that portend a crisis, e.g., a diabetic being able to recognize the signs of oncoming sugar shortage or insulin shock, or an epileptic being able to recognize an oncoming convulsion. In a sense, this is a form of self-diagnosis.
- The ability to respond to the crisis of the moment . . . the diabetic who carries sugar or candy or insulin, or the epileptics who stuff handkerchiefs between their teeth just before convulsions. This is, in a sense, a form of self-treatment. An aspect of this self-treatment is to carry it out in a manner that keeps "one's symptoms as unobtrusive as possible . . . [e.g.] emphysema sufferers

learn to sit down or lean against buildings in such a fashion that they are not mistaken for drunks or loiterers."

- The ability to establish and maintain a regimen. The extent to which a person is able to do this depends on his or her belief in the efficacy of the regimen, the effectiveness of the regimen without producing distressing or frightening side effects, and the guaranty that important daily activities, either of the patient or of the people around him/her, can continue relatively uninterrupted.

SELF-INITIATED BEHAVIOR CHANGE

Contrary to popular belief, there is a growing body of evidence that many people overcome addictions and related disorders *on their own*. Considerable research demonstrates that obesity and drug use have responded to nonprofessional intervention in which the individuals themselves are the key agents.

Stanley Schachter reports, in opposition to overwhelming professional pessimism, that most addictive disorders, such as opiate use and cigarette smoking, are responsive to long-term self-cure in a high percentage of cases. In his studies of self-cured smokers, he found that 63.6 percent of those who attempted to quit smoking had succeeded. On the average, successful quitters had not smoked for 7.4 years. Some 87.8 percent of these quitters had been nonsmokers for a year or more. This is consistent with the surgeon general's report in 1979 that over 30 million people had given up smoking on their own since 1964. Schachter summarizes: "These data suggest that a considerably larger portion of the general population may have given up smoking for long periods of time than has heretofore been suspected from estimates based on studies of therapeutic success. The process appears to be relatively painless for light smokers and painful for many heavy smokers, but the two groups are equally successful at quitting."[15]

There is evidence that narcotics addiction, too, may not be the intractable condition it has long been believed to be. Robins's 1974 study of returned Vietnam-veteran drug users indicated "a surprisingly high remission rate for heroin addiction" without benefit of professional treatment.[16]

Schachter's studies also indicate that 62.5 percent of obese individuals successfully reduce their weight on their own.[17] He notes that people can and do cure themselves of smoking, obesity, and heroin addiction and they do so in large numbers and for long periods of time, in many cases apparently permanently.

He observes that most of the reported results on therapeutic interventions relate to a single attempt to quit smoking or lose weight. This is quite different from the self-initiated efforts, which take place over a long period of time or a lifetime.

There is also considerable new data reported by C. Steven Richards et al. indicating that many college students successfully deal with academic problems, depression, overeating and sexual problems through self-initiated, self-controlled behavioral approaches.[18]

SELF-HELP MUTUAL AID

John Naisbitt, in his best-selling book *Megatrends,* lists self-help as one of the ten major trends in our society.

> During the 1970s, Americans began to disengage from the institutions that had disillusioned them and to relearn the ability to take action on their own. . . . Self-help has always been part of American life. In the 1970s it again became a movement that cut across institutions, disciplines, geographic areas, and political ideologies.[19]

Today, 500,000 self-help mutual-aid groups provide help to over 15 million people.[20] The special significance of mutual aid is that the person in need is converted into a help-giver. Thus, instead of 22 million arthritics being viewed only as people in need, they can be seen as resources. Their special "inside," experientially based knowledge of living with the illness gives this help a qualitative dimension as well as the quantitative one.

Not only has there been growth in the numbers, but also in the range of problems addressed by the self-help groups. There are self-help groups for nearly every disease category listed by the World Health Organization, as well as groups concerned with a wide variety of psychosocial problems through literally the gamut of life crises, from birth to death. Groups have developed for couples who are infertile, parents of newborns, parents whose child has died, single parents, divorced persons, adolescents and their parents, older persons having difficulties with their children, and the widowed. There are groups for parents who abuse their children, for isolated older people, the handicapped, drug abusers, suicide-prone people, smokers, drinkers, overeaters and patients discharged from mental institutions.

Self-help groups are also developing among those with care-taking responsibilities—parents of children with handicaps, parents or relatives of individuals who have been institutionalized, those taking care of sick or older parents, and spouses of those who have had strokes or other disabling conditions.*

The U.S. Department of Health and Human Services predicts that the number of persons reached by self-help mutual-aid groups needs to double by 1990 to reduce the gap in mental-health services.[21]

Mutual-aid groups are inexpensive, highly responsive and accessible to the consumer who is her/himself a service-giver as well as receiver. Such groups can expand greatly to deal with the ever-growing need. As the need arises, so does the response or potential for response.

The self-help modality expands services not only quantitatively by creating a large number of service-givers, but qualitatively as well since the service-giver/helper obtains new benefits from playing this help-giving role. Moreover, peer help is less likely to produce dependence than the standard client-professional relationships. Finally, because the peer is nearer to the problem and shares it in an experiential fashion, he or she is able to provide another dimension of help.

Self-help groups have two unique preventive features: They provide social support to their members through the creation of a caring community; and they increase members' coping skills through the provision of information and the sharing of experiences and solutions to problems.

There are countless other examples of self-help and mutual aid, which we can only mention: the neighborhood approach to crime

---

* It should be noted that many self-help groups may provide advice and help that is counterproductive, resulting in unanticipated difficulties as well as prolonged dependency. This may also be true for the various forms of informal help described above. Needless to add, professional intervention sometimes takes the form of malpractice, as in medicine, and various other iatrogenic effects such as the disease spread in hospitals, etc.

reduction, where reports indicate that the reduction in crime in 1982 was primarily due to the involvement of citizen groups in anticrime programs;[22] the rapid expansion of bartering and cooperative groups; the huge explosion of self-help books and videotapes (if you own a video cassette recorder, you can now learn the fundamentals of photography, magic, Chinese cooking, tennis, golf, crocheting, ballroom dancing, dog training, blackjack, massage, weight lifting, plumbing, car repair, Spanish, speed reading, how to grow roses, etc.).

THE CONSUMER IS THE KEY

We have delineated a variety of consumer-based lay forms of help-giving: (1) the lay help-givers—neighbors, friends, hairdressers, etc. —providing help to other people of similar background; (2) the individual giving help to him/herself in giving up smoking or other addictive behavior and otherwise improving his/her health; (3) the individual providing and receiving help in a mutual-aid support group for people with a similar problem.*

In the informal help-giving affecting millions of people daily, it is worth noting that the help-giver is probably helped as well. This is consistent with the considerable data supporting the helper therapy principle[23]—that is, the person giving help is helped in turn. Thus the hairdressers, bartenders, lawyers and supervisors who are providing help are also probably being helped, and this extends the range of help obtained in the mutual-aid support groups, where the members are both helpees and helpers and benefit from both roles.†

In the self-initiated behavior, it may also be true that the person who helps him/herself benefits not only from receiving that help but from the independence and empowerment achieved by giving it. This

---

* There are, of course, a large number of other help-givers that we are not considering: psychics, astrologers, people who lay on hands, groups such as est, the clergy, etc. It would be useful to map all the different kinds of help-giving that take place, the help-giving processes that are operative, and to develop a typology and assessment of these help forms. These help-giving systems go far beyond the obvious direct professional care that is generally assessed.

† In education it is striking that peer tutors typically benefit as much or more than their tutees in peer-tutoring programs. (See Alan Gartner, Mary Kohler and Frank Riessman, *Children Teach Children,* Harper & Row, 1971.) Similar findings are reported for peer counseling and peer caring where high-school youngsters are trained to provide help to other youngsters.

is more difficult to assess, but it is a hypothesis worth considering. An individual who gives up smoking may feel good from the strength derived in providing that help as well as from receiving the help. This may also be true of self-care that individuals obtain and give in dealing with their own health. Certainly there is a reduction of dependence in playing this self-help-giving role, and there may be other factors that are related to the helper-therapy principle. This merits further investigation.

What these examples seem to have in common, in addition to the fact that they are inexpensive, is a special involvement of consumers —patients, students and clients—so that they become a force in the increased productivity of the service. *The consumers are actually operative in the delivery of the service;* it is not some general form of participation. And there is a definite increase in the output.

Victor Fuchs points out that, unlike goods production, in the services "the knowledge, experience, honesty, and motivation of the consumer affects service productivity."[24]

Human services are consumer-intensive. The more the productivity of the provider depends on consumer behavior, the more consumer-intensive is that activity. Here, then, is a decisive factor that can affect education or any other human service. If we see students, for example, not as the passive recipients of teaching but as workers in the production of their own learning, then the organization of those learning activities takes on quite a different focus.

What is key in efforts to increase children's learning, then, are those activities that can enlist the student as a more active and effective learner/worker. *Engaging students in a program such as peer tutoring, where they learn through teaching other students, makes most efficient use of the student/worker.*

All of this may be conceptualized under what Alvin Toffler calls the "prosumer"—in effect, the consumer functioning as a producer.[25] In essence, consumers in various roles—in mutual support groups and in self-initiated behavior change—are adding enormously to the help provided by the society.

The critical question is how to relate this to the professionally led formal care-giving system.* There are a number of possibilities. These

* It would be valuable to describe and enumerate the various forms of help-giving that are in fact taking place. Second, it would be useful to conduct research evaluating

include activities such as the development of materials by professionals for lay use, training of lay group leaders, sponsorship of self-help groups, referrals, etc. It also includes having professionals learn from self-help groups and other forms of lay help by attending self-help-group meetings, by including lay people in training sessions for professionals, and by having professional curricula in social-work schools, and health-education programs include information on the various forms of lay help.

THE FORMS OF INTEGRATION

The seeds of integration are beginning to sprout. There are, at present, twenty-seven regional self-help clearinghouses that bring professional expertise to bear upon the building of mutual-aid groups. These local clearinghouses typically provide the following services: publication of a directory of local self-help groups; a hotline for information and referrals; provision of technical assistance to existing groups; conducting of conferences and fairs; publishing relevant self-help materials.

Some further examples of integration:

- The American Hospital Association has developed a whole self-help resource packet directed at assisting and encouraging health professionals in hospitals in working with and developing self-help groups.
- The American Association of Retired Persons (AARP) has developed a series of programs relating to self-help groups for widows.
- New York City's Department on Aging operates a program involving lay people in monitoring hypertension.
- The Florida Mental Health Institute piloted a program where patients were trained in self-help approaches in connection with their planned deinstitutionalization.
- In Holland a "duo" system has developed where patients with chronic illnesses are helped by a combination of a professional and a lay person who has the problem him/herself.[26]

---

the various help-giving forms and to investigate the processes underlying them. For example, how do people go about giving up smoking by themselves? What preceded the self-initiated act? What factors affected the quitter?

- Reevaluation counseling, an approach that is widespread in the United States, utilizes a trainer to teach lay individuals how to counsel each other.
- The self-care project directed by Lowell Levin at Yale is concerned with empowering self-help groups in the community by providing technical assistance, etc., but always relating this assistance to the mode, style and skills that already exist in the client or consumer population.[27]
- Peer-counseling approaches in schools and colleges typically utilize a professional psychologist to train students in counseling other students.
- Eugene Gendlin, who developed the focusing technique in psychotherapy, is concerned with transferring the skills involved in that approach to a consumer population who can then do it themselves. (Most self-help books are written by professionals to give lay people the skills and approaches they use in helping themselves.)
- Weight-watchers and Smokenders use trained experts to help the client population achieve the desired effect, and they also utilize lay people and members of the client population itself.
- In Westchester, professionals attached to that county's self-help clearinghouse have been training natural helpers in the community, adding skills and techniques to their already existing repertoire, but being careful not to violate the natural approaches and the strengths they possess.
- Various alternative services—including runaway houses, drop-in centers, free clinics, hotlines and hospices—typically include a combination of professional and lay help.

Thus a new, expanded service system should be able to provide technical assistance, training, resources and other kinds of support to build on and expand the vast help-giving processes that exist.

But the new integration need not work only one way, expanding the resources of the help-giving system by benefiting the self-helpers. It can also provide the needed revitalization of the human services. As the ethos and style of the more natural self-help system begin to rub off on the professional system, it may become less distant, more humane and more informal. The result could be a very different service-delivery system, one that is more participatory and appealing to a public that often has been critical of bureaucratic, wasteful and inefficient service delivery. Not only would the new service system be dramatically expanded, but the services provided would be more people-based and personalized.

The news media generally depict self-help quite attractively, and the public sees it as an inexpensive, nonbureaucratic, participatory expansion of services that makes people less dependent in general. These services are therefore likely to win the much needed support against conservative budget-cutting.

The new prosumers are no longer dependent consumers nor public critics, because they are involved directly in the production and delivery of services. Since they are not employed workers, however, they are not subject to the same bureaucratic controls that might apply to the paid employee. Their more direct involvement with services may somewhat reduce a supercritical public stance, to say nothing of the possibility that the new restructured services may actually be less deserving of criticism or attack.

At the present time, two vastly different human-service systems exist side by side, with only occasional articulation: the self-help system and the professional system. Each has its weaknesses and strengths. A dialectic integration of the two may provide not only a useful balance that gives them the chance to learn from each other, but a vastly expanded, restructured and cost-effective production of human services that is responsive to the growing human-service crisis in our society.

In building the human-service system of the future, we need to restore what has been cut, but in a new fashion, because, as we have seen, the present system cannot possibly fulfill the enormous unmet needs in our society. What we have proposed is a fuller integration of the vast informal help-giving structures with the professional formal system. This integration should help each system, with the added bonus of consumer involvement in help-giving activities. The consumer, then, is the hidden resource that needs to be mobilized for a new dimension in service productivity.

Notes

1. Alan Gartner and Frank Riessman, *The Service Society and the Consumer Vanguard* (New York: Harper & Row, 1974).
2. Donald I. Warren, *Helping Networks: How People Cope with Problems in the Urban Community* (University of Notre Dame Press, 1981).
3. Emory L. Cowen, "Help Is Where You Find It," *American Psychologist.*
4. A.H. Collins and D. L. Pancoast, *Natural Helping Networks: A Strategy for Prevention* (Washington, D.C.: National Association of Social Workers, 1976).
5. Lowell S. Levin, "Self-Care in Health," *Annual Review of Public Health,* 1983.
6. J.M. Last, "The Iceberg: Completing the Clinical Picture," *Lancet,* 2:28–31, 1963.
7. J. Horder and E. Horder, "Illness In General Practice," *Practitioner,* 173:177–85, 1954.
8. K.L. White et al., "International Comparison of Medical Care Utilization," *New England Journal of Medicine,* 1967.
9. Audrey Gartner, "Self-Help/Self-Care: A Cost-Effective Strategy," *Social Policy,* Spring 1982.
10. Jay W. Gillenwater et al., "Home Urine Cultures by the Dip-Strip Method: Results in 289 Cultures," *Pediatrics,* Oct. 1976.
11. Harvey P. Katz and Robert R. Clancy, "Accuracy of a Home Throat Culture Program: A Study of Parent Participation in Health Care," *Pediatrics,* May 1974.
12. Simon Rottenberg, *Self-Medication: The Economic Perspective* (Washington, D.C.: Proprietary Association, 1980).
13. Alan D. Haas, "The Trend To Self-Help Medicine Grows," *Newsweek,* 23 Aug. 1983.
14. Anselm Straus, "Chronic Illness," *Society,* Sept./Oct. 1973.
15. Stanley Schachter, "Recidivism and Self-Cure of Smoking and Obesity," *American Psychologist,* Apr. 1982.
16. L. Robins, "The Vietnam Drug User Returns," Special Action Office monograph, May 1974.
17. Schachter, op. cit.
18. C. Steven Richards et al., "An Investigation of Naturally Occurring Episodes Of Self-Controlled Behaviors," *Journal of Counseling Psychology,* 1977.
19. John Naisbitt, *Megatrends* (New York: Warner, 1982), ch. 6.
20. National Self-Help Clearinghouse, Estimates of the NSHC, Graduate School, City University of New York, 1982.
21. "Promoting Health, Preventing Disease: Objectives for the Nation," (Washington, D.C.: U.S. Department of Health & Human Services, 1980).
22. Reported in *USA Today,* 20 Apr. 1983.
23. Alan Gartner and Frank Riessman, *Self-Help in the Human Services* (San Francisco: Jossey-Bass, 1977), ch. 4.
24. Victor Fuchs, "Health Care and the United States Economic System," *Milbank Memorial Quarterly,* L, 2, Apr. 1972, 229.
25. Alvin Toffler, *The Third Wave* (New York: William Morrow, 1980).
26. M. Bremer Schulte et al., "Oorspronkelijke Stukken," *Ned. T. Geneesk* 126, nr. 45, 1982.
27. Cynthia Savo, "The Yale Self-Care Education Project," *Social Policy,* Fall 1983.

7

A Sea Change in Schooling

Theodore R. Sizer

Beyond Reagan, what might lie ahead for education?

Despite recent posturing, Reagan, as well as his presidential predecessors, has had little to do with the schools. They sail before different winds, and the most important contemporary fact of American elementary and secondary education is that there is a sea change under way, a subtle, slow, ill-defined but inexorable shift in public priorities and perception about formal schooling. The institution of the school (as contrasted with learned competence itself) is losing the central place in American iconography that it has held since World War I. The future will reflect these tides more than anything else.

School is now just one of a number of places for "growing up," all too often primarily a place for enjoyment, a place for rituals, and all too rarely a place for serious, sustained commitment of intellectual energy by students. School as an institution is no longer above serious challenge. The alliance of parent and teacher (and sometimes clergyman) in the rearing of a child is the exception today. Parents and teachers are rarely colleagues in the nurturing of the young, and more frequently are antagonists.

Because spokesmen for the schools don't want to acknowledge this sea change and wish to think that the declining public interest is but a brief aberration, its existence is pushed into the background of national discussion. A gaggle of reports, particularly focused on high schools, has emerged in the early 1980s, clacking with diagnoses of "rising tides of mediocrity" and the essential need for a recommitment to education.[1] Few serious citizens question these reports' argument that a far higher level of competence in our young people is needed,

---

Theodore R. Sizer is Professor of Education at Brown University and author of *Horace's Compromise: The Dilemma of the American High School.*

but similarly few believe that the schools, even buoyed by fresh infusions of money taken from tax revenues, are unquestionably the best vehicles for delivering that higher competence. Skepticism is deep in public consciousness, and it is new.

As the shift in public attitudes has been gradual, the evidence of disaffection has lacked commentators, even as the tone of the press has, from the mid-1960s, changed from hopeful to critical about schools. And the virtual silence about educational issues in political agendas during federal and state electoral campaigns in the 1970s was striking. The emergence of schooling as a likely issue for the 1984 presidential campaign and the attention paid to it by some governors, especially in the Southeast, seem to indicate a renewed attention, but when one looks beyond the speeches of candidates, one finds no fundamental reassessment of the ways we keep school or much attention paid to careful planning of educational strategies. Furthermore, given the scale of the school systems, pitifully few new moneys are proposed to be applied to the enterprise. Thus, while schools may have become a freshly popular topic, they have drawn to their cause little more than rhetorical support and promises of more regulation and standardization, those familiar political tools that simulate action without investment.

There are other sorts of signals, however oblique. Since the late 1960s, no university has reinforced or seriously reconstructed its programs affecting the schools; indeed, withdrawn support has been the rule, justified by the teacher "glut." The universities have readily accepted their obligation to the school world as merely one of turning out professionals. Careful educational research and development is a peripheral concern. Childrens' issues lack prestige, and the critical questions about their learning get short shrift. Ironically—since it depends on their products—academia despises schools.

Apart from the relatively trivial bureaucratic exercise of creating a Federal Department of Education and the passage of well-lobbied bilingual and special-education legislation, few federal initiatives were seen during the Nixon, Ford and Carter years. Programs from the 1960s were funded at marginally lower or higher levels under all four of the post-Johnson presidents; while some were repackaged, few were seriously restructured. Very simply, the national educational scene over the last twelve years has been boring: No one really cared enough to ask the tough questions. Save within the educational establishment,

Reagan's and Senators Packwood and Moynihan's tuition-tax-credit idea created few sparks. Even at their most expansive levels, these proposals were of limited financial scale and were often focused more as tax-relief measures than ones concerned with school improvement. In all, the structures and initiatives from the late 1950s and 1960s persisted; the schools, drifting, were neglected.

The Gallup polls tell a story. Since 1974, pollsters have administered questions to assess attitudes toward the public schools, and the results "show a steady decline in the public's regard for the schools."[2] Asked to rate their local public schools, 18 percent of people in 1974 gave them an "A," but in 1982 only 8 percent did. The more popular "grades" were "C" and "D"; these accounted for 27 percent of the "votes" in 1974 and 47 percent in 1982. In 1982, almost half of the respondents said that, tuition costs aside, they would prefer to send their children to private rather than to public schools.[3]

The least understood and most telling evidence of the decline in the public perception of the importance of schools is found in the schools themselves, in the docility of students and the demoralization and disengagement of teachers. Save for certain special groups of kids in high schools—the honors sections, the athletes, the "special" students of one sort or another—many adolescents go to school in an obliging but strikingly detached way. They value the diploma and know they can get it by dutiful attendance. Their principal quarrel with their experience is that it is "boring"; school is supposed to be entertaining. Given the often illogical way that their school days and weeks are organized, many students conclude that the adults teaching them don't really care either. The husk of the ritual is what is important, not the nourishing core within.[4]

Faced with daunting tasks (such as teaching algebra to 175 often truant and highly distracted students a day), teachers lose heart, or make treaties with their students in order to survive.[5] "I'll not push you very hard if you don't push me." The result all too often is a functionally illiterate fifteen-year-old who has already been "taught" in school for well over 10,000 hours. Periodically, university leaders, who wouldn't allow a freshman English writing teacher to carry more than fifty students, rail at the schoolteachers for their incompetence —without ever crediting their heavy student load. They are joined by business spokesmen—whose company training programs deliberately use few of the pedagogies embedded in the schools and whose workplaces, such as those for stenographers, are far more congenial to thoughtful work than those found in a typical school. The teachers recognize these discrepancies between what their critics see as lacking in the schools and what these same people provide in their own institutions. Few critics, they accurately conclude, really care about what goes on in schools.

Perhaps they never did. However, whatever the high-water mark of public belief in the schools may have been, it surely must have been close to or at it in 1965, with the passage of the Elementary and Secondary Education Act. The rhetoric of the *Brown* decision by the Supreme Court in 1954 sketched out the high ground. Education, it ruled, "is required in the performance of our most basic public responsibilities . . . it is the very foundation of good citizenship . . . it is doubtful that any child may reasonably be expected to succeed in life if he is denied the opportunity of an education."[6] By the late 1950s, after *Sputnik,* the schools were commissioned as a key weapon in the War Against Poverty. It has been downhill since then.

FORCES FOR SEA CHANGE

As soon as schools were given very specific social roles—as central instruments for social justice or weapons in the battle to eliminate poverty—the expectations for them became equally specific, something that the feisty young field of social science asserted it could measure. That is, the importance of schooling was not only going to be displayed by philosophical assertion (a tradition going back to Jefferson and Horace Mann); it was now going to be scientifically proved. The problem was, in fact, that schools might not work at all as their propagandizers had long asserted.

The most influential social-science survey was that mandated by Congress under the Civil Rights Act, essentially to "prove" the worth of integrated schools. This "Equal Educational Opportunity" report, prepared by a group led by James S. Coleman and published in July 1966, both legitimized in a scholarly manner the effort to understand what schools do and made respectable the criticism of schooling.[7] Daniel Patrick Moynihan, then a professor of education and urban politics at Harvard, correctly saw the potentially explosive influence of Coleman's work, calling it, privately, "the most dangerous document in the history of American education." He and a Harvard statistician, Frederick Mosteller, organized a seminar to reanalyze Coleman's voluminous data, and from this effort more reports emanated, most notably a summary volume by the seminar participants and Christopher Jencks's influential study, *Inequality: a Reassessment of Family and Schooling in America.* [8] Also involved with Moynihan's and Jencks's group were the radical economists Samuel Bowles and Herbert G. Gintis; their *Schooling in Capitalist America: Educational Reform and the Contradictions of Economic Life* appeared in 1972 and also drew on Coleman's and other social-science data. [9]

These books—all challenging many much-revered conventional wisdoms—caused a storm of controversy and a newly skeptical political climate for the consideration of education legislation and budgets. By the end of the 1970s, the expectation that schooling was to be routinely subjected to rigorous inquiry by social science was widely acknowledged and accepted. That some of the schools' old claims now seemed hollow was inevitable. Mouse hairs had been found in mom's apple pie.

Concurrent with the new heights of importance bestowed on education by statements such as that of the Court in *Brown* and those surrounding ESEA in 1965 was the final practical realization of mass secondary education. In 1940 barely half of American seventeen-year-olds finished high school; by 1970 over three-quarters had their diplomas. The numbers of young citizens in elementary and secondary schools almost doubled. The schools now included, and held for substantial periods of time, young people previously ignored or who earlier had dropped out of the system—the poor, minorities, kids with special needs. That the schools—especially the high schools, which had been designed for a selective, motivated clientele in the 1890s—did not always serve this broad and diverse student population very well is no surprise. The public heard about it largely through a clutch of angry books, exposés for the most part: *Death at an Early Age, The Way It's Spozed to Be, Our Children Are Dying,* and others. [10] The authors were given sustained attention from the press, and the problems their books highlighted were widely discussed. As with social science's entry into schooling, the enduring result was both to raise questions in the public's mind about the efficacy of schooling and to legitimize criticism of the schools.

Ralph Nader's *Unsafe at Any Speed* was about the Chevrolet Corvair, but its procedural message had substantial impact on promoting an adversarial attitude among consumers. Combined with the increased use of the courts to force social change, early and well used by the advocates of civil rights, it provoked manufacturers and those who purported to deliver some kind of service to pull up their corporate socks; at its worst, it brought out the trustless selfishness of Americans. Ultimately, the effect was for folks to "look out for number one." Public education had long depended on the majority of Americans being interested in and willing to be taxed for the schooling of other people's children. Some of that generosity melted in the presence of this new climate of consumerism, skepticism and distrust.

The public schools' growth had always depended on the happy coincidence of a broad coalition of proeducation political advocates and a rapidly rising economy. Two of the greatest school growth spurts happened during economically strong periods—the pre–World War I era and the post–Korean War years. The 1950 coalitions included all of organized education and some of corporate America—teachers, school administrators, college presidents, school-board members, senior business executives. They met regularly at summit meetings such as those of the Educational Policies Commission of the National Education Association and the American Association of School Administrators. Dwight Eisenhower and James B. Conant were members of the commission. Time Inc.'s Roy E. Larsen, Procter & Gamble's Neil McElroy and others of the Fortune 500 elite chaired White House conferences and led national organizations to abet the objectives of schools. Professional educators from the university schools of education moved easily among these folk, greasing the machinery. As the schools' political leverage was never very large, they depended heavily on this coalition, which reached its acme in the early 1960s. Organized teachers and school administrators (and the school boards that hired them) soon were to be antagonists.

With the breakup of the coalition, school politics fractionated into enclave politics; each group set its own agenda and fought just for that. Pieces of the old coalition might temporarily reconnect at congressional budget time, but the old idea of an undifferentiated Crusade for the Schools was replaced by infrequent, but often clever, coalitions when it appeared that cooperation might mean that each group's chances could be enhanced. Special-interest lobbies mushroomed in

the late Sixties and Seventies—teachers' groups (the two most important ones, the NEA and the American Federation of Teachers, yap-
ping almost as much at each other as at government); administrators'
groups; coalitions of private schools; advocates for handicapped kids,
or gifted kids, or Hispanic kids, or for computers; the professional
educators' groups fighting for their research moneys or consultancies.
Ed biz depended on a hustle focused on particular legislation or
federal or state budget lines. Coalitions had little to offer to these
special closed circles; the demise of the broadly based school lobby
was further evidence of the take-care-of-number-one mentality. The
public lost the voices of the old coalition, and the assurance and uplift
that it provided.

A further cause of the sea change was the apparent ideological
inconsistency of many of education's public advocates. Milton Friedman, Richard Nixon and Christopher Jencks all were for education
vouchers. The Left, on the whole, favored all sorts of mandated,
regulated school services: Where, people asked, was the Left's commitment to individual freedom in all this? The Republican Reagan
and the Democrat Daniel Moynihan both wanted tuition tax credits.
No coherent and consistent philosophical or practical policy positions
emerged from either major party, or even from individual educational
pundits. One was never sure just where James Coleman or Albert
Shanker might come out on any issue. Their tentativeness is laudable
in the abstract, but it added to the confusion, to the signal that no one
really had thoughtful, consistent, persuasive views of what schools
should be and should do. The confusion added to the public's unease.
The schools, buffeted by fresh criticism from the late 1960s on, were
left by confused and usually inattentive politicians to go on essentially
as before. If school doesn't work, why not change it? the thoughtful
citizen wondered. There has been no compelling reply.

Paradoxically, public respect and support for the schools may have
decreased because of this same public's growing respect for learning,
the putative substance and *raison d'être* of schools. When one's life
chances appeared relatively little affected by whether one learned
one's mathematics or not, and when a rising economy meant that
most citizens could improve their lot in life without much apparent
dependence on their formal education, the substance of school was not
taken all that seriously. Keeping adolescents happy, off the labor
market and in a safe and reasonably constructive environment was

enough. Friday-night basketball was far more important than Tues-day-morning physics. It is different today; a significant segment of the public perceives that its offspring really have to *know* something and be able to exhibit and use it in order to "make it." Americans perceive the future as troubled and difficult; a good hook shot is no longer all that is needed from a high-school senior. People increasingly take their childrens' intellectual competence and competitiveness seriously and thus find the schools of the early 1950s, with their rituals and mindlessness (to use Charles Silberman's indictment), seriously want-ing.[11] This is difficult for educators to swallow: Just as the public appears ready to take the central stuff of schooling seriously, it turns on the teachers who wanted such a focus all along. The bitterness of rejection runs deep in the teaching profession.

THE PROSPECTS FOR SCHOOLS

What, then, are the prospects for American schools in the latter 1980s, seen from this perspective of sea change? No longer are the schools accepted, unchallenged. No part of them is above criticism. At the same time, the traditional image of the school doughtily contin-ues, however misplaced or demonstrably inefficient school practice is. Age grading will continue, although we know that young people develop at different rates at different times. Achievement will continue to be measured largely in terms of time spent ("three years of mathe-matics"), silly though this practice is. Schools will be seen as places where adults give knowledge to children, even though we know that significant learning is accomplished only by the learner herself or himself; the teacher must be helper and cajoler, not some sort of vat attendant transferring knowledge to individual new bottles. We will continue to offer classes in groups of twenty-plus, at the high-school level in fifty-minute snippets, even though we know that learning is much more efficiently pursued in a variety of groupings. The basic structure of the academic disciplines—English, mathematics, French and so forth—will persist, each isolated from the other, even though we know this is clumsy, inconsistent with emerging modern scholar-ship and often practically dysfunctional. We'll run our schools basically with a discipline of threat (compulsory education—defined as serving time—being but the first instance) even though we know that positive incentives promote learning and negative ones repress it. We'll continue to treat our teachers as interchangeable parts, with the fifteen-year able veteran having essentially the same responsibility as a clumsy beginner, even though we know that such practice is wasteful. Schools will be empty most of the hours per year, at vast cost; they'll be actively used for their prime function but 1,100 hours out of the total 8,760 hours available.

In sum, there will be criticism, but at the same time there will be little energy for fundamental reengineering of the schools' structure, inefficient, costly and unproductive though it demonstrably is. Criticism and tradition will be in a sort of balance, or trance; the indecisiveness and wallowing of the early Eighties will persist, with no reform group gaining a sure enough handle to get on with the clearly required fundamental reconstrual and redefinition of schooling.

The handwringing will continue. Reports on the status of schools will continue to be issued; all will be critical, though few will propose radical policies. The tone of the rhetoric will continue, however, to be apocalyptic, with predictions of America's decline if the schools are not improved. The contrast between this hot rhetoric and the pallid vigor of the proposed remedies will be striking. There will continue to be recommendations for changes in the curricula, personnel and organization of schools, but these will be limited, at least in the near range of years, by the political strength of particular constituencies. The most persistent one of these recommendations will be for "choice"—that a family should have options among schools. However, whether the vehicles proposed for this purpose are tax credits (likely to have little impact), tuition vouchers (unlikely to get political support) or magnet schools in the public sector, they will little affect the basic structure of schooling. Magnet schools are likely to increase in number, since they keep control—jobs, contracts, curriculum— within the existing bureaucracy.

The mainstream prescriptions growing out of well-publicized national commission reports will be focused on the high schools and will argue for reinforcement of the "mainline," traditional college-preparatory curriculum—English, mathematics, history and social studies, and science, primarily—and the reassertion of adult control of the schools' program.* The most interesting characteristic of these prescriptions is their conservatism: They accept the schools' mission, structure, central curriculum, even their governing metaphors (schools are "service-delivery systems"). They seem to say, Let's take the programs that (apparently) produced the Successful People of the 1930s, 1940s and 1950s, and slap it on all. This state of reform will argue that such a conservative approach is realistic, being what the public wants, needs or will accept. Much effort will go into the propaganda of change—the blue-ribbon committee encyclicals, the corralling of key media people, the stage-managing of various kinds of announcements of proposed reform. By comparison, the substance of reform will get short shrift. How to implement change even through this conservative perspective is not on the agenda. Where interpretation is the focus, it is in so-called backward strokes. Back to Basics seems visionary; certification a radical endeavor.

This counsel to oil up the status quo is ironic at a time when the country is being swept by a communications revolution. In the face of new technology, the organization and functioning of even such conservative institutions as commercial banks are being profoundly revamped, but the schools, unaffected (it seems) by market pressures, are left standing as designed almost 100 years ago. Most "reformers" will continue to argue that it is "unrealistic" to suggest otherwise.

The mainline secondary-school curriculum now being reasserted has been the staple of the high schools since the 1890s and is in fact now "taken" by many of the students over whom the critics currently grieve, although the way it is presented in schools flies in the face of what we know about adolescent learning. These facts, however, will be overlooked, as most of those prescribing for the schools are little acquainted with the complicated realities of learning and schoolkeeping, and thus these mid-1980s reform reports calling essentially for more of the same will get plaudits. Pressure will be put on schools, course titles will change, a few electives not protected by powerful lobbies (such as that guarding the gates of vocational-technical educa-

* The term *main line* is that of Charles W. Eliot, the chairman of the NEA's "Committee of Ten" on secondary-school studies, which reported in 1893 and whose influence has thereafter been profound. The arrangement and time allotment in Eliot's "English" curriculum and that of the 1983 Commission on Excellence in Education are almost identical. Eliot's report is reprinted in full in my *Secondary Schools at the Turn of the Century* (New Haven: Yale University Press, 1964). See also *Horace's Compromise*, part 2.

tion) will disappear, and a few teachers will get awards and even "merit" supplements to their salaries. Not much else will happen.

Disproportionate attention will be paid to the federal government's role in schooling. The call for "national leadership" will continue; this call for "leadership," however, really hides an abundance of public and professional confusion. The Department of Education will not be dismantled. There will be legislation that any president will sign to "improve" the teaching of mathematics and science, but the dollars attached will be insufficient for even those parts of the task amenable to such intervention. By the late 1980s, when a teacher shortage is seen in some form in every congressional district, a fresh version of the now-defunct Education Professions Development Act of 1967 will be seen. The politics behind even this modest national legislative effort will be the politics of special interests: The science/business/technology group will get their bill; ed biz will hold on to its research funds; the NEA will get teacher-training funds. The key leadership for education will be fractionated among special interests, enclaves and political bases. There will be attempts to rally a broad coalition again, but they will fail.

Simply, the schools will change little in the latter 1980s, in spite of increased palaver on their behalf. Citizens will continue to worry about the quality of learning of the younger generation, and a growing number of attentive parents will continue to seek superior alternatives to the traditional schools for their children—to "magnet" schools, private schools, public schools in wealthy, homogeneous suburbs. The bulk of the funds for the schools' support will continue to flow from state and local coffers, allocated in familiar ways. The basic rituals of schoolkeeping will be safe, untouched yet by powerful tides.

By the 1990s the continuing sea change will produce further recognition of the limits of school as inherited and modified in eras preceding the post–World War II equity and opportunity agenda. The difference between *education* and *schooling* will become more obvious as large coteries of ambitious young people demonstrably succeed in their learning *outside* of schools. A painful shortage of teachers will force many issues about schools back onto local and state agendas; the old ways of employing and deploying staff will come under new scrutiny. Cheap, flexible computing equipment and imaginative software, multichannel television and, most important, an economy that rewards young people who are intellectually competent and aggressive will spur parents and older students to end-run the schools. The often boring routine of the traditionally structured high school will be a poor match for these new opportunities. The impatience of ambitious kids and their families will cause growth in the public magnet and private schools, thus siphoning off aggressive citizens into a special enclave of "experimental" exceptional schools, ones that reward students' initiative, use home-based technologies and adhere little to the traditional 1980s fifty-three-minutes-per-day, five-days-a-week curriculum.

In essence, a new kind of school system will evolve, defended as an alternative but in fact an ultimate replacement. But it will serve only those who push for it; unambitious or ill-informed families will get the old gruel. The education gap between the rich and the poor will widen. This fact ultimately will be noticed by the political Left, and a new generation of books on inequality will be published by the mid-1990s.

Parallel to this, and more important, will be the full extension of a national communications system, cementing the cultural homogeneity that has grown with television. As now, entertainment will dominate it, and its base will be commercial: What will go out to millions of Americans will be what those of them who are the spenders of money want. The quick-fix imaging of *People* magazine and the TV advertising spot will be ever more ubiquitous. Sophisticated, interactive communication will be cheap, flexible and therefore powerful. The teachers with their chalk and textbooks will be no competition, and the values of a commercial, consuming society will be more powerfully pervasive than ever. In many ways, such a culture replaces school, or what the nineteenth-century school was designed to provide—an opening to a world beyond a child's own little community, a conversation across time and space, exposure to the ideas and skills that govern the culture. In the subtle, often masked way that democratic societies work, many Americans will increasingly see the power of this evolutionary reality and, comparing it with the productivity of the schools, find the latter wanting. Those families who want something more effective than the traditional schools and more decent and wholesome than the fare disgorged by commercial media will patronize the new "experimental" schools. Their members will be increasingly significant.

In spite of this trend, the old constituencies will go on much as before. The game in Washington over who will testify to what committee, the perils-of-Pauline politics of the overly bureaucratized school systems that serve poor kids, the periodic but brief forays of university influentials into a concern for the arena of mass schooling will continue. But the sea change will assure that these will be trivial matters. The important directions for American education will be found in those ambitious youth who, both within and without the public sector, insist on an end run of traditional education.

Given the fact that broad coalitions for education (sadly or happily) are politically dead in America, those who sense the sea change must seize the opportunity provided by those ambitious citizens intent on the end run of the existing school system. The shape of these "end runs" is where the key, long-term design of education rests. They will be small at first, and apparently tangential—just as public high schools were in 1890 and as commercial television was for the whole culture in 1950.

An enlightened public policy would welcome this trend without regret for the demise of the traditional school. Comprehensive school education had its day and was appropriate for it: *Requiescat in pacem.* Conditions in the 1980s will demand new approaches, and the sensible time to start with the experimental engineering of these is during the Eighties.[12] If broad education-political coalitions are a thing of the past, at the least there might be a new special-interest lobby to attract public and philanthropic support, political and financial, for some fundamental, radical experiments. Wise policy-makers would look beyond the current catfights over merit pay, diploma requirements and tuition tax credits to the far more pressing problem of creating an educating system that is structured in line with the needs and realities of the twenty-first century. The way to do this is to encourage small experiments, to nurture the best of these and to promote the successful. Any temptation to shift all the schools at once to some new model should be resisted; such an effort surely would fail, and the "new" schools need an experimental phase. So policy-makers should think small, but very carefully.

As for practicing schoolpeople, the sooner they join this movement, the better. Their most difficult task will be to assure that poor children are not left behind by this sea change; these children above all must benefit quickly from effective new ways of helping students learn. The temptation will be, as always, to leave them behind, and the teaching profession is perhaps the key lobby to see that this does not happen.

It would be nice in 1993, upon the centennial of that Bible and blueprint of the traditional high school, the NEA *Report of the Committee of Ten on Secondary School Studies,* to find an effective new form of schooling emerging for young Americans, one that started as an end run but eventually became the main track of a modern American education.

Notes

1. For example, the National Commission on Excellence in Education, "A Nation at Risk: the Imperative for Educational Reform" (Washington: U.S. Government Printing Office, 1983); and Ernest L. Boyer, *High School:* A Report of the Carnegie Foundation for the Advancement of Teaching (New York: Harper & Row, 1983).
2. Stanley M. Elam, ed., *A Decade of Gallup Polls of Attitudes Toward Education, 1969–1978* (Bloomington: Phi Delta Kappa, 1978), 2.
3. George H. Gallup, "Gallup Poll of the Public's Attitude Toward the Public Schools," *Phi Delta Kappa,* Sept. 1982, 39, 47.
4. See the forthcoming study by Arthur G. Powell, David K. Cohen, and Eleanor Farrar (Boston: Houghton Mifflin, 1984); and Diane Hedin, Paul Simon and Michael Robin, *Minnesota Youth Poll: Youth's Views on Schools and School Discipline,* Minnesota Report 184 (Agricultural Experiment Station, University of Minnesota, 1983).
5. The teacher's lot is sketched out in detail in my book *Horace's Compromise: The Dilemma of the American High School* (Boston: Houghton Mifflin, 1984).
6. *Brown et al. v. Board of Education of Topeka et al.,* reprinted in David B. Tyack, ed., *Turning Points in American Educational History* (Waltham: Blaisdell, 1967), 306–7.
7. James S. Coleman et al., *Equality of Educational Opportunity* (Washington, D.C.: U.S. Government Printing Office, 1966).
8. Frederick Mosteller and Daniel P. Moynihan, *On Equality of Educational Opportunity* (New York: Random House, 1972); and Christopher Jencks, *Inequality: A Reassessment of Family and Schooling in America* (New York: Basic Books, 1972).
9. Samuel Bowles and Herbert Gintis, *Schooling in Capitalist America: Educational Reform and the Contradictions of Economic Life* (New York: Basic Books, 1976).

10. Jonathan Kozol, *Death at an Early Age* (Boston: Houghton Mifflin, 1967); James Herndon, *The Way It's Spozed to Be* (New York: Simon & Schuster, 1968); Nat Hentoff, *Our Children Are Dying* (New York: Viking, 1967).
11. Charles Silberman, *Crisis in the Classroom* (New York: Random House, 1970), 10ff.
12. See *Horace's Compromise,* especially parts 2 and 4; and John Goodlad, *A Place Called School* (New York: McGraw-Hill, 1963).

8

Understanding Bilingual Education

Raul Yzaguirre and Lori S. Orum

For most of its short history, federal bilingual-education policy has been involved in some sort of tug-of-war between political expediencies and educational needs. The policy has never been comprehensive enough to meet the needs of all children with special language needs; still, substantial gains have been made since the days when schools could, and did, ignore the educational civil rights of language-minority children with complete impunity. The gains of the last decade, however, have been steadily eroded since 1980 as the Reagan administration has attempted to reshape federal bilingual-education policy. The administration has tried, with some success, to reduce the availability of bilingual-education funds, to direct federal assistance to English-only approaches, to reduce by definition the population of children eligible for services, and to transfer some of the federal government's responsibilities to the states. This approach has met with resistance from those who do not share the president's vision of "educational new federalism" and believe that continued federal direction is necessary both to safeguard civil rights and to design a language policy that addresses national needs.

Although the Reagan administration has not been able to enact all of its policy proposals in bilingual education, those changes that have been made have curtailed enforcement of civil-rights laws affecting language-minority children, significantly cut funding and reduced the number of students receiving services.

While policy directions are difficult to reverse, future federal bilingual-education policy need not follow the course charted by the current administration. There are a series of compelling reasons why this

Raul Yzaguirre is president of the National Council of La Raza. Lori S. Orum is senior education policy analyst for the Council.

should not occur, and a variety of forces that will push policy in different directions. The changing demographics of the public schools are an increasingly important force in shaping this policy. Public opinion, positive and negative, and the political weight of the various constituencies most directly affected by bilingual education will also play a part in determining what sort of policy evolves. It is still too early to predict which of several suggested directions will prevail, but the federal Bilingual Education Act must be reauthorized this year, and some policy changes are certain to be reflected in the new legislation.

The National Council of La Raza's vision for the future of bilingual education is contained in the policy recommendations that follow. This vision is based on the belief that bilingual education is one of the major civil-rights issues of the 1980s and that the educational attainment of Hispanic-American children must be dramatically improved. However, bilingual education remains one of the most poorly understood of all federal education programs.

Like other emotion-laden issues, bilingual education is more often surrounded by myths and misperceptions than by simple, factual information. Unfortunately, many discussions on this issue never move past the myths to the facts. Positions on bilingual education are intimately connected to individuals' views of whether a pluralistic American society is desirable or even possible. There is also the fear that bilingual education may lead to widespread bilingualism and create "another Quebec" in the United States. Although the political and language situations in Quebec and the United States are not analogous, this fear is repeatedly voiced in the media and before congressional committees.

Simply defined for our purposes, bilingual education is the use of two languages, one of which is English, as a means of providing instruction. Federal bilingual-education policy dates from 1968 with the passage of the Bilingual Education Act, Title VII of the Elementary and Secondary Education Act, which provided some limited federal assistance for districts choosing to implement bilingual-education programs. The type of bilingual education supported by Title VII is designed chiefly to teach English to limited-English-proficient (LEP) children, and to use the native language to provide temporary access to other subjects while the children are learning English. These programs include a structured English language component and use the native language of the child only to the extent necessary to teach basic skills so that children do not fall behind their peers in other content areas while they are learning English. Other types of bilingual programs financed by state and local funds may include the broader goals of developing a child's capabilities in both languages, and have less emphasis on the quick transition to an English-only curriculum. Title VII initially supported these types of programs as well, but current policy is to support only the "transitional" form of bilingual education.

Title VII is a discretionary program and funds are available only by successful competition for a grant. Funding is very competitive due to the small Title VII budget and the large number of children needing services. In fact, the Office of Bilingual Education and Minority Languages Affairs (OBEMLA) is able to fund only approximately 50 percent of the applications it receives. Local educational agencies (LEAs) design their own bilingual programs and submit proposals to the federal government requesting funds for their particular brands of bilingual education. Programmatic requirements are quite flexible; federal regulations require only that English and some amount of the children's native language be used in instruction. Because of these limited requirements, programs funded by Title VII vary tremendously.

One of the few federal constraints on program design is that districts must avoid the unnecessary separation of limited-English-proficient students from other students. LEP children are to be separated from other children only for those portions of the school day where such grouping is a bona fide educational necessity. To avoid segregation, local districts are also allowed to design programs in which up to 40 percent of the students are fluent English speakers.

Title VII also supports efforts to train bilingual teachers, and provides funding for bilingual vocational training, research and supportive services. Support services include centers that develop and disseminate curricular materials and offer training and technical assistance to teachers, paraprofessionals, administrators and parents. These activities have not always received federal support, however. Teacher training was not added until 1974, and funds were not available for research until 1978, so some aspects of this young program are embryonic. The newness of the research component has contributed to the scarcity of high-quality evaluations of bilingual programs and has left

TItle VII vulnerable to the charge that it is difficult to determine whether or not these federally funded programs are being effective.

The other major aspect of federal bilingual-education policy emanates from Title VI of the Civil Rights Act of 1964, which specifies that no person in the United States shall, on the basis of national origin, be subjected to discrimination in any activity receiving federal assistance. The Department of Health, Education and Welfare's interpretation of Title VI as prohibiting the denial of access to education programs because of a student's limited English proficiency was set forth in a guideline known as the "May 25, 1970, Memorandum" and was upheld by the U.S. Supreme Court in *Lau* v. *Nichols* in 1974. After the *Lau* decision, HEW developed a set of guidelines for school districts interpreting their responsibilities to language-minority children. These guidelines, known as the "Lau Remedies," were the basis of some 500 compliance agreements negotiated with school districts.

The Lau Remedies required that limited-English-proficient children be taught English as rapidly as possible and that these students be provided with instruction in locally required subjects in a language they could understand while they learned English. Although HEW used these guidelines for several years to negotiate compliance with districts, the Lau Remedies were never published as regulations. As a result, an Alaska school district brought suit, and in 1978 a federal court decree required HEW to promulgate regulations defining its standards for enforcing Title VI. This ruling led to the 1980 notice of proposed rule making, by the newly created Department of Education, of the Lau Regulations, which were based largely on the previous Lau Remedies and were the subject of much congressional debate. Finally, Congress passed a resolution delaying the implementation of the regulations until June 1, 1981, to allow study of the issues raised during debate. However, on February 2, 1981, President Ronald Reagan's secretary of education, Terrel Bell, withdrew the proposed regulations.

Although Secretary Bell initially pledged to issue new regulations in response to the 1978 court order, to date none have been promulgated, and thus there are currently no regulations or guidelines defining the responsibilities of school districts to language-minority children. Instead, the Department of Education returned to the Lau Remedies for a time, and finally announced that even these would no longer be enforced. Districts were invited to renegotiate their previous

Lau compliance plans on the basis of the department's new flexible approach to negotiating compliance, with little federal protection when local districts do not seriously attempt to meet the needs of these children.

The Reagan administration's attempts to redirect federal bilingual-education policy have not been limited to changes in civil-rights policies. Title VII has also been the subject of a series of attacks. Ostensibly as part of the president's overall commitment to reducing budget deficits, the Reagan administration has, until its fiscal year 1985 request, proposed cuts in the Title VII budget at every juncture in the budget process. Some of these requests have been approved by Congress, although the last two proposed cuts were rejected. Still, the administration has succeeded in reducing the federal funds available for bilingual education from a high of $172 million in fiscal year 1980 to $138 million in fiscal year 1984. The president requested $94.5 million for Title VII in 1984, which, if approved, would have represented an overall reduction of 45 percent in the Title VII budget since 1980.

Although initial budget cuts were defended solely on the basis of the need to reduce the federal budget deficit, more recently the administration has contended that there are not really as many limited-English-proficient children as initially believed, and therefore less funds are necessary to serve them. This is based largely on proposed changes in the definition of children in need. The attempt to define the need away is consistent with the administration's policies in other areas as well. Interestingly, language projection studies funded by the Department of Education actually predict substantial increases in the number of LEP children. Since approximately 70 percent of these children are Hispanic and 1980 census data indicated a considerable growth in the number of Hispanics, census data also appear to contradict the administration's assertion that the number of LEP children is smaller than previously thought.

A CLIMATE FOR CHANGE

Despite the policy directions previously described, positive changes still could occur in federal bilingual-education policy. Sometime during the current Congress, Title VII must be reauthorized. The reauthorization process provides an important forum to evaluate the progress of programs and make any adjustments that are necessary to respond to changing needs. In addition to the administration's proposals, which would extend the bill through 1985, legislation has been introduced in the House simply to extend Title VII as it is currently written until 1989. In spite of the Reagan administration's outlook on bilingual education, this may well be a good time to reexamine and refine federal bilingual-education policy.

Since the legislation was last amended in 1978, several important changes have occurred. The numbers of limited-English-proficient children of U.S. citizens have increased, and there are growing numbers of immigrant and refugee LEP children in need of special educational services. The large number of refugees from Southeast Asia, Central America, Haiti and Cuba all postdate the last amendments.

In addition to the growing numbers of children needing bilingual education, there has also been an increasing recognition that American public education in general could use some adjustments. The public is aware that the current system is not adequately preparing students to be workers in a highly interdependent and technological world. Many educators and policy-makers have recently decided that it may no longer be sufficient simply to be able to speak, read and write English, and many of the recent studies on the state of American education have called attention to the need to improve both computer literacy and foreign-language education. If we as a nation are seriously committed to promoting multiple language learning, bilingual education is a logical beginning for a national language policy for all American children. If the quality of education available in public schools needs substantial improvement, then the quality of education available in Title VII bilingual programs must also be carefully examined and upgraded where necessary. The call to improve U.S. public education must be a call to improve education for all children, not just the "average" child profiled in most of the recent reports on the state of public education.

Public-school demographics have changed the picture of the "average" schoolchild. Census data have dramatically illustrated the changes in the shape and complexion of the public-school population and the fact that many large city school districts are now "majority minority." Given the youthfulness and larger family size of Hispanics, the Hispanic share of the public-school population will continue to increase over the coming decades. These changes in the makeup of the public-school population are especially important since demographers have also signaled the coming "age gap"—when the two largest groups of Americans will be the elderly and the children. Within this sort of demographic structure, strategies to improve the educational outcomes and employability of the large numbers of Hispanic school-children are crucial, since these children will be a large part of the work force ultimately called upon to support the Social Security system. Demographic changes have made bilingual education a national necessity.

The final positive factor is that Hispanics are an increasing political and economic presence in the United States, and Hispanics overwhelmingly support bilingual education. Population increases and reapportionment have contributed to the presence of sizable Hispanic constituencies for many congressmembers who had never had a particular interest in "Hispanic issues." Hispanics have also made their presence felt at the ballot box. This year there are more Hispanic congressmembers than ever before and Hispanics are now the swing vote in five of the ten largest states. The rate of Hispanic political participation is on the upswing, and a nationwide voter-registration drive is under way to register 1 million Hispanic voters before the 1984 election. Hispanics are also an important economic force in the United States, possessing over $60 billion in annual purchasing power. It is becoming difficult and foolhardy for politicians to discount the policy preferences of Hispanics.

VISIONS FOR THE FUTURE

The federal government has both an opportunity and a responsibility to provide leadership and guidance to help schools better educate limited-English-proficient children. In order to adequately meet the educational needs of these children, and be a part of an overall strategy to improve American education, federal bilingual-education policy in the 1980s must contain the following features:

- a commitment to increase the number of highly qualified bilingual teachers and other school personnel;

- a commitment to provide understandable instruction in locally required subjects while children learn English;
- a definition of language learning that moves beyond oral proficiency to full literacy;
- an emphasis on parent and community involvement; and
- a commitment to decrease the isolation of language-minority students.

During the 1980s, the United States should also move toward a national language policy that recognizes that bilingualism is in the national interest for all Americans. Title VII programs can be a part of this policy but should not be the only catalyst. Each of the above features is important to improving and expanding the educational opportunities available through bilingual education.

Increasing the Number of Highly Qualified Bilingual Teachers and Other School Personnel

Probably the most important long-term changes in bilingual education will come about because of the availability of well-trained teachers. One of the most pervasive problems in bilingual education to date has been the absence of adequate numbers of properly trained personnel to implement programs. The need to train bilingual school personnel is still with us, despite the administration's contention that we now have enough teachers and can begin to phase out training programs. A recent study on teacher language skills showed that of 55,000 teachers using a non-English language for some part of their teaching day, 35,000 (over 63 percent) have absolutely no special academic qualifications to be using that language. Only 21 percent of all those teachers have both academic qualifications and the ability to use the non-English language competently enough to teach subject matter through that language. Among teachers of English as a second language (ESL), the situation is even more dismal: Of all those teachers currently teaching ESL, only 17 percent have ever had even one course in how to teach ESL. This figure should cause great concern to those who advocate replacing bilingual education programs with ESL programs. It is dangerous to assume that on-the-job-training will adequately compensate for this abysmal lack of adequately trained personnel.

It is also important to realize that bilingual classroom teachers solve only one part of the problem. Other instructional personnel also need to be trained to work with LEP children. The new math-science teacher-training initiatives should call our attention to the fact that these teachers should also be trained in the techniques of teaching math and science to LEP students. Special programs also need to be available to LEP children. Without bilingual special education, and gifted and talented teachers, these programs are not accessible to LEP children. Additionally, there is a tremendous need to increase the numbers of bilingual school counselors, school psychologists, principals and administrators. We have not done the whole job simply by training bilingual classroom teachers.

Ensuring Understandable Instruction in Subject Areas

This concept is the cornerstone of bilingual education and is a feature that must not disappear from federal bilingual-education policy. It is important that policy-makers remember that American education does more for monolingual English-speaking children than just work on their English skills, and bilingual education must do the same. No parent would place his or her elementary-aged child in a school that offered instruction only in English-language skills. The central purpose of federal bilingual-education policy must be to provide children with equal access to education, and education entails comprehensible instruction in math, science and social studies in addition to English-language arts.

Given the multilingual character of some school districts, there may be instances when it is not possible to offer this instruction in the child's native language. However, bilingual education is practical in the schools that the overwhelming majority of language-minority children attend. In instances where bilingual education is not possible, districts have the responsibility for bringing their best resources to bear to make full and comprehensible instruction available. While federal assistance in this endeavor would certainly be beneficial, such assistance must not come about at the expense of bilingual programs. No federal assistance should be provided to programs that do not provide for comprehensible instruction in content areas.

Literacy

Our society has long passed the days when literacy could be defined simply on the basis of ability to write one's own name. Nor does the qualification of having completed the fifth grade adequately prepare individuals for full political and economic participation; deciphering rental agreements, bank statements, job applications and ballots requires more than that level of literacy. To work in technical and professional fields, the level of literacy demanded is even higher.

Given the importance of literacy in our society, bilingual educational programs must be as accountable as every other education program for teaching children how to read and write in English. Merely concentrating on oral language skills—i.e., teaching children to speak English—is woefully inadequate, and yet that is the focus of many programs. It is important to move beyond a definition of English proficiency that is so heavily based on speaking. To be English-proficient, to be an English *user,* means being able to understand, speak, read and write English.

Illiteracy is a special problem in the Hispanic community. Recent research from the University of Texas at Austin suggests that 56 percent of the Hispanic population may be functionally illiterate. Although Hispanics living in integrated areas become English speakers at about the same rate as everybody else, there is not an automatic shift in written language. The absence of good educational programs designed to help children become proficient language users has caused many children to be illiterate in both Spanish and English. Children should not be "graduated" from programs as soon as they speak a few words of English; they must be able to read and write English before they can compete equally with monolingual children in English-only classrooms. Federal bilingual-education policy must reflect that necessity.

Parent Involvement

Meaningful parent participation in bilingual programs must continue to be a part of federal bilingual-education policy. Although parent participation is closely correlated with student achievement, interaction with the schools was all but impossible for the parents of LEP students before bilingual educational programs. In many schools, the advent of a bilingual program brings the first school staff able to communicate with the parents of limited-English-proficient students. Without bilingual school personnel as a bridge to the LEP community, parents are unable to communicate with the schools in emergency situations, let alone participate as classroom volunteers, join parent organizations or help their children with homework. Parent participation must remain a central component of any federally supported bilingual educational program.

As districts with multilingual student populations struggle to develop and provide appropriate language programs, they must also devise ways to provide parents with access to school information and encourage parent participation. Admittedly, this is more challenging in multilingual situations, but it is not impossible.

Decreasing Isolation

Last, but certainly not least, federal bilingual-education policy must expand its efforts to ensure that children are not isolated within schools on the basis of language, and that bilingual programs are not used as an excuse for segregation. A good start has already been made in this direction since federally funded bilingual programs may contain up to 40 percent fluent English-speaking children. However, because need is usually greater than funding, districts have been hesitant to let fully English-proficient children be a part of Title VII programs when this might mean that limited-English-proficient children would have to be excluded. Indeed, it is difficult to argue that already inadequate resources should be stretched even further to provide fluent English speakers with bilingual education. However, with additional funding, integrated, reciprocal bilingual educational programs that help all children learn two languages have the most potential for meeting our dual needs of improved educational opportunities for language-minority children and increased language resources for the nation as a whole.

CONCLUSION

Although the term *bilingual education* is emotional, the concept and practice are logical, necessary and beneficial to all Americans. Perhaps, in the interest of better public understanding, the name needs to be changed. However, the number of these "dual language" programs needs to be increased, and the quality improved to keep pace with other national efforts to upgrade public education. These programs, whatever they are called, are necessary if public education is to respond to our changing national needs and continue to address the need for improved educational opportunities for language-minority children.

9

Revisioning Public Responsibility

Peter B. Edelman

About 35 million Americans—over 15 percent of us—live in families with incomes below the federally defined poverty line. This is the highest percentage since 1967 and the highest absolute number since 1965.

The Reagan administration's budget cuts and recession have exacerbated the situation considerably, but the fact is that it has been gradually worsening, with some ups and downs, since 1973, when the poverty percentage was 11.1 percent, or around 23 million people.

It is the purpose of this essay to ask what might be done, after Reagan, to reverse the trend of the past decade and move toward significant reductions in the incidence of poverty in America.

It would be easy but wrongheaded to advocate "solving" the problem by transfer payments. It would be wrong because it is more expensive than our politics are likely to support, because it would represent a continuing drain on public resources that an employment and training strategy would avoid, and because it would likely continue a pattern of destructive and debilitating dependence that is already too prevalent in our currently inadequate structures of assistance to the poor.

I hasten to stress that transfer payments, both cash and in kind, have been and remain critical elements of policy. Many Americans cannot work. Many other Americans cannot find work. The transfer payments we have in place are preventing a far higher incidence of poverty. Sheldon Danziger of the University of Wisconsin estimates that more like 50 million people would be poor without the assistance currently provided in the form of welfare, SSI, food stamps, subsidized housing, Medicaid and a few other programs.

Peter B. Edelman is professor of law at Georgetown University.

Nor is the assistance provided by current transfer programs anything like adequate. Aid to Families with Dependent Children—
"welfare," in popular parlance—provides average benefits at about
half the "official" poverty line, and these benefits were in fact reduced
in terms of real purchasing power by about 30 percent between 1969
and 1981. Food-stamp assistance is worth about $10 a person a week,
an average of about 47 cents per person per meal.

Public policy has shifted the demographics of poverty over the past
decade. The elderly are no longer as poor as they used to be. The
indexation of Social Security and the growth of SSI have brought
poverty among the elderly down to the point where the percentage of
the elderly that is poor is the same as that for the rest of the population. While segments of the elderly do remain disproportionately poor
—specifically, women and minorities—the dramatic increase in poverty over the past decade has occurred elsewhere: among female-
headed households, to be precise. Over half the children who live in
female-headed households in America now live in poverty.

Yet even this figure is misleading, because, at least in the minority
communities, the male counterparts of the households—the fathers of
the children—often do not show up in the statistics at all. They have
stopped looking for work, and they are not counted by the census.
Some of them do appear in our crime statistics, and some of those in
turn live in our prisons. If an epidemic of teen-age pregnancy visibly
characterizes the young women in minority poverty areas, a continuing epidemic of heroin addiction grips the young men of those areas.
Poverty has been "feminized," to be sure, but one should make no
mistake: The feminization of poverty has a male counterpart.

If the "old" poor are worse off than they were a decade ago, there
is of course a new phenomenon in the current decade, a "new" poor
composed of workers displaced by the multiple effects of international
competition and the flight of jobs abroad, automation and the recession. Warnings abound that many of those laid off in the current
recession will never be called back to their old plants.

In the past, the litany of programmatic response to the foregoing
would have been a platform of training and retraining, with the bigger
spenders also advocating large-scale job creation. The more "liberal"
advocates would have insisted that the "old" poor be fully involved
as participants along with the newer category of displaced workers.

As an isolated strategy, this will no longer wash. Full employment is simply not achievable by making the government the "employer of last resort," not when there are well over 10 million people out of work and we already have a $200-billion deficit. The public sector cannot resolve the extensive employment problems in this economy. The answer has to begin with macroeconomic policy. The economy will not get well and stay well when it is running $200-billion deficits. Deficits of that magnitude become inflationary when recovery is well enough along not to be assisted by the stimulative effect of big deficits. Lenders know this, and they will continue to demand high interest rates to cover the eroding of the dollars they will receive down the road after the continued big deficits have their inflationary effect. And when private borrowers begin wanting credit again, they and the government will be competing for it, driving interest rates up further. High interest rates will prevent sustained recovery, so full-employment advocates must begin by doing everything possible to get interest rates to come down and stay down—and that means attending to the deficit.

But attending to the deficit is hard going. It means collecting more revenues and spending less. On the spending side, about the only area left for serious belt-tightening is defense. (We can and probably should tighten up on railroad retirement, federal retirement and veterans' pensions, but the dollar figures involved aren't large. And we have to tighten up on health care, but that isn't to save money—it's to prevent a bigger drain down the line.)

Revenue-raising is not very popular. A fair amount can be raised by broadening the base, as the reformers have come to call it, but much of the base-broadening will be opposed by powerful special interests, and even a high degree of success in broadening the base will probably not restore enough of the lost revenue. Reagan's enduring contribution has been to destroy the federal revenue base.

The honest politician's guide to restoring America's economic health and reaching full employment begins, therefore, with serious and unpleasant measures to close the deficit, the tax portions of which would go into effect once the recovery is well under way and before it is choked off by continued high interest rates. (It should also include an "incomes" policy to moderate the price and wage increases that resurgent inflationary pressures presage.)

The next problem is that the most intelligent macroeconomic policy will, according to the most optimistic macroeconomists, reduce unemployment only to 6 percent, with the usual far higher numbers for minorities. The problem is deeper than was previously understood by structural-policy enthusiasts, but structural policy is essential.

Throughout, the ultimate complication to be faced is that while the outcome of an "industrial policy" that works may be healthy enterprises, all right—revitalized American auto and steel industries and other industries getting to new international market frontiers on an accelerated basis—they may be healthy only because they are highly automated. They may turn a big profit and employ very few people.

This is not an argument for refusing to produce in the most efficient way possible. That is a choice that is unavailable. Deliberately continuing on a high-cost, labor-intensive path in order to save jobs will destroy the jobs and the enterprises at the same time.

On a sustaining basis, the commitment to fairness can come only from a healthy economy. A shrinking pie cannot produce enduring fairness; expanding the pie must become everyone's business.

In that context, structural policy must involve much more than the "industrial policy" everyone is talking about. It must encompass the full range of education and training policies, stronger antidiscrimination enforcement, measures to enhance workplace satisfaction and safety, and the rebuilding of vitally needed infrastructure.

And this is where the use of some of the profits from the modernized, automated economy can be critical in putting people to work in new public-service roles. Recent studies by the Urban Institute and the American Institute of Research have identified nearly a million and a half useful jobs that could be performed by nonprofessional workers—in education, caring for the elderly and the severely handicapped, energy, environment, conservation, family services, day care, and law enforcement and corrections. This is to say nothing of the possibilities for fully trained professionals in those fields if the financing were available.

Everything I have mentioned is an essential part of a strategy to reduce poverty. Everything is necessary. No one thing is sufficient.

MINORITY EMPLOYMENT

Nonetheless, there is one element on which I wish to focus especially. The story begins with the absolutely abysmal performance of our society in bringing minority young people into full participation in our economy. That abysmal performance, I suggest, has a great deal to do with why we tend to keep relying on an income-maintenance approach to "entitlements," which in turn perpetuates a dependency from which too many of its clients cannot escape.

For the longer run, it is imperative that we arrive at a new perspective on the idea of entitlements. We require a new design that uses the concept of "entitlement" as a force to bring people to self-sufficiency as functioning, taxpaying participants in the economy. Lest I be misunderstood, I would stress again that the entitlement I am about to advocate will have less than full impact if its participants cannot graduate into unsubsidized employment—i.e., if the economy is unhealthy. But we dare not wait on the needed amalgam of policies to restore growth before pursuing greater equity in how the current pie is shared. Indeed that emphasis should stimulate and guide our search for a healthy economy.

The demographics of this decade pose mounting problems if we do not act. The number of eighteen-year-olds will decrease by about 12 percent during the rest of this decade, which would be good news for youth-employment trends except for the fact that the number of black and Hispanic eighteen-year-olds is on the upswing and will shortly constitute about a 33-percent larger portion of the cohort of entry-level workers.

Some history is in order. Federally financed welfare assistance (i.e., AFDC) was created in the 1930s as a relatively minor part of the Social Security Act. The expectation was that as the nation came out of the depression, welfare would be a residual program of fairly modest size for those who were unable to work, including the rather small number of widowed or divorced mothers of small children who were not in a position to work because of their child-caring responsibilities. It was assumed that economic growth would produce full employment. (Of course, full employment assumed that most women would be married, have children and stay home. Adult female labor-force participation at the end of World War II hovered at about 33 percent.)

In the postwar period, however, enormous and unforeseen social and economic changes began to occur. A baby boom of unprecedented proportion took place, creating an inevitable problem down the road for absorption of this larger group into the labor market. And, shortly, women began to enter the labor market in increasing numbers.

Meanwhile, the rural-to-urban migration that had begun in the 1930s had been accelerated by the demands of the war production effort. With barely a pause for absorption of the previous arrivals, the newest phase of the agricultural revolution began. The twin miracles of mechanization and chemicals drove thousands more off the farms, a process given added stimulus later on by repressive measures in the South taken against blacks during the civil-rights movement.

In the West and Southwest, the reduced need for migrant agricultural labor brought a large Chicano population to the cities, as did a fair amount of illegal immigration. The crushing poverty in Puerto Rico drove many Puerto Ricans to New York and other cities in the East.

There were not enough jobs to absorb the huge and continuing stream of immigrants, and many of them lacked even the most basic skills to do other than farm work. At the same time, a process of structural economic change was under way, making jobs for the unskilled much less prevalent. In addition, these new immigrants encountered widespread discriminatory treatment. The only government assistance generally available was welfare, which was primarily limited to families that had split apart.

Unemployment in the major urban areas climbed steadily. Black teen-age unemployment—always the highest relative to other groups —was less than 15 percent in 1950. It is now over 50 percent, with most of that increase coming in the last twelve or thirteen years, in tandem with the general increase in unemployment over that time.

In the late 1950s and early 1960s, public debate began to acknowledge the poverty and racial discrimination in our midst. But the half-loaf that the economy, supplemented by the government, offered in response was not good enough.

Some good things did happen. The demolition of discriminatory legal barriers, along with the extraordinary burst of prosperity of the 1960s, produced an emerging black middle class and, not far behind, a considerable new Hispanic middle class. In some areas, access to better-paying jobs occurred on a wholesale basis—think of transit workers in many cities and of automobile assembly lines. But the new pool of potential workers was not being fully absorbed. Limited job-training efforts were undertaken, to be sure, but these were insufficient in scope and consisted too often of training people for jobs that did not exist. Many jobs moved to the suburbs and became relatively inaccessible to residents of the inner city. Although some inner-city residents certainly managed to get such jobs and move closer to them, too many remained behind.

We now see that an iron vise was tightening—schools and other institutions that didn't convey sufficient work skills, and jobs that weren't there. The more aggressive, resourceful and talented were able to escape its grip. For the rest, help came to consist primarily of cash assistance rather than aid in reaching self-sufficiency.

In the mid-1960s, a new set of phenomena appeared: the poverty program, the welfare-rights movement and the development of legal advocacy for the poor. The welfare rolls started to grow. Food stamps became a major factor in the early 1970s when the unlikely interplay of George McGovern and Richard Nixon caused that program to be expanded into an important source of income maintenance. But these constructive steps were not coupled with a sufficient effort to bring skills and employment to the young in areas of high unemployment.

The economy was in general quite successful in absorbing new workers during this period. But women were seeking and competing for jobs across the board, while the baby boom, too, was being assimilated. As a result, low-income minority young people found that their situation was on the whole getting worse rather than better. Too many others were ahead of them in the queue.

The most recent symptom of this circumstance is the "feminization" of poverty. A change in family structures has been occurring throughout the society, but the lack of economic opportunity for low-income young people has been an important factor in the current wave of adolescent pregnancy in the minority communities. This has been a significant force in bringing about the increased number of minority female-headed households, and a very large number of these, in turn, live in poverty.

The imperative to contend with what has become a continuing process of decline and stagnation is complicated by a sick economy and a general loss of faith in its capacity for strength and equity, too.

How do we break out of this vicious cycle?

The keys for minorities are jobs and training. Even the much-needed improved macroeconomy will require a perception of these as "entitlements" if the cycle is to be broken. The necessary strategy is more complicated than any we have undertaken previously. The complexity is dual: the many different kinds of activity that will be required, and the many different institutions, both public and private, that will need to participate.

THE ROLE OF THE SCHOOL

Beyond the absolutely fundamental need for a sufficient number of jobs, one institution is critical. It is the school that is at once a provider of knowledge and skills, a center of personal development and citizenship awareness, and a bridge to the job market.

Something like half the age cohort of eighteen-year-olds each year do not enter a postsecondary institution of any kind. Most of these enter the labor market. Thus the issue of the school as "bridge" occurs almost everywhere. Employers are widely dissatisfied with the preparation given by the school to their entry-level workers.

Efforts to improve our schools are nothing new. And the educational side of the agenda here is certainly not confined to the "regular" school system. But it is also the case that employment and training initiatives over the past two decades tended to look at just about everything except the "mainstream" high school for the required educational component. High schools, especially those serving large concentrations of low-income students, have received scorn by the bookshelf and not a fair share of the efforts of either educational or employment strategists. A look at two of the approaches of the 1960s illustrates why.

One was the creation of alternative schools—street academies, community schools and other entities that circumvented the inner-city high school or picked up its dropouts. The idea was, in part, that these alternatives would be yardsticks against which to compare the performance of the "regular" high school, and the contrast would spur changes in the mainstream system, much as the TVA showed the nation what was lacking in the performance and pricing structure of private electric-power companies. Many young people benefited from these alternative institutions, but little change occurred in the mainstream high schools along the more efficacious lines identified by these efforts.

The second was the Elementary and Secondary Education Act of 1965, and in particular Title I thereof, which provides aid for disadvantaged children in the development of basic skills. The problem here is that, in operation, nearly 90 percent of the aid has been concentrated below the ninth grade. No doubt, this is for the good and logical reason that one spends limited resources where one thinks they will do the most good, and getting a child early certainly will tend to be more cost-effective. But the side effect has been that the high schools have largely been untouched by any direct federal stimulus.

The time is absolutely ripe for a new initiative. Test scores seem to be rising in the elementary grades and also, although to a lesser extent, in junior high. This suggests the value of school intervention and the potential of a major push for improvement in our senior high schools. Why the recent gains in younger children's test scores? The years of investment in Title I probably are one reason. Another reason may be that many of the larger urban school systems serving high concentrations of minorities have, after years of turmoil and division, settled down in the past decade with new leadership. With a minority person in the top slot, and with significant minority representation throughout senior management and on the school board, schools have begun to face minorities with dignity and deep commitment.

This new leadership is beginning to turn its attention to the high schools—often with the assistance of other units of government and aided by partnership and cooperation with the local business community. This is beginning to occur in dozens of cities.

How can these new consortia operate most effectively? First, they must approach the problems with a sense of strategy geared to the practical needs and economic possibilities in the community and its environs. Second, there must be a major concentration on reinforcing at the high-school level the basic skills that have been receiving attention for some time in the lower grades. Computer literacy and mathematical and scientific groundwork for participation in the newly emerging "high-tech" industries should be especially stressed in the schools that serve low-income students.

The business community—particularly those corporations that

have education "systems" of their own—can help in the design of basic skills curricula. Their role is vital to the practical and central task of building better bridges to the job market. This means getting better labor-market information into the schools. This, in turn, will influence job-related curriculum design and choice of program direction by students. School systems and local Private Industry Councils, established under recent federal legislation, should work together on these tasks, and PICs should play the key role in involving the business community in the effort. Regular visits by Employment Service people to the school would be of major value, too. Also important is attention to developing readiness for negotiating entry to the job market—teaching students how to fill out applications, how to deal with interviews, how to respond to supervision and how to keep a job, once secured.

If many high-school students literally or almost literally do not know how to go "downtown" and look for a job, or even what possible jobs there are downtown, it is also true that all too often downtown employers consciously avoid considering the graduates of certain high schools. This is partially due to discriminatory attitudes, but it is also due to long experience with the poor preparation of many graduates of urban high schools. It becomes easier to create a blanket policy of exclusion than to examine candidates on a case-by-case basis. This has to change. It has been a vicious cycle, because the more avenues to the job market are closed, the more defeated and defeating some high schools are going to be. Every employer who hires high-school graduates as entry-level employees must be persuaded to make a renewed and special effort not only to recruit in every high school but also to work with those schools to ensure that there are qualified candidates for jobs.

As the young people get slightly older, the education agenda becomes a training agenda. In other words, the education agenda is much more than the issue of improving the public high schools. The community college has a key role. Regional vocational-technical high schools, where they exist, can be important. And when the young people have already dropped out of school, there is the long-standing question of just what entities are the best ones to get the job done. The answer will vary from community to community. For too long, policy initiatives on work and training have stopped at the water's edge with regard to school dropouts. They are a difficult clientele to serve, often reading poorly or not at all and exhibiting serious problems of behavior and attitude, so it is understandable that programs have tended to "cream," or "triage," helping those who are easiest to help with the limited dollars available. Nonetheless, in a renewed effort to break into the cycle of poverty by providing intensified training and work opportunities for people when they are chronologically ready for the labor market, those who have special needs do indeed merit an extra effort.

Recognizing that the education agenda slides over into the training agenda helps delineate another function for the business community in the locality, with the PIC playing a catalytic role. That function is the mutual, shared design and implementation of training programs for specific jobs. To the extent that public funds subsidize business and industry for part of the cost of training employees in order to get training to people who would ordinarily not get trained and hired, the employers should be willing to help design the program and make a commitment to hire the graduates. This notion of a shared public-private responsibility for training is at the heart of the recently enacted Job Partnership Training Act, so it is one piece of the strategy that is at least partially in place.

An employment strategy for young people, however, must go beyond education and training. It must include provision for private-sector work experience. A major problem young people—especially low-income minority young people—face when they look for a job is that they have never worked. They have no experience. CETA experience—i.e., work experience in a created public- or nonprofit-sector job —was looked at skeptically, and in any case it is now no longer available. A critical element in easing the entry of a young person into the labor market is the demonstration that he or she has worked for a private employer. It is a key credential.

We must develop new forms of experiential education—cooperative education and other forms of work experience that are integrally a part of the schooling process. This is an area that overlaps with the need to subsidize work experience for many young people as a part of their training, since it may well be that the kind of quasi-apprenticeship experience that would be valuable for the student is not one where he or she is going to be sufficiently productive to justify an unsubsidized wage.

All of the education agenda will unfold and develop more quickly if federal policy stimulates and encourages it. Even over President Reagan's objection, which is sure to be interposed regardless of his recent verbal expressions of interest, the Congress could enact the framework now and begin with modest funding.

An important component of a youth jobs/education/training strategy would be subsidized work experience in the private sector, with the private training slots concentrated in small businesses so that a personal supervisory relationship could be established. Five years ago such an initiative would have been much harder to contemplate as a practical matter than it is today. The creation and gradual sophistication of the PICs make it possible to develop a public-private structure at the local level, which, with sufficient staff, could develop enough placement sites to make private-sector work experience and training workable.

If there were ample jobs available on a fully nondiscriminatory and geographically accessible basis, the only issue would be how to produce properly trained workers most efficiently. Under those circumstances, classroom training and on-the-job training for a job already committed are proven strategies. However, well-designed work and training combinations are also effective, and that fact seems particularly important in the current circumstances. With the barriers that exist for low-income minority young people in particular, and the general state of the economy, on-the-job training is less likely to be available to them, and classroom training by itself may not be attractive enough without being connected to a paycheck.

I argued earlier that this should be structured as an entitlement. How would this be done? It would be designed on a means-tested basis. The entitlement would assure young people from low-income families a substantial period of training and "quasi-apprenticeship," which would have the effect for many of preventing a lifetime of welfare dependency. Practically speaking, fiscal realities, as well as the time needed for effective implementation, are likely to dictate that some years would pass before the program could be put on an entitlement basis. But when that time came, it would be an investment well worth the cost. It is an investment that many other countries regularly make. It is an investment that we would need to make even when the economy recovers, because we are talking about the people who were suffering a depression even when there was no recession.

The entitlement I propose would at a minimum be an entitlement to a part-time job during the school year, full-time during the summer, for low-income students during their last two years of high school. Returning to school (or participation in a high-school-equivalency program) would be a condition of participation for dropouts. Staying in school would be a condition for those in school at the outset. Minimum age would be sixteen; maximum, the twentieth birthday. There would be a preference for private-sector placement, but public-sector and nonprofit agency placement would be permissible.

This model was in fact the subject of an impressively successful demonstration in seventeen locations during the Carter years. It was called the Youth Incentive Entitlement Pilot Projects (YIEPP). The Manpower Development Research Corporation of New York City conducted a systematic evaluation of the demonstration and found that it helped many students stay in school and was of value in terms of transition to next steps in their lives.

The costs of the program (in addition to the costs of schooling) are low, about $4,300 annually per participant. This is because the jobs created are mainly part-time jobs.

This is by no means a full-scale youth employment and training strategy. The educational policy measures outlined above are critical as well, and there is a serious issue as to what happens to the "graduates" of the entitlement program if they cannot find unsubsidized work. A significant investment in a variety of public-jobs initiatives, from so-called soft public works to human services, is necessary to respond to the continuing lack of enough jobs to go around and the inequitable distribution of the jobs that do exist. An annual investment of $10 billion for a near-term jobs program, to be carried out at the local level by people most familiar with local tasks, is the minimum that is required.

At the same time, public policy should make a greater effort to create more private-sector jobs especially accessible to low-income people. The track record here is mixed, to say the least, but it is worth saying that if a "modern Reconstruction Finance Corporation" becomes a major initiative of public policy, it should among other things be charged with directing an appropriate portion of its attention to the economic development of areas and jobs that would be particularly responsive to concentrations of unemployed people.

What we need after Reagan, in summary, is a new framework of federal policy revolving around education, training and jobs. Indeed, it should be enacted now and provided with start-up funds, looking toward public-private, school-employer-labor-civic-governmental partnerships at the local level to create new job and training opportunities directed especially at those who need extra help in becoming fully productive participants in our economy.

Nor is the private-sector component proposed as a panacea, but rather as an added element that, with training efforts, might make a significant difference. With an appropriate level of commitment from local civic and business leadership and an appropriate subsidy geared to making up for the trainee's initial lack of productivity, job developers attached to the local PIC should be able to find enough sites to make the program work.

PART III

NATIONAL SECURITY

Editors' Introduction

While boastful, the comment of a Reagan administration official captures their basic intent. "When we came into office, one of our primary missions was to get Americans out of the 'Vietnam syndrome' and get them accustomed again to the idea that projecting power overseas can help the cause of peace. Well, it's worked. There's a consensus on Capitol Hill in favor of keeping American troops in a battle zone."

Although the troops deployed were in Lebanon, it was Russia's shooting down of a South Korean airplane that led to what Tom Wicker called "a breakdown of mature diplomacy." George Kennan, commenting from his half-century of experience with Soviet-American relations, described "the relations between two highly armed great powers" as having "the unfailing characteristics of a march toward war—that, and nothing else."

While sudden shifts in foreign relations are not unknown (e.g., the Nixon overture to China), and the consequence of leadership changes not unimportant (viz. Androprov's death and the rise of Brezhnev's protégé, Chernenko), the basic agenda of the coming years must be to reverse this mad drive toward confrontation. And while matters of North-South relations may in the long run turn out to be more fundamental, it is East versus West that must hold our attention in the coming years and which is the topic of this section's first essay.

During the last few years, a broad-based peace movement has emerged in the United States. Town meetings across the country have been the turf of debate from which resolutions calling for nuclear freeze have resulted. Einstein's warning after Hiroshima—that after so devastating an event "our modes of thinking" will have to change —has finally proved right, at least among ordinary citizens, as they have begun to reclaim control of their government's decisions, which have put them at greater and greater risk. Massive marches, a new genre in books and media events, numerous citizen-to-citizen visits between U.S. and Soviet citizens, all underscore the effort of people at large to say "no" to nuclear annihilation. When Jonathan Schell's *Fate of the Earth* flew to best-seller status, readers were excited by his warning and by the native American ideal of the stewardship that one generation owes another. Religious groups, aroused again as they were in the struggle for civil rights, have echoed the call for sanity and long-term responsibility.

All this is not to call for no national defense. Rather, as Gordon Adams spells out in our second essay, it is to replace the current wasteful and risky defense system with a more prudent and sensible one.

National security is not just now; now is the was of what will be, hence future security is on the agenda. It is at once a narrow military question and a wide-scale question affecting how we use our environment and the people in it: devastation of our land, seas and skies by chemicals, nuclear power, acid rain and the like are national-security questions, too. National security does not conventionally carry this baggage, but it is appropriate nonetheless, as Kazis and Grossman write, for we live at risk as a result of the assault on the environment and the mentality of innovative immediate defense against today's enemy at whatever cost. So, too, entrepreneurship drives our culture beyond the specific question of arms control. But arms control is fundamental. And so, too, the issues it points to—military spending, rash international engagements, ideological posturing. These threaten the very democracy we are told we must protect against demonic foes.

We need to become stewards of our physical and moral trusts—the planet, the environment, the democratic quality of life. The ideal of stewardship is not, however, a simple panacea even if we could be inoculated with it quickly. There are those who worry about future generations from a somewhat different point of view—that is, from the point of view of who will make up this nation, whose children will be privileged to work in decent conditions, and what languages our offspring will be speaking. Too often, this concern for the future leads to efforts to control who shall enter the U.S. and to overprotect those already here or those who are admitted as specially chosen because they are highly skilled and English-speaking. Others see the future built by the vitality and hard work of newcomers as has been the case before—indeed, since the beginning. It is, in fact, the essence of the U.S.

So all the tough, hard, short-term shoves against the fortress gate are in opposition to a more open, flexible readiness to recognize the dangers to all, pointed out by Greer and DeWind, from the severe controls entrusted to bureaucratic officers and the strict censorship that comes from frightened, defensive spirits.

Stewardship as the framework of national security offers a route to a future for our children. But to try to limit who our children might be, whom they go to school with and how many may be exploited will compromise our promise to future generations, compound the problems in our relations with developing countries and—in this nuclear age—foreclose on the future entirely.

10

Beyond the New Cold War

Roy Bennett

Second only to recovery from the current recession, the American electorate in virtually every national poll expresses its deepest concern over the threat of nuclear war. Despite this, America finds itself today in a new cold war bearing comparison with the "Red" hysteria of 1917 and the cold war immediately following World War II.

Why this is so is the subject of this inquiry. It seeks to answer the questions why U.S. policy developed as it did; why the first serious attempt at detente after Vietnam failed; and whether there is a feasible alternative to the mindless escalation that today so frightens the American people.

THE NATURE OF U.S. POLICY

Most standard texts on foreign policy agree that since the early twentieth century U.S. policy with regard to Europe has been characterized by a consistent pattern:[1]

1. to support a general balance of power in Europe to prevent the emergence of a single major power that could dominate the continent;
2. to be the balancer of last resort if Great Britain, the dominant European power, failed in the task of maintaining the balance.

America's late intervention in both World War I and II was the consequence of this policy, when Britain and France twice failed to contain the "Greater Germany." With the Soviet army's unexpected destruction of the Nazis and Russia's consequent emergence into Central Europe, America was faced with the single great power it

Roy Bennett is a former United Nations correspondent for the London *Tribune*.

thought potentially capable of dominating the continent.

With all Europe prostrate economically and militarily, the United States assumed Great Britain's historic nineteenth-century role of dominant balancer of the European balance of power.

THE ORIGINS OF THE COLD WAR

When it became clear that Russian postwar aims included turning the prewar *cordon sanitaire* (the belt of hostile East European nations bordering the Soviet Union) into a buffer zone of contiguous nations, the basis for the first cold war and the consequent policy of containment was laid.

But what gave the cold war its urgency, over and above the traditional and historical conflicts, was the introduction of a fanatic ideological element. The conflict was seen by both sides as a systems challenge. This was not a conflict between two capitalist imperiums, but a struggle between two opposing worlds that could never coexist. As noisy as the anti-Communist crusade was on our side, the Soviets, through the Cominform, successor to the Comintern, hastened to assure the world the struggle was indeed between the "two worlds."

Containment, as refined in the furnace of the cold war, aimed at confronting and defeating what the United States perceived as Soviet expansionism—first in Eastern Europe and then using it as a springboard for the invasion of the whole of war-ravaged Western Europe. Containment theory was based on the gross miscalculation that if totally confined, politically and economically, the Soviet system would collapse.

Thus, the cold war in its first stages was a product of America's actions to prevent Soviet consolidation in Eastern Europe and Soviet determination to reap the fruits of its military victory by extending its suzerainty over the nations of Eastern Europe on its borders.

For the Soviet Union, American actions in almost immediately unleashing the cold war to prevent the Soviet consolidation of a sphere of influence in Eastern Europe confirmed that America aimed to obstruct Soviet recovery from the war and recognition of their legitimate right—as they saw it—to a bordering sphere of influence spelled out at Teheran and later with Churchill.

The view from America was obviously markedly different. The

absorption of Eastern Europe into the Soviet sphere was followed in quick succession by the Czech coup, the blockade of Berlin and the establishment of East Germany. Within a year Chiang Kai-shek's China collapsed (erroneously seen as the handiwork of Moscow) and Red China emerged. Less than twelve months later, Communist North Korea invaded South Korea. This series of events convinced Washington that the Soviet Union was indeed on the march.

The first cold war peaked when the United States took over the war in Korea and found itself as a consequence in direct war with Red China. The result was a spiral of interaction where the action of one became the mirror image of the other, contributing to continuing symmetrical misperceptions of the other's policies and signals.

INTERREGNUM: 1955 TO 1970

For the next fifteen years, following the Korean War acute phase of the cold war, the tide of U.S.-Soviet relations ebbed and flowed. This period saw three major efforts to ease tensions, but each step forward was nullified by crisis events that followed.

The Vienna Summit of 1955 was the first. It followed the end of the Korean War, the expulsion of France from Indochina and the death of Stalin. The Summit unexpectedly resulted in the Soviet Union unilaterally withdrawing from its occupation of Vienna, permitting the neutralization of the whole of Austria—a settlement successful to this day.

This short period of good feeling exploded in 1956, less than a year later, with the invasion of Egypt by Israel and the simultaneous Soviet intervention in the Hungarian revolt.

The second effort, Eisenhower's 1959 Camp David meeting with Khrushchev, an even more promising attempt than Vienna, collapsed on the eve of a planned summit, with the crisis over the shooting down and capture of the American U-2 spy plane and pilot far in the interior of the Soviet Union.

The third effort, the most promising, was the successful negotiation under President John Kennedy of a partial test-ban treaty in 1963. However, the expectation of a major summit was aborted—first by the assassination of President Kennedy and then by the Vietnam War.

THE NIXON DETENTE

Two factors, after fifteen years, produced the series of comprehensive agreements and treaties between the U.S. and the USSR on arms control, trade and cultural relations that became known as detente—the most promising forward step by both powers since the end of World War II.

The first and most powerful was enormous domestic pressure for an end to the cold war from a Vietnam War–weary population. "We had to end a war in Indo-China in the midst of a virulent domestic assault," complained Henry Kissinger. "We were on the edge of a precipice."[2]

The second was the political profit of a popular international settlement six months before the presidential elections. Nixon's rating, after signing the detente treaties in May 1972, precipitously increased from 10 to 15 percent, virtually assuring his reelection.

Out of these necessities came an agreement, although with fundamental and contradictory flaws.

Detente, as Nixon saw it, expressed itself in accepting the demand of the times—moving toward the area of peaceful coexistence, a politically profitable position, while simultaneously pursuing the traditional role of dominating the international balance of power.

Indeed, the Nixon-Kissinger policy in practice did not change the fundamental principle of containment. It was the administration view that in exchange for recognition of strategic military parity (SALT I) and most-favored-nation trade relations (the latter never delivered), *Soviet leadership would concede that the political situation around the world be frozen, or, if it were not, the Soviets would voluntarily withdraw, damp down or not respond to political events outside their immediate East European sphere of influence.*

The Soviet Union's view differed in two important ways. One, it considered these agreements the first step toward its eventual recognition as an "equal" superpower. *In the Soviet perception, this meant Soviet participation in all major settlements in which it had an interest.* And two, following from the first, *this also meant recognition that the Soviet Union had an equal right with the United States to respond when called upon for moral and material support by legitimate governments in the developing world.*

As a result of the two nations' conflicting perceptions and also domestic differences in the United States, detente ran quickly into trouble. The Jackson Amendment to the Trade Treaty nullified granting the Soviet Union equal trade status with all other nations (most favored nation), considered by the Russians second in importance only to SALT I. In addition, detente came under fierce attack from the media as soon as the next conflict arose. Soviet and Cuban arms support to the Ethiopian and Angolan governments—in their view legitimate activity—and political support to Sadat after his defeat by Israel in 1973 also served to vastly undermine the tenuous detente settlement. The final burying of detente took place in the Carter administration with its failure to secure Senate ratification of SALT II, which the administration itself had signed.

Zbigniew Brzezinski, in his memoirs, describes how he virtually created the panic over the secret "Soviet Brigade" in Cuba, a brief *cause célèbre* threatening to rival the Cuban missile crisis of 1962. Knowing it was (in his words) a "phony" issue, he nevertheless urged that "the president should use the crisis to establish his credentials as a tough-minded Truman-type leader. . . . "Admittedly," Brzezinski modestly conceded, "this could have the effect of further reducing the chances of SALT ratification."[3]

The tortuous conflict inside the Carter administration between Secretary of State Cyrus Vance, who vigorously supported SALT II and normalization of relations with the Russians, and National Security Adviser Brzezinski, who fervently opposed both, became academic with the Russian invasion of Afghanistan.

The detente experiment ended in 1980 with a return to the cold war under the Reagan administration in a new and more virulent form. The failure of detente underlines the continuity of containment in U.S. foreign policy.

FOREIGN-POLICY AIMS

Baldly stated, the central aim of Washington's containment policy is not war, as some have charged, but *finally to convince the Soviet Union that it must come to terms with the position of a junior relationship in the superpower race.*

This relationship means agreeing that American interests and American power are paramount and worldwide (Brzezinski); that settlements and negotiations will be directed and managed by the United States (Kissinger); and that Soviet efforts to counter by support, material or ideological, to Third World countries constitute Soviet expansionism and violate de facto recognition of U.S. hegemony.

What of the Soviet side? Professor Stanley Hoffman, director of Harvard's Center for European Studies, saw Soviet aims as follows: "Is Soviet policy," Hoffman asked, "a deliberate planned and masterly march toward world domination" (as it is almost always depicted), *"or more plausibly, is it a relentless attempt at achieving equality with the U.S.—at breaking the American monopoly of the high seas or of the means for it to intervene all over the world—and at imposing Soviet participation in the settlement of all major disputes?"*[4] (My emphasis—R.B.)

What stands in the way of considering, at least as a negotiating position, U.S. acceptance of the USSR as a political equal?

The biggest obstacle facing acceptance of Soviet claims to equality and consequent mitigation of American global hegemony is the superior economic status of the U.S. and the exaggerated perception of its relative power compared to the Soviet Union's. Stated simply, the administration and people of the U.S. believe the Soviet system is a total failure. The perception is of an economically staggering, helpless giant, virtually unable to feed its own people without the help of the U.S.

The U.S. also believes the fate of the Soviet economy depends on American and Western technology, which, if withheld, condemns the Soviets to little better than the future of a huge, less-developed country. This belief has led to trade and grain boycotts and bans on shipment of so-called high-technology equipment. But most of all it has led to the myth that a gigantic competitive arms race will drive the Soviet economy into the ground.

As long as the American people believe the Soviet economy does not work—that without American food and technology, it will stagnate—it is not hard to see why they would conclude that a detente recognizing the Soviet Union's equality would be making a huge, unrequited concession. Indeed, it would appear in this view that a detente would solve most acute Soviet problems with no quid pro quo.

If, on the contrary, the American people saw a growing viable economy with a standard of living beginning to approach their own —something not yet true in the Soviet Union—it would be difficult, whatever administration were in power, to convince people of the economic myths now being circulated.

Therefore, it is important to see the Soviet economy relative to the West in realistic perspective. In short, if it is true that Soviet society is in the shambles we portray, there is little prospect of a new, more equitable detente. If, however, the current picture is distorted and in addition there is the prospect of a narrowing of the economic gap, one's expectation for a new detente relationship may be possible.

Thus, it would be useful to take an objective look at some present broad indicators of the Soviet economy to see where they are now and, in rough terms, how they compare to the West.

THE SOVIET ECONOMY

A thumbnail sketch from exclusively Western sources shows the following:

On Soviet agriculture:
Probably the most distorted picture of all. As long ago as 1973, the Joint Economic Committee of Congress, in a study entitled "Comparative Farm Output" (page 348), estimated Soviet gross crop output as 87 percent of the United States'. Thomas B. Larsen, former director of Soviet Research for the State Department, estimated the figure at 80 percent in 1975.[5]

Since that time, U.S. grain production has grown from 200 million metric tons to 270 million metric tons—compared with Soviet production of 205 million metric tons during the same period. However, nearly 40 percent of the U.S. grain crop is exported or stored, making domestic grain consumption approximately the same for both countries.[6] The U.S. Foreign Agricultural Service in 1979 noted that the socialist countries' "per capita consumption of calories and protein no

longer differs from the advanced capitalist countries."* This results
from the Soviets' large dairy and fishing industries, since meat production still lags behind the West (80 percent of Western Europe's, 60
percent of the U.S.'s per capita). Total Soviet milk production is
70–75 percent higher than in the U.S.,† and the nation's fish catch is
3.5 times as large.[7] While less than the West's, Soviet meat consumption exceeds that of Japan, Sweden, Finland and Norway, also large
fishing nations.

When meat and fish production are taken together, Soviet production was 70–75 percent of the United States' in 1980 and reasonably
close to Western Europe's.[8]

On stability:

The CIA in its 1983 analysis showed Soviet GNP growth as averaging
4.7 percent for thirty years, although growth has slowed in the past ten
years. Respectable as this figure is, the same report noted that other
Western researchers show markedly higher rates: from 5.5 to 7.7
percent—the latter, however, over a fifteen-year period. This compares
with slightly over 3 percent for the United States over the same
period.‡

*   *U.S. Foreign Agricultural Services,* agricultural circular, FLM-4.79 (Washington,
D.C.: U.S. Government Printing Office, July 1979); *Prospects for Soviet Agriculture,
1980–85* (Paris: OECD, 1979).

    Karl Eugene Wadekin, Giessen University, West Germany, author of 1982
OECD report on Soviet agriculture, notes: "In terms of calories the average Soviet
citizen consumes as much per head per year as the average West European and only
slightly less than the American."

    See also *Challenge* magazine, interview with Bob Berglan, secretary of agricul-
ture in the Carter administration, Sept./Oct. 1978:

    "I was in the Soviet Union recently. They are the world's largest wheat producer,
the largest cotton producer. I saw building for housing livestock enterprises everywhere. They are expanding these and they are well managed, very sophisticated,
productive and efficient. I was impressed, frankly. Their situation was better than
I expected."

†   Professor Karl Wadekin, Giessen University, explains why the U.S. produces more
meat than the Soviet Union with similar grain production: It is due to a combination
of cold climate, poor soil and inadequately housed cattle, requiring more feed than
normal. The best feed—corn and soybeans—cannot be grown in the Soviet Union.

‡   *USSR: Measure of Economic Growth,* 1950–1980, CIA for Joint Economic Committee, 8 December 1982, p. 15. This study shows a slowdown in GNP, falling in
1976–80 to 2.7 percent. Soviet data claiming much higher growth is disputed, as
are results of independent American researchers. (Official figures from the Soviet
Union for the first six months of 1983 show an increase to 4.1 percent. *Wall Street
Journal,* July 25, 1983.)

On output:

A look at the CIA-selected figures for actual output (since the analysis concedes GNP estimates require a high degree of speculation) is revealing. Out of thirty-three indicators reported, the Soviets led in seventeen, the Americans in sixteen. These included such basic commodities as steel, oil, gas, fertilizer, tractors, cotton and wool fabrics, in which the Soviets led; and electricity, autos, grain, coal and plastics, in which the United States led.[9]

While the CIA gives no dollar industrial-production comparison, the Russians officially estimated in 1981 that their industrial production was 80 percent of the U.S's.[10] That this is a reasonably credible figure is confirmed by an estimate by Thomas B. Larsen, in his *Soviet-American Rivalry*. Says Larsen, "The USSR in 1950 produced about 30% of U.S. production; by 1975 this was in the neighborhood of 75%."[11]

On Consumerism:

The Soviets' weakest link in any East-West comparison. Although the Soviet citizen today appears, for the first time, nearly as well dressed as his Western counterparts, there is a very noticeable difference in the quantity and assortment of light consumer goods available. Soviet department stores have nothing resembling the plethora of soft goods in American shopping malls or Oxford Street in London. However, the output of 7–8 million television sets, refrigerators and washing machines annually has been sufficient so that in the near future almost every family will be supplied with these now essential consumer durables.

While the lack of light consumer goods is the most noticeable difference, the most significant gap in comparing standards of living is in personal and public services. Retail distribution is poorly served, while restaurants and public catering in general are in noticeably short supply.

For the past twenty-five years, the Soviets' main consumer effort has gone into an unprecedented housing program. Around every Soviet city are huge belts of housing estates built since 1960 and made up of over 50 million modern high-rise apartments with kitchens and bathrooms, unheard of in pre–World War II Russia. Before the end of the decade, they will have rehoused the entire population.*

These few observations might be classified as a "best case" report. However, the judgment of two respected Soviet specialists tends to confirm these observations. Professor Seweryn Bialer, director of the Columbia University Institute on Social Change, in his *Stalin's Successors,* puts it this way: "The crucial sphere is the domestic economy. . . . By this standard the regime's performance can be judged a success. . . . The Soviet Union has solidified and strengthened its position as a great industrial power. The Soviet regime has, by and large, been able to deliver the goods; it has generally been able to satisfy popular expectations for higher standards of living."[12]

Professor Stephen F. Cohen, chairman of Russian Studies at Princeton University, observed:

> The most misleading assertion is that the Soviet Communist system has utterly failed to deliver on its basic domestic promises over the years. Nothing I have learned in years of studying and visiting the Soviet Union and talking with sober minded dissidents truly supports that picture. . . . Despite important inadequacies and official exaggeration, a comprehensive welfare system now provides free secondary schooling, health care, pensions and subsidized housing and food for virtually all citizens. . . . Instead of dangerously deceiving ourselves about the Soviet Union's "crisis" . . . we should ask why a system with so many problems is so stable.[13]

What are the "inadequacies" to which Professor Cohen refers? Their foremost problem lies in the acknowledged rigidity and complexity of their central planning system, a problem that biases the economy against innovation and risk-taking. Inflexible pricing often results in excessively low prices of desired goods and therefore shortages, or high prices of inferior goods and consequently oversupply. Second to the overcentralization problem are the twin problems of poor motivation and low productivity resulting from guaranteed full

* "In 1975 housing units per 1,000 of population reached 80% of the American level . . . although smaller and less well equipped. . . ." Official plan figures for each five-year period since 1960 have provided for 2.2 million apartment units annually, or, by 1990, 66 million units. Even with possible shortfalls, this figure should be adequate. It does not include usable prewar housing, early poor postwar construction, renovation, or vacation (dasha) housing. Thomas B. Larsen, *Soviet American Rivalry* (Norton, 1978), p. 53.

employment with life tenure. Finally, despite steady improvement in the standard of living, the society still suffers from a skewing of the economy toward heavy industry, continued high investment in infrastructure (pipelines, railroad, highways, etc.) and the burden of a huge military budget.

Assessment

Given all of the above, the figures scarcely present a picture of the economic basket case so assiduously portrayed in the United States. How then, on the basis of a more objective observation, might one assess the present situation and consider its effect on the future of relations?

If one accepts the fact that the Soviet Union is an *industrial* power with perhaps 75–80 percent of the capacity of the United States which produces at a rate probably 60 percent of the American GNP, there is still a substantial gap to be overcome before something approaching economic parity can be achieved. One cannot expect this gap to be narrowed or closed in the short term; but it is feasible—especially if the economic reforms about which much has been written are successful—that the Soviet standard of living can reach 65–75 percent of that of the United States during the 1990s.*

If this were to be achieved, its impact would be enormous. For what will be recognized, hostile propaganda notwithstanding, is that Soviet

---

* The *New York Times* printed excerpts from a confidential memorandum (6 August 1983) on Soviet economic reorganization outlining structural problems in the Soviet Union with suggested solutions. It was the most searching, frank analysis ever made. It was produced by an official commission of Soviet economists from the Novosibirsk branch of the Academy of Sciences with the State Planning Commission's approval.

In brief, it called for decentralizing power to the enterprise level, wiping out intermediate levels of bureaucracy "who now occupy warm places with ill defined range of responsibilities but with quite respectable salaries." They suggest, among other proposals, using market forces and a "profound re-structuring of state economic management" involving "disbanding of many department trusts and corporations that have been mushrooming in the past decade." They predict resistance to their proposals from "the more inert group of older workers" as well as managers and functionaries whose soft jobs will be eliminated.

Some of the criticism is startling in its harshness. Whether their proposals, which go to the heart of their economic society, will carry the day cannot now be told. What is clear is that they have identified what most Westerners agree are their major problems. Whether the political power exists for implementing their solutions remains to be seen.

society is here to stay. We would have to face the inevitability of living for the long term with a different social system that is not going to decay or be overthrown. We would have to find a way to make living together far more tolerable and less dangerous than it has been in the past or is today.

The shooting down of the Korean passenger plane that admittedly violated sensitive Soviet borders in the late summer of 1983 does not so much underline the trigger-happy fingers of the Soviet military as it presents to the world a classic scenario of how an accidental nuclear war could occur so long as the adversary relationship continues to exist without restraint.

The basic premise of this paper is that military parity is the basis for partial arms control but not significant arms reduction. Economic parity or at least near-parity is a necessary basis for the political equality the Soviets seek and that is the precondition for real arms reduction and a new approach to global political relations.

But what of democracy and freedom inside the Soviet Union? Do they not play an important role in achieving a normalization of relations? Of course they do. But the reason for the economics emphasis in this review is the conviction that the growth of democracy in the internal political system of the USSR will follow, or at least parallel, the easing of tensions, rather than precede it.

This is true for at least two reasons. First, because a society that considers itself under siege (as Soviet society does) for its entire existence—and with some justification—is not likely to fundamentally change internally before it sees a corresponding change externally. Second, while it would make the task of rapprochement easier if the "garrison state" mentality, as the Soviets' historian Roy Medvedev calls it, did not dominate policy and diplomacy, it would not change the fundamental fact that political equality, recognized political parity, will be forthcoming only when approximate economic parity can be seen.

In short, without in any degree underrating the difficulties inherent in resolving conflicts between two differing political systems, the fact remains that before a long-term new type of political relationship is possible, the people of the rest of the developed world must be able to see a Soviet economic system that is working. At a time when the economies of the developed West are showing signs of uncommon difficulties, there could be nothing more impressive than a manifestly stable, growing economic society in the East. This is, of course, their task, and one that even they consider basic.

THREE CHOICES

In the near future, three choices will face the United States: first, continued heightened confrontation, even leading to the brink (typical of the late Forties and early Fifties); second, resumption of an ebb and flow of relations, but never reaching stable self-enforcing agreements (typical of the Sixties and Seventies); or, third, a totally new view of detente as a historical probability *in a world in which nuclear parity rules out resort to military solutions and near economic parity rules out domination based on economic superiority.*

If the third option is a possibility, what are the elements of a new approach?

Detente II—A New Approach

In this view, a new detente is most likely to emerge in two stages. The first would be at minimum a return to the 1972 detente: (a) a mutual arms freeze during which a SALT III or its equivalent would be negotiated, not only putting a cap on arms but taking the first step toward reduction; (b) a comprehensive total test-ban treaty, automatically putting a ceiling on new technology developments, all of which require testing; (c) a trade treaty; and (d) a series of cultural-exchange agreements.

These familiar steps would constitute a near-term goal. For the longer term, a fundamental reorientation is required—something that in four decades the United States has avoided facing. This would involve (a) United States policy coming to terms with the imperative of living with the Soviet Union on the basis of political equality; and, following from that, (b) establishing a system that might be called "codification of coexistence."

What does *equality* mean in practice? It means involving the Russians in settlements, especially where their interest is involved. It means accepting a Soviet presence in negotiating conflict resolutions. It means recognizing the legitimacy of Soviet involvement in the settling of major problems around the world.

"Codification of coexistence" starts with the premise that an end has been put to the automatic hostile adversary relationship characteristic of the past. It seeks to establish rules and standards for mutual relations. Instead of political, military confrontation in every small or large crisis, the superpowers, their allies and the relevant regional organizations will consult and negotiate *along previously agreed-upon ground rules.* It takes for granted that the Soviet Union will refrain from exacerbating or escalating, for its own advantage, conflicts in which the United States is involved, just as the U.S. will not automatically characterize as "Soviet-inspired" every conflict or social change of which it does not approve.

What is at issue in codification is the task of defining and accepting social change without disrupting a stable balance of power.

To project U.S. acceptance of the Soviet Union as a political equal, to hope to achieve a code of coexistence, is clearly not suggested as a current probability. It may take several or more new administrations to reorient and replace political leadership and to secure public support for such a major change. The opinion polls over the past decade consistently record overwhelming support—70–30 percent—for arms control and better relations with Russia, notwithstanding an equal percentage recording continued strong hostility toward the Soviet system. This suggests the public, despite suspicion of the Soviets, is more ready than recent political leadership—Democratic and Republican—for an unprejudiced change in policy. The mountainous waste and acute danger derivative of the newly heightened cold war are increasingly a burden on the developed powers and prevent any comprehensive approach to growing critical Third World problems.

The coming years will demonstrate how well the United States and the Soviet Union have coped with the problems of their respective economic slowdowns. Seldom has the time been more advantageous for a significant turn in policy, one that will permit concentration on urgent problems at home so necessary for both superpowers.

Notes

1. See F.S. Northedge, *The Foreign Policy of the Powers* (London: Faber & Faber, 1968), 42–43; John Spainer, *Games Nations Play,* 2d ed. (New York: Praeger, 1976), 10–11; Hans J. Morganthau, *A New Foreign Policy for the U.S.* (Council on Foreign Relations, 1969); and Inis L. Claude, Jr., *Power and International Relations* (New York: Random House, 1962).
2. Henry Kissinger, *Years of Upheaval,* (Boston: Little, Brown, 1982), 235.
3. Zbigniew Brzezinski, *Power and Principle* (New York: Farrar Straus & Giroux, 1983), 347, 350–52.
4. Stanley Hoffman, *Dead Ends: Foreign Policy in the New Cold War* (Cambridge, Mass.: Ballinger, 1983), 99.
5. Thomas B. Larsen, *Soviet American Rivalry,* (New York: Norton, 1978), 46. "In 1950 Soviet Agriculture produced roughly $\frac{3}{5}$ of the output produced in the U.S.; a quarter century later this had risen to $\frac{4}{5}$" (80 percent in 1975)— R.B.).
6. *CIA Handbook of Economic Statistics* (Washington, D.C.: U.S. Government Printing Office, Nov. 1981), table 146, p. 168.
7. *CIA Handbook of Economic Statistics,* 1981, tables 155 and 156, p. 178; and Kenneth R. Grey, *Soviet Consumption,* bulletin of the Association for Comparative Economic Studies (Arizona State University, Summer, 1981); Harry B. Schaffer, *Soviet Agriculture* (New York: Praeger, 1976).
8. *CIA Handbook of Economic Statistics,* 1981.
9. *Ibid.,* table 8, p. 22.
10. *Statistical Yearbook: USSR,* Norodno Khozraistvo SSR, 1922–82.
11. Larsen, *Soviet American Rivalry.*
12. Seweryn Bialer, *Stalin's Successors* (Cambridge, Mass.: Cambridge University Press, 1980), 149.
13. *Nation,* 6 Aug. 1983, 103.

11

Restructuring National Defense Policy

Gordon Adams

American military spending has doubled since 1980. If the Reagan administration has its way, the defense budget will triple by 1988. Americans will spend $3,200 per household on the military in 1984; the bill will be over $20,000 per household between 1985 and 1989. Military spending now consumes 50 cents of each income-tax dollar; this bill will be over 60 cents by 1988. In 1985, Americans will spend more on defense in peacetime than at any point, peace or war, since the end of World War II (see Fig. 1).

As military spending grows, so does our national insecurity. We seem ever closer to war—nuclear or conventional—and the Pentagon and its budget appear out of control, unaccountable to citizens or their elected representatives. The search is under way for an alternative as criticism of the Reagan military buildup grows.

- A bilateral nuclear-weapons freeze, once a fringe issue, is supported by 75 percent of the American people, was approved by popular referenda in nine states and many cities, has been endorsed by the U.S. House of Representatives and will be a central issue in the presidential election.
- The MX missile program was nearly stopped in Congress and may yet die.
- Though the Reagan administration scorned arms control, it was forced by public opinion to open talks with the Soviet Union.
- Europeans are severely divided over the deployment of Pershing 2 and ground-launched cruise missiles on their soil, creating uncertainty in NATO.

Gordon Adams is director of the Defense Budget Project at the Center on Budget and Policy Priorities.

167

- A spate of reports on defense contracting have exposed waste and inefficiency, from the M-1 tank, which has mechanical problems, to the Bradley amphibious infantry fighting vehicle, which doesn't float, to $110 diodes for F-18 simulators, which should cost 4 cents each.[1]
- Critics, ranging from the Heritage Foundation, through the Department of Defense, to the Brookings Institution, warn that the defense budget is out of control.[2]
- Many Americans are concerned about the impact military spending is having on federal budget deficits, interest rates, capital supplies, future industrial investment and the creation of new jobs.

THE SEARCH FOR AN ALTERNATIVE

The Reagan military buildup has brought into question thirty-five years of U.S. national-security policy. The American people are widely debating matters once left to the experts, but a realistic alternative defense policy has not yet been defined. This essay lays out the framework for such an alternative.

The thrust and rationale for the Reagan buildup are clear. U.S. strategic forces must be able to deter the Soviet Union and have the capacity to "prevail" in a "protracted" nuclear war. The MX missile, the Trident submarine and second-generation missile, the B-1 bomber, 7,000 cruise missiles (land, sea and air versions), a stealth bomber, ballistic missile defense, *Star Wars* devices in space, and civil defense are all part of this program. Conventional military spending is equally important to the administration. There has been a dramatic increase in spending for antiarmor missiles, tanks, armored personnel carriers, helicopters, fighters, airlift, battleship reactivation, aircraft carriers, and a 600-ship navy. These systems are designed to serve the demands of expanding U.S. military commitments in the Middle East, Latin America and the Pacific, as well as the "modernization" of NATO forces.[3]

Partial defense alternatives have begun to appear in response to the budgetary explosion, excessive rhetoric, unreal objectives and wasteful spending the Reagan policy has spawned. A congressional "mili-

PEACETIME MILITARY BUILDUP
The Historical Context

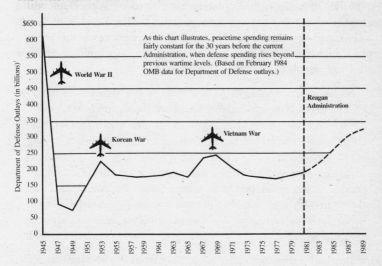

As this chart illustrates, peacetime spending remains fairly constant for the 30 years before the current Administration, when defense spending rises beyond previous wartime levels. (Based on February 1984 OMB data for Department of Defense outlays.)

[Chart axis label: Department of Defense Outlays (in billions)¹]

Reagan Administration

World War II

Korean War

Vietnam War

¹In constant 1985 dollars
Defense Budget Project, 236 Massachusetts Ave. NE, Suite 505, Washington, DC 20002

tary reform caucus," ranging from Senator Gary Hart (D-Colo.) to Congressman William Whitehurst (R-Va.), has focused on weapons performance as the centerpiece of an alternative policy. Weapons, Senator Hart has argued, are the core of the problems caused by the buildup:

> The overall result of these policies will make the defense problems under previous Administrations seem trivial. Reagan's defense legacy will be a crippled military, with equipment that won't operate, troops that haven't been trained and, ultimately, to pay the soaring bills, huge cuts in force structure—ships, divisions and aircraft wings. This is a sorry future for a military that was to have been "second to none."[4]

The military-reform prescription, however, does not include any analysis of what national security actually requires. There are no "military reform" views about the Soviet Union, the military balance in Europe, or rapid intervention in the Third World. Big spenders and budget-cutters can rally to this flag, but it does not constitute an alternative direction for national-security policy that might cost less and provide greater real security.

Another, overlapping alternative, supported by such Democratic defense analysts as Senators John Glenn (D-Ohio) and Sam Nunn (D-Ga.), and the Center for National Policy, focuses on the need to replace nuclear security with a conventional military buildup. Senator Glenn has put this alternative succinctly:

> Nuclear arms would not have to play such a significant role in Europe if NATO's conventional forces were adequate in their own terms. NATO's conventional forces do not now match those of the Soviets and Warsaw Pact, though they are sufficient to make a Soviet attack very costly.
>
> . . . Conventional forces deserve more emphasis in our defense effort because to the extent that conventional forces are able to head off threats to the peace, the danger of nuclear war is diminished. Conventional forces that were adequate in an era of nuclear monopoly are not adequate now.[5]

This alternative does not differ noticeably from the administration in viewing of the international scene as hostile, overshadowed by a Soviet threat and requiring major increases in U.S. military spending. As an alternative policy, it would divert but not slow the arms race.

A third, fledgling alternative grows out of the arms-control, nuclear-freeze, and peace movements. The ingredients of this view include serious negotiations on European nuclear forces and strategic arms; a U.S. declaration of "no first use" of nuclear weapons; measures to reduce the likelihood of accidental nuclear war; negotiations on a bilateral, verifiable nuclear-weapons freeze between the United States and the Soviet Union; the elimination of chemical weapons; nonintervention overseas; and, for some, steps toward comprehensive disarmament.

These goals are desirable, but the arms-control/freeze alternative is not a coherent alternative national-security posture. Its supporters have not described the framework within which a freeze would be included. Supporters address only peripherally the details of defense budgets, spending or conventional forces. Too often, the advocates of this position assume that human interaction between Russians and Americans is enough to eliminate the arms race. While human interaction is an important ingredient, it is an inadequate tool in a real and dangerous world of nations with conflicting definitions of their interests.

A coherent alternative national-security vision needs to start from clear principles that many Americans share. These principles should redefine national-security aims and the missions of the armed forces. New goals and missions should in turn determine the weapons being purchased and the forces required for national defense. The defense budget, in the end, should be based on the costs of this commonsense alternative.[6]

The framework for a reformulated national defense policy presented here is based on the following five premises:

1. The United States and the Soviet Union will have to live with each other; the alternative is mutual suicide. They share an interest in stabilizing the nuclear-arms race, reducing strategic weapons and moving economic resources to productive investment.

2. The military balance in Europe remains stable. NATO has a more-than-adequate nuclear and conventional capability to deter war; NATO and the Warsaw Pact are in a stalemate. More important, neither pact wants a war in Western Europe, and, despite their military spending, neither *expects* such a war. Increased military stability, a reduction in the risk of nuclear war, and serious bilateral negotiations on conventional force reductions and on chemical weapons are needed.

3. In the Southern Tier of the globe, over 100 new nations have emerged from the shadow of colonialism to face serious problems: starvation, inadequate resources, unbalanced and uneven development, a lack of investment capital, untrained populations, ethnic conflicts, irrational boundaries. Neither the United States nor the Soviet Union helps solve these problems by expanding oceangoing navies, increasing rapid-deployment forces, or foreign arms sales. Political and economic attention must focus on the area's real problems, with military forces playing only a residual peacekeeping role.

4. Pentagon weapons purchases cost far more than necessary, and there is no incentive for cost control in the Defense Department or the defense industry. The alternative is to eliminate wasteful spending, ensure that weapons choices are linked to national-security goals and not to the survival of bureaucrats or corporations, open up the decision-making machinery to make it accountable.

5. National security requires a healthy economy. The rapid growth of defense spending makes it more difficult to solve our economic problems by increasing federal borrowing requirements, draining capital markets, keeping interest rates high and contributing to deficits. It diverts productivity-enhancing research investment away from commercial business, and weakens our ability to create new employment. The alternative includes careful defense-budget planning, with attention to its impact on the economy, alternate uses of military production facilities and workers, and careful research and development planning for maximum economic benefit.

THE UNITED STATES AND THE SOVIET UNION: IS THERE A WAY?

The Reagan administration has used the Soviet "threat" to justify its military buildup:

> For twenty years the Soviet Union has been steadily accumulating enormous military might, most of which is designed for offensive actions. For much of that period the United States restrained its own military spending; in fact, investment in our defense actually declined in real terms during most of the 1970s. The result was a dangerous shift in the military balance, which threatens our ability to deter and, if deterrence fails, to defeat aggression.[7]

This administration is not the first to exaggerate Soviet military capabilities as a way of greasing the skids for the defense budget in Congress and the country. The global military power of the Soviet Union has unmistakably grown; it would be naïve to assume otherwise. Yet a "threat" from the Soviet Union is a slender and fraying justification for defense budgets, based as it is on a series of military myths:

Myth #1
"From 1970 to 1981, the Soviets outinvested the U.S. in defense by about half a trillion dollars in constant 1984 dollars."[8]

The spending gap is a myth. Data on Soviet defense spending is thin and concealed.[9] Since the ruble is not convertible to the dollar, there is no way to know directly how much the Soviet Union spends *in dollars.* The CIA end-runs this problem by counting Soviet troops and Soviet military equipment and estimating what it would cost us to reproduce the same troops and equipment. Higher U.S. wages and prices are applied to Soviet personnel and equipment, creating an overestimate of what the Soviet Union spends.[10] Every U.S. military wage increase or weapons-cost overrun means the estimate of Soviet military spending automatically rises.*

These comparisons also avoid directly comparing NATO and the Warsaw Pact. Even given the inadequacies of the methodology, a comparison of NATO defense spending over ten years with Warsaw Pact spending for the same period shows NATO outspending the Warsaw Pact by $250 billion.†

Myth #2

"While our principal adversaries engaged in the greatest buildup of military power seen in modern times, our own investment in forces and weapons continued to decline until very recently."[11]

The decline in U.S. military spending is a myth. Figure 1 traces U.S. defense spending since 1940 in constant (uninflated) dollars. U.S. defense spending did indeed decline, in real dollars, each time the United States ended its involvement in a war (World War II, Korea, Vietnam). These declines say nothing about U.S. military strength. Peacetime defense spending has remained fairly constant from Korea to Vietnam and from Vietnam to 1980. The sharp upswing in the Reagan years is the most rapid increase in peacetime military spending in U.S. history.

* The intelligence establishment recognizes the weakness of its methodology. In the spring of 1983, CIA and Defense Intelligence Agency analysts reported that they had overestimated the real dollar growth rate of Soviet military spending by at least one-third over the past eight years. See Leslie Gelb and Richard Halloran, "CIA Analysts Now Said to Find U.S. Overstated Soviet Arms Rise," *New York Times,* 3 Mar. 1983; also Fred Kaplan, "Soviet Arms Budget Stirs Debate in U.S.," *Boston Globe,* 16 Feb. 1983 and Gordon Adams, "Moscow's Military Costs," *The New York Times,* 4 Jan. 1984.

† Franklyn Holzman, "Are We Falling Behind the Soviets?" *Atlantic,* July 1983. Another comparison, using figures from the respected International Institute for Strategic Studies, concludes that "the United States and its NATO allies outspent the Soviet Union and its Warsaw Pact allies on defense by more than $300 billion in the last decade." See Richard Stubbing, "The Imaginary Defense Gap: We Already Outspend Them," *Washington Post,* 14 Feb. 1982.

This myth focuses on strategic forces in particular. U.S. spending on strategic forces *was* lower in the 1970s than in the 1960s, yet these forces cost over $100 billion from 1970 through the last budget of the Carter administration (fiscal year 1981). This spending completed deployment of 550 Minuteman III missiles, fitting each with three warheads and more accurate guidance; continued research and development on the MX missile; provided new electronics, engines and wings for the B-52 (at a cost equal to the original cost of building the B-52 fleet); redesigned specific B-52s to carry cruise missiles; developed and produced the air-launched, sea-launched and ground-launched cruise missiles; developed and produced the Trident submarine and its C-4 missile; and researched and developed the Trident D-5 missile.

The logic of the nuclear arms race seems inexorable—the United States invested heavily in the 1960s; the Soviet Union expanded its forces in the 1970s; the United States has begun a new generation of weapons in the 1980s.

Myth #3

The Soviet Union has achieved a "definite margin of superiority" over the United States.[12]

With respect to strategic forces, this assertion is meaningless. The standard comparisons of strategic nuclear forces—"bean counting" of delivery vehicles, warheads, throw-weight and accuracy—indicates parity between the superpowers.*

Bean-counting will not suffice in comparing conventional forces. One has to look as well at a country's strategy, history of warfare,

---

* The Soviet Union holds a lead in "delivery vehicles," with nearly 2,500, while the United States has just under 2,000. The United States leads in strategic warheads, with over 9,000, to roughly 7,000 in the Soviet arsenal. Moreover, the United States added 5,200 warheads to its arsenal during the 1970s, while the Soviet Union added 4,200. The Soviet Union leads in "throw-weight," having heavier, more explosive warheads. U.S. nuclear planning in the 1960s permitted this to happen, since the U.S. lead in accuracy led strategic planners to decide that a larger number of less-explosive warheads could reach their targets more accurately. Although the initial strategic arms negotiating position of the Reagan administration made an issue of this imbalance of throw-weight, a summer 1983 interagency study on the question concluded, according to the *New York Times,* that "a highly accurate warhead is found to be almost as effective against a target hardened by concrete, such as a missile silo, as a larger, less accurate warhead." See Leslie H. Gelb, "Aides Say U.S. May Ease Arms Stance at Geneva," *New York Times,* 11 Aug. 1983.

military readiness, foreign-policy objectives and, especially, geographic situation for adequate force comparison. U.S. and Soviet forces should look different from this perspective. The Soviet Union has a larger armored force, coastal navy, and air defense system (fighters and missiles) than the United States. This is to be expected, given the Soviet history of repeated invasion by other nations, Soviet occupation of potentially hostile countries on its western frontier, long borders with unfriendly nations, little naval experience and the risk of a two-front war in Europe in Asia.

The United States has clear superiority in air transport, long-range bombers, oceangoing naval vessels, sea transport, longer-range fighters, and antitank weapons. This, too, is predictable, given few invasions of U.S. territory, a history as an oceangoing power with military involvements overseas, and a focus on advanced-technology weapons.

Neither military force is automatically superior to the other, and U.S. defense analysts would not trade for Soviet forces. General John W. Vessey, Jr., chairman of the Joint Chiefs of Staff, for example, testified that he preferred U.S. forces: "Overall, would I trade with Marshal Ogarkov? Not on your life."[13]

Myth #4

U.S. Strategic forces face a "window of vulnerability."[14]

The real meaning of *window of vulnerability* has always been the alleged vulnerability of up to 90 percent of the 1,052 U.S. land-based strategic missiles to a totally successful Soviet missile first strike. This worst-case analysis stimulated Air Force support for the mobile, land-based MX missile. It is unlikely, however, that the Soviet Union would have a surprise advantage, given U.S. space-monitoring capabilities, and it is unlikely that all Soviet missiles would behave as projected.

It is even less likely that the U.S. would sit idly by and fail to respond. The capability for such a response is more than ample since only 23.2 percent of U.S. strategic warheads are on land-based missiles. The remaining 75+ percent are on bombers and submarines, unaffected by the worst-case scenario and able to respond. By contrast, 70 percent of Soviet warheads are on land-based missiles, offering a "window of vulnerability" to more accurate U.S. forces.

Myth #5

In a "protracted" nuclear war, the United States should plan to "prevail." In other words it is possible to imagine fighting, controlling, winning and surviving a nuclear war.

To close the "window of vulnerability," the Reagan administration plans for nuclear forces capable of responding to a Soviet attack, sustaining such a response over an extended period of time and, in the end, prevailing. The MX, Trident D-5, cruise missiles, accurate warhead guidance, survivable command and control capabilities, ballistic missile defense, space weapons and civil defense all fit into this strategy of limited nuclear war. The goal is selective targeting, as Arms Control and Disarmament Agency adviser Colin Gray has noted: "We have to target, as discreetly as we can, the Soviet state as opposed to the Russian people. Now we can only do that to a limited degree —the state is to a large degree co-located with the Russian people, unfortunately. But we think we're talking into the Russian value structure."[15]

A significant number of strategic analysts—including former defense secretary Robert McNamara, former national security adviser McGeorge Bundy, and retired NATO and U.S. military officers— argue, however, that a nuclear war, once started, would quickly become uncontrollable.

A commonsense alternative must move away from these myths and their logical extension—a destabilizing next stage of the arms race with the Soviet Union. *Stability* is the key concept in this alternative. Americans and Soviets need not be alike, they need even like each other. Both sides need only agree that the next step in the arms race would be a mutual suicide pact.

The technology exists to implement and verify arms-control agreements such as the SALT II treaty (still not ratified by the United States), a comprehensive ban on all nuclear tests, and a bilateral nuclear-weapons freeze.[16] Nor would these agreements freeze the United States at a level of inferiority.[17] Rather, they would close the door on the nuclear arms race, shutting out fast, silent, invisible, accurate, long-range missiles, space-based high-energy lasers aimed at each other's forces, accurate satellite-assisted targeting on both sides and massive civil defense expenditures, all destabilizing.

The next step must be mutual reductions. Fewer strategic nuclear weapons would actually enhance security. "Nuclear superiority," by contrast, is impossible. It is easy, and relatively inexpensive, to deny superiority to another country; it is practically impossible, and prohibitively expensive, to achieve it oneself.

A decision not to build the MX, Trident, cruise missiles and the B-1 would not affect the military value or survivability of existing strategic weapons. The U.S. submarine force will remain survivable for many years, given U.S. submarine and antisubmarine warfare technology. With a stable parity assured, arms control talks can focus on mutual trade-offs. The U.S. lead in warheads, accuracy and submarine warfare could be bargained against Soviet leads in "throw-weight" and megatonnage. So long as the reductions do not threaten either side's deterrent, they can continue until the nuclear deterrent itself is negotiable.

A decision to move toward stability with reductions, halting new nuclear programs, would reduce the 1984 defense budgets by roughly $15 billion in budget authority and would provide greater security by reducing the risk of nuclear war.

CONFLICT IN EUROPE: IS IT LIKELY?

A divided Europe, the legacy of World War II, is armed to the teeth, as if war were expected at any moment. The Reagan administration extends the term *window of vulnerability* to include the European military balance; many Democrats worry publicly about the strength of conventional forces in Europe. More than 250,000 U.S. soldiers are stationed in Europe, with considerable armor, munitions, fighters and over 6,000 nuclear warheads. U.S. airlift and sealift planning focuses principally on European contingencies.

Roughly half of the U.S. military budget is spent with Europe in mind. The new U.S. weapons programs—the F-16 fighter, M-1 tank, Pershing 2 missile and ground-launched cruise missiles, Bradley armored personnel carrier, antitank weapons—have been designed with a European war in mind. The administration, and even many of its critics, contend that this rebuilding effort is urgently needed lest the Soviet Union and its Warsaw Pact allies be tempted to sweep across central Europe, pushing NATO forces aside in a rush to the Atlantic.

Current national security policy for Western Europe has a yawning credibility gap. NATO and the Warsaw Pact have both made it abundantly clear that they do not desire a war in Europe. More important, there is no evidence that either alliance actually expects such a conflict; neither appears to plan such a conflict today, and both acknowledge it would be a disaster. It has been more than twenty years since the Berlin Wall crisis, the last time such a conflict seemed possible.

The military balance in Europe, moreover, is far from unfavorable to NATO. Former Secretary of Defense Robert McNamara has described the "threat inflation" commonly used in discussing Europe:

> Soviet conventional strength is not as great as many state it to be, and the NATO conventional weakness is not as great as it is frequently sad to be. Therefore, the conventional balance is not as favorable to the Soviets as is often assumed.
>
> . . . we overstate the Soviets' force and we understate ours, and we therefore greatly overstate the imbalance. This is not something that is new; it has been going on for years.[18]

NATO spending on defense has, as noted, surpassed that of the Warsaw Pact for the past decade. In terms of combat forces, setting aside 800,000 Soviet soldiers on the Chinese frontier, NATO actually has slightly more personnel under arms in Europe than the Warsaw Pact (2.8 million versus 2.6 million). The Soviet tank advantage (27,000 versus 12,000) is countered by a NATO antitank weapon advantage (190,000 versus 70,000). Soviet coastal and medium-range shipping is surpassed by NATO forces. NATO has 485 surface combatant ships, while the Warsaw Pact has only 195. NATO naval combat aircraft total 1,820; the Warsaw Pact, 870.[19] According to data released by Senator Carl Levin (D-MI), NATO actually built more warships in the 1970s than did the Warsaw Pact (200 versus 109).[23] Even in the significant category of attack submarines, where the administration argues the Soviet Union has an advantage, NATO outbuilt the Warsaw Pact 87 to 70 in the 1970s.[21]

Bean-counting, added to the earlier discussion of strategic history and geography, suggests that Warsaw Pact military superiority is a myth. William Kaufmann, Brookings Institution defense analyst, contends that a much more satisfactory way to determine the adequacy of U.S. forces, and of the programs to improve them, is to estimate the extent to which they are capable of reaching realistic objectives. When that test is applied, U.S. capabilities come much closer to adequacy than is suggested by the current wisdom, and the improvements required to increase their effectiveness tend to be somewhat different from and less demanding than the programs proposed by the administration.[22]

For Kaufmann, NATO's greater need is to improve its ability to resupply troops once war is under way; the scenario of a sudden Soviet rush to the sea he considers virtually impossible.[23]

The root of an alternative policy for Europe, then, is how to reduce the risk of a war nobody wants or expects. Here, too, *stability* and *force reductions* are the key concepts. Theater nuclear forces are the first problem. The Soviet Union has been deploying SS-20 missiles while it retires the older, less mobile SS-4s and -5s. On the other hand, total NATO nuclear warheads, short- and medium-range, outnumber those of the Soviet Union, 6,000 to 3,000. The Pershing 2 and ground-launched cruise missiles add incentive for new Soviet deployment. Neither side requires new nuclear weapons; stability would be served by reductions on *both sides.* The commonsense alternative includes a U.S. declaration of "no first use" of nuclear weapons (the Soviet Union has already done so), serious negotiations on an agreement to reduce nuclear forces, and the gradual withdrawal of nuclear weapons from Europe.*

A denuclearized Europe does not require massive increases in conventional arms spending for its security. Instead, conventional force reductions (and the elimination of all chemical and biological systems) would enhance mutual stability and security. In the short term, a balance needs to be struck between force improvements, training, readiness spending, and supplies for NATO, on the one hand, and negotiations between the two pacts to reduce forces in a mutual way, on the other.† Depending on the progress of theater nuclear and

---

* In *The Military Balance, 1982–1983* (London: IISS, 1982) 134, the International Institute for Strategic Studies has noted the risks of escalation in the continued buildup of theater nuclear forces in Europe: "Even a modest exchange of nuclear warheads in Europe would, in all probability, escalate rapidly to the strategic nuclear level."

† There are signs that the ten-year-old Vienna negotiations on mutual and balanced force reductions between NATO and the Warsaw Pact could make significant progress in the near future. See Jonathan Dean, "Soviet Shift in Vienna," *New York Times,* 1 Aug. 1983.

conventional force reductions, as much as $15–20 billion could have been avoided in the fiscal year 1984 U.S. military budget.

THE SOUTHERN TIER: WHAT CREATES SECURITY?

The most dramatic global geopolitical change in the twentieth century has been the emergence of over 100 independent new nations, carved out of European colonial empires. The legacy of colonialism has been the severe vulnerability of these countries to shifts in global trade, investment, and currency values; a paucity of educated personnel; continued poverty and disease; inadequate resources for housing, health, transportation and employment; and frontiers laid with attention only to colonial history.

The result has been inevitable social upheaval and territorial quarrels. These upheavals are likely to continue for decades, with uneven economic development, social violence, limited growth of democratic politics, and international disputes. The first requirement of an alternative national-security policy is to accept and understand the inevitability of these changes.

The direct intervention of each superpower—the Soviet Union in Ethiopia and Angola; the United States in Chile and the Philippines —influences short-term changes. Despite efforts to portray changes in El Salvador, Ethiopia, Angola, South Africa or the Lebanon as the result of Cuban and Soviet meddling, neither the United States nor the Soviet Union determines the long-term flow of events in the Southern Tier.

The course of resistance to change pursued by the Reagan administration leads inevitably to repeated U.S. military intervention in the Southern Tier. The administration is committed to a major increase in U.S. capabilities for such intervention, including two new carrier battle groups (beyond the current thirteen), a 600-ship navy (up from the current 500+), and a rapid deployment force (RDF) capable of global mobility. Originally a proposal for a force of roughly 110,000, under Reagan, the RDF has grown to over 225,000, including a command headquarters, an additional 50–100 cargo aircraft, new sealift, and pre-positioning of equipment overseas.

Aggressive arms sales policies add to the military nature of current U.S. policy toward the Southern Tier. While the Carter administration restrained arms sales for a time, under President Reagan U.S. foreign sales have risen to nearly $20 billion a year.

Each element of an increasingly militarized policy is decreasing American national security; the inevitability of change will almost certainly lead to repeated deployment of U.S. forces overseas for combat purposes. Public reaction to the Middle East or Central American crises suggests that Americans understand the need for an alternative policy that accepts and works with the changes taking place. Time and economic growth are the ultimate solutions to the stresses and strains of the Southern Tier. American security policy needs to focus on diplomatic and economic initiatives that will help the process along as smoothly as possible.

There is a place for military forces in this alternative. A 600-ship navy, however, is unnecessary and highly costly.* The United States already has overwhelming oceangoing naval superiority. Most of the Soviet navy is coastal; the first two Soviet aircraft carriers are still under construction, while the U.S. Navy has thirteen carriers and plans to build two more. With NATO naval forces, the alliance fleet is superior in virtually all respects. Open sea-lanes can be maintained with the forces at hand.

The rapid deployment force is also an excess. Airborne and marine forces already give the United States the world's most powerful mobility force, with airlift second to none. If mobility forces require additional funds, they would best be spent on additional sealift, training and supplies. Where intervention may be needed—to support NATO allies, to protect American lives or to participate in international peacekeeping efforts—current forces, properly maintained, are more than adequate.

Foreign arms sales directly reduce American national security. Though defended as support for friends, the result is to make the inevitable Southern Tier conflicts more deadly and to risk their expansion. Moments of significant socioeconomic change contain the greatest risk of wider war, as the experience of World War I demonstrates.

---

* In a contradictory way, buying new ships is so costly it is forcing the Navy to retire a larger number of usable, older vessels early to save the expenses of operating them and transfer the funds to purchase the new ships. See Dina Rasor, ed. *More Bucks, Less Bang,* 3–4.

Rapidly expanding foreign arms sales will pull both the United States and the Soviet Union into similar conflicts unnecessarily.

In sum, a restructured U.S. policy toward the Southern Tier could save another $10–15 billion in fiscal year 1984 military spending.

ARE WE GETTING THE BEST SECURITY FOR OUR MONEY?

National security also depends on the quality of decisions being made in the Pentagon. In 1983, a number of investigations, several inside the Defense Department, have focused on the degree to which defense spending is out of control: underfunding of the defense budget, inefficiencies and waste in the contracting process, and actual fraud by contractors.[24]

National security requires ready armed forces and efficient spending of defense dollars. In contrast, as one recently retired general put it, "Their approach has been to assign a high priority to everything. It's not a well-thought-out buildup, just more of everything."[25]

The spending spree has created serious readiness problems. The fastest-growing part of the defense budget has been for "defense investment"—i.e., researching, developing and producing weapons and military construction. The share of the defense budget going to readiness, particularly personnel and operations and maintenance (O&M), is actually declining (Figure 2). Although these measures are rough, the changing proportions have created concern that a rapid buildup will actually decrease readiness.

> O&M will have to support larger forces, more installations and activities, employ a greater number of civilians, maintain a growing inventory of equipment while maintaining readiness and increasing sustainability. And there is real concern that if the O&M base proves to be too limited to support this burden, it can be corrected in the face of a growing "outlay bulge" created by the production of the increasing number of weapons we have authorized over the past two years.[26]

To solve this dilemma, either O&M spending has to be increased, pushing the whole defense budget even higher, or there will have to be deep cuts in the weapons systems being bought. Congressional and public pressure is unlikely to permit the budget to grow more rapidly. Moreover, a restructured security policy eliminates the need for many of the new weapon systems. Cutting weapons is the most appropriate solution.

Establishing weapon priorities will also help solve another major national-security dilemma: the high failure rate of many new systems. Here the military reform group makes a contribution, noting that the M-1 tank has engine and drive-train problems, the M-2 personnel carrier is too small, the F-18 fighter is too costly and is below its intended range, the Copperhead missile is less accurate than the contractor stated, and the AH-64 helicopter could be a suicide vehicle for its crew.

Tax dollars can also be saved by serious reforms in the way the Pentagon buys its weapons. The Reagan administration has totally failed to control weapons costs. Its procurement policy reforms (the so-called Carlucci initiatives) do not even focus on the cost problem. Instead, such contractors as Lockheed and Rockwell, both of which have had cost problems in the past, have received new production

WEAPONS *V.* READINESS
Where Is the Denfense Dollar Really Going?

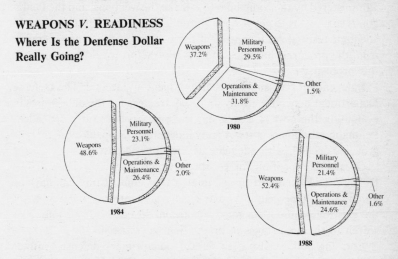

[1]Weapons include research and development, procurement, military construction and nuclear warhead programs in the Department of Energy.
[2]Military Personnel includes personnel and retirement pay.

Based on February 1983 Office of Management and Budget data for budget authority for the national defense function. Totals may not add up to 100% due to rounding.

contracts for C-5A and B-1 aircraft, respectively. To cite another example, the July 1983 Grace Commission report on Defense Department management notes that instead of seeking to reduce costs through greater competition, the Pentagon awards more than 90 percent of its contracts in dollar value without competitive bidding.[27]

A restructured national security policy must make major changes in the way weapons and military budgets are planned. If readiness is an important goal, then readiness, not weapons, should be the focus of the budget. The framework set out here suggests the ingredients of such readiness: a stable, lower level of nuclear deterrence; a capable, smaller presence in Western Europe; and oceangoing and mobility forces adequate to protect the United States and its citizens, keep sea-lanes open and provide for international peacekeeping. Dramatically lower purchases of new equipment will make this readiness goal easier to attain.

Several basic reforms are also needed in the procurement process. For example, many major weapons are inadequately tested and fail to perform once they are operational; the testing programs are usually administered by the companies that make the weapons, and the Pentagon is so anxious to get weapons into the inventory that it, too, shirks adequate testing. An independent testing agency, working separately from the procurement office and the contractor, would help mitigate this problem.*

Independent cost analysis is also desperately needed. The Defense Department depends entirely on its contractors for the data it uses in evaluating the cost of a weapon; there is virtually no independent Pentagon estimate of costs. A truly independent, capable cost analysis group is needed, with adequate access to basic cost data.

Greater competition for contracts would also reduce costs. The Defense Science Board has estimated that competition can save as much as 15–20 percent in an average contract. Strong enforcement of the existing requirement for competition, stretching from initial research to the final stages of production, is essential.

Auditing policies also need reform. The primary defense contract auditor, the Defense Contract Audit Agency (DCAA), has been hamstrung. For example, "indirect costs" on a contract—the large administrative overhead of a contractor for secretaries, managers, paper

---

* Such an agency was legislated by Congress, over Defense Department opposition, in 1983.

work, auditing, legal and other expenses—are rarely audited, and auditors are denied essential data in this area. The DCAA needs greater access to records and should participate in the final negotiations between the contractors and the services when costs they have questioned are being discussed.[28]

The criticism of Defense Department practices has done little to change spending practices. A House Armed Services Committee briefing suggests why procurement reform is so difficult:

> O&M is handicapped when competing against highly organized Washington lobbies actively seeking more dollars for various procurement and R&D programs. . . . [A] Washington representative for a procurement program would have little problem conveying to you the effect [of a cut] on his program. . . . This constituency for procurement and R&D works independently of the services, while the troops in the field are almost wholly reliant upon service sponsors.[29]

The simple truth is that the Defense Department's work is only partly designed to serve national security. The defense market is one of the largest in America—over $100 billion in defense contracts are awarded each year. It is a concentrated market—the leading twenty-five contractors to the Defense Department regularly receive 50 percent of all prime contracts, in dollar value. It is also a stable business—the top twenty-five firms have been there for years (Boeing, Grumman, General Dynamics, Lockheed, Rockwell, McDonnell Douglas, and Hughes Aircraft, to name only a few). For some of these, defense contracting is their basic business: Lockheed, Northrop, General Dynamics, McDonnell Douglas and Grumman depend on government contracts for over 60 percent of their sales.

Defense contractors have powerful political allies. As a general rule, members of Congress who come from districts with defense plants or who sit on key committees support higher defense spending, as do Defense Department bureaucrats who rely on higher budgets and new weapons to ensure their institutional survival and enhance their authority.

Together, defense contractors, key members of Congress, and Pentagon bureaucrats make up an "iron triangle"—a network of policymakers, linked through information, access, influence and, above all, money.[30] Defense contractors are quite self-conscious about their political role and have been innovators in developing techniques for influencing government policies and weapons decisions.

Contractor influence begins at the research-and-development stage, where contractors and Defense Department officials create and evaluate new weapon systems and future defense plans. Early access and influence are reinforced by membership on federal advisory committees and by company hiring practices. In the 1970s, for example, nearly 2,000 individuals moved between the Defense Department or NASA and eight leading defense contractors—Boeing, General Dynamics, Grumman, Lockheed, McDonnell Douglas, Northrop, Rockwell International, and United Technologies.[31]

Most major contractors also maintain Washington offices to monitor and to influence congressional and Defense Department decisions. Audits in 1976 by the Defense Contract Audit Agency of the Washington offices of five leading contractors—Boeing, General Dynamics, Grumman, Lockheed, and Rockwell International—show that each company spent an average of $1.5 million a year on its Washington presence. The bulk of this was billed to the companies' defense contracts.[32] Defense contractors also make considerable use of political action committees (PACs) to maintain access to key members of Congress. Defense contractors operate some of the largest corporate PACs. The same eight major contractors, for example, spent over $2 million through their PACs in the late 1970s, most of it in contributions to key members of Congress.[33]

Contractors can also stimulate their local "constituents"—employees, stockholders, communities and subcontractors—to support their defense business. In its campaign for the B-1, for example, Rockwell spent hundreds of thousands of dollars mobilizing its 114,000 workers, the holders of its 35 million shares of common stock, local officials, and suppliers to support its lobbying effort. Grumman mounted a similar effort in 1977 and 1978 when production of its F-14 was threatened.[34]

A restructured national security policy needs to deal with the persistence of the iron triangle. Even limited steps would help, ranging from making it more difficult for contractors to hire former Pentagon employees, to requiring greater disclosure of information on subcontracting (in order to track the emergence of political constituencies for new weapons), to limiting contractor PAC contributions.

At the root of the triangle lies the heavy dependence of some firms on defense contracts. It may be necessary to reexamine the structure of ownership in defense production. Some defense manufacturers are already inefficient; public ownership of these facilities could hardly be less efficient. At the very least, direct public accountability for the contracting process could increase the potential for major reform.

THE ECONOMY AND THE MILITARY BUILDUP

National security is not only military—it depends as well on the state of the American economy. World War II seemed to end the depression of the 1930s, and many view today's military spending as crucial to the nation's economic activity. Today, budget *deficits* are out of control, American *productivity* has declined, and new *jobs* are hard to find, while 12 million Americans remain unemployed. Rapidly expanding military spending today, however, may make it *more difficult* to solve these economic problems.

Defense spending, the only federal program growing in real dollars, has a direct role in the growing budget deficit, which the Congressional Budget Office says will aggregate $1.3 trillion between 1984 and 1988. As Harvard economist Benjamin Friedman has noted, "substantially all of the increase in the projected deficit for the 1980's is due to a reduction in revenues and an increase in defense spending in relation to gross national product."[35]

Since defense dollars are drawn from tax dollars (and not from separate trust funds), the role of defense spending in the deficit problem is more direct. Trust funds for Social Security, unemployment and Medicare are not in deficit, while the part of the federal budget funded by tax revenues is. Defense spending takes up over 40 percent of general revenues. Combined with military programs in the Department of Energy, NASA and the Veterans Administration, defense's share rises to over 50 percent. Future control over budget deficits will depend on controlling defense spending.

Federal borrowing to fund the deficit, moreover, creates upward pressure on interest rates and reduces the supply of capital available for private investment. Businesses investing in productivity improvements or new industries find capital scarce and expensive. This in turn hinders improvements in U.S. productivity.[36]

Furthermore, the federal government spends 70 cents of each of its research-and-development dollars on military research. The Defense Department argues that its research investments are good for economic productivity, yet defense technology has now become so sophisticated and expensive that its commercial applications are declining. Direct federal research spending to enhance productivity and create new jobs would be preferable.

Even job creation may be hampered by rapid growth in defense spending. The defense budget is often defended as a jobs program. Many American workers and communities depend on the defense dollar. From Los Angeles to Long Island, well over 2 million Americans work on defense contracts. Within the defense industry, however, the power of the defense dollar to create new jobs is declining. For example, although McDonnell Douglas does four times the dollar value of defense contracting today that it did in 1970, its labor force has shrunk from 92,000 to 72,000 over the same period.[37]

Gradually, the defense business is becoming more "capital intensive," with a greater proportion of the defense dollar going into raw material, research, technology and machinery, and less into new jobs. Moreover, the defense industry does not employ groups suffering from the highest unemployment rates in America: minorities, females, the less skilled and less educated. Almost any other federal spending program—housing, health, education—creates more jobs for these Americans. If new employment is an important national-security goal, defense spending may be frustrating that effort.

An alternative policy should focus on military spending that maximizes national security while minimizing its harmful effects on the economy. Budget planners should seek consistency between defense-spending plans and overall national economic policies. Defense-spending planners should be conscious of balanced regional spending goals, employment needs, environmental and natural resource effects, national research and technology goals, and policies for corporate diversification and small-business development.

If the broader alternate policy proposed here saves resources in the defense budget, it must also include a defense-conversion program. This program should involve plans for specific defense facilities; a joint planning process between localities and the federal government; aid to communities that depend on the defense dollar; legislation to ensure that defense workers have pension and health-benefit portability, retraining and relocation assistance; and federal support to help diversify and convert defense plants.

CONCLUSION

The Reagan military buildup has clearly failed to achieve the one goal it promised: a feeling of national security. As military spending grows, new weapons are piled into the arsenal, the NATO alliance comes unraveled, arms sales expand, the risk of American military intervention overseas grows, money is wasted, economic health is frustrated, and Americans become noticeably less secure.

The need for an alternative national security policy is clear. That it has not emerged in the political process is a testimonial to the complexity of the issue and to the fear among politicians that they will appear "soft" on the defense of the United States. Yet the framework for a realistic alternative is at hand, drawing from common sense about our relationships with the Soviet Union, Europe and the Southern Tier and from practical thinking about efficiency in government and the health of the American economy. This restructuring of national-security policy needs to start from clear principles and can lead to savings of as much as $50 billion in 1984.

The contribution of this alternative to current national-security policy would be substantial:

1. A stable, less risky relationship with the Soviet Union, in which real threats, conflict and competition could be managed with lower risk of nuclear war.

2. Closer harmony with our NATO allies in a less militarized Europe facing far lower risks of war.

3. Realistic acceptance of change in the Southern Tier, with reduced risk that those changes will stimulate regional or global conflict and with improved possibilities for the kind of economic development that can benefit all nations.

4. Leaner, more efficient military forces, with greater readiness, tailored to meet real national-security missions: the defense of allies, sea, land, citizens and borders, and peacekeeping.

5. A procurement process that wastes less money, establishes clear

priorities, buys more appropriate equipment and is accountable to and controllable by the Congress and the taxpayer.

6. An opportunity to restore the American economy to health without the harmful side effects of runaway military budgets.

Clarifying real national security and the means to achieve it will strengthen America politically, economically and militarily. The alternative—a growing risk of confrontation and war—has lost its credibility.

Notes

1. On the M-1 tank, see contributions by Patrick Oster, Bruce Ingersoll, and John Fialka in Dina Rasor, ed., *More Bucks, Less Bang: How the Pentagon Buys Ineffective Weapons* (Washington, D.C.: Fund for Constitutional Government, 1983), 34–50.

    On the Bradley Infantry Fighting Vehicle, see William Boly, "The $13 Billion Dud," in Dina Rasor, ibid., 13–28.

    On the diode, see "Millions Found Wasted in Buying Military Spare Parts," *Chicago Tribune,* 11 July 1983.

2. See George Kuhn, "Department of Defense: Ending Defense Stagnation," in Heritage Foundation, ed., *Agenda '83,* 69–114; Franklin C. Spinney, *The Plans/Reality Mismatch and Why We Need Realistic Budgeting,* Defense Department Briefing Paper, Dec. 1982; U.S. Air Force Systems Command, *The Affordable Acquisition Approach Study* (Washington, D.C.: U.S. Air Force Briefing, Feb. 1983; William Kaufmann, "The Defense Budget," in Joseph A. Pechman, ed., *Setting National Priorities* (Washington, D.C.: Brookings Institution, 1983).

3. See, for example, Nautilus Research, *Pacific Command: The Structure and Strategy of the U.S. Military in the Pacific* (Leverett, Mass.: Nautilus, July 1983); and Richard Halloran, "Military Forces Stretched Thin, Army Chief Says," *New York Times,* 10 Aug. 1983.

4. Gary Hart, "Reagan Policies Will Cripple Military," *Los Angeles Times,* 24 Feb. 1983.

5. John Glenn, "Rethinking Defense," in John Glenn, Barry E. Carter, and Robert W. Komer, *Rethinking Defense and Conventional Forces* (Washington, D.C.: Center for National Policy, 1983), 12–13.

6. Although every administration would argue that it has prepared defense budgets in this clear and straightforward manner, in reality the defense budget frequently emerges on the basis of last year's numbers, the desire of Pentagon officials to have more, and industry and congressional pressures for greater spending. For more detailed discussion of this process, see below, and also Gordon Adams, *The Politics of Defense Contracting: The Iron Triangle* (New Brunswick, N.J.: Transaction Press, 1982); Adams, "Disarming the Military Subgovernment," *Harvard Journal on Legislation* 14, no. 3, (Apr. 1977): 459–503; and Adams, "The Iron Triangle: Defense Contracting as a Case

Study in Closed Circuit Policy-Making," in Frank Fischer and Carmen Sirianni, *Critical Studies in Organization and Bureaucracy* (Philadelphia: Temple University Press, 1984).

7. U.S. Department of Defense, *Your Defense Budget: Fiscal Year 1984* (Washington, D.C.: U.S. Government Printing Office, 1983), 1.

8. White House, Office of Policy Information, *Fairness II: An Executive Briefing Book* (Washington, D.C.: 1 May 1983), tab V.

9. Official Soviet data show a defense budget of only 17 billion rubles. The artificial conversion rate is $1.37 per ruble.

10. See Franklyn Holzman, "Are the Soviets Really Outspending the U.S. on Defense?" *International Security* 4, no. 4 (Spring 1980): 86–104; and "Soviet Military Spending: Assessing the Numbers Game," *International Security* 6, no. 4 (Spring 1982): 78–101.

11. Caspar Weinberger, *Annual Report to the Congress, Fiscal Year 1983* (Washington, D.C.: U.S. Government Printing Office, 1982), I–4.

12. President Ronald Reagan, Press Conference, 31 Mar. 1982.

13. Testimony, May 11, 1982, quoted in Holzman, *Atlantic,* 14.

14. President Ronald Reagan, Press Conference, 1 Oct. 1981.

15. James Lardner, "The Call of the Hawk's Hawk," *Washington Post,* 14 May 1983.

16. See Federation of American Scientists, *Public Interest Report,* Sept. 1982.

17. Randall Forsberg, "A Bilateral Nuclear Weapons Freeze," *Scientific American,* Nov. 1982.

18. Robert Scheer, "Fear of a U.S. First Strike Seen as Cause of Arms Race," *Los Angeles Times,* 8 Apr. 1982.

19. John Collins, *U.S.-Soviet Military Balance: Concepts and Capabilities, 1960–1980* (New York: McGraw-Hill, 1980).

20. Senator Carl Levin, *The Other Side of the Story,* monograph issued by Senator Levin, May 1983.

21. See *Washington Post,* 8 Apr. 1983.

22. Kaufmann, in Pechman, 57.

23. Ibid., 63–64.

24. See Gordon Adams, *Controlling Weapons Costs: Can the Pentagon Reforms Work?* (New York: Council on Economic Priorities, 1983); Richard Halloran, "Admiral Says Shoddy Work Adds 50% to some Arms Cost," *New York Times,* 26 June 1983; Department of Defense, Office of the Inspector General, *Draft Report on the Audit of the Procurement of Aircraft Engine Spare Parts,* 21 June 1983. See also Kuhn, Kaufmann, Spinney, and U.S. Air Force, all op. cit. (note 2).

25. *Wall Street Journal,* 6 July 1983.

26. U.S. Congress, House, Armed Services Committee, *Staff Briefing on the FY 1984 DOD O&M Request,* March 1983, 7.

27. *Newsweek,* 11 July 1983; and *Time,* 11 July 1983.

28. See Adams, *Controlling Weapons Costs.*

29. U.S. Congress, House, Armed Services Committee, op. cit., p. 5.

30. See Adams, *The Politics of Defense Contracting,* ch. 1.

31. Ibid., ch. 6.

32. Ibid., ch. 9.

33. Ibid., ch. 8.

34. Ibid., ch. 13.

35. Benjamin M. Friedman, "Managing the U.S. Government Deficit in the 1980's," preliminary draft article, Apr. 1983, 6.

36. See, for example, the Bipartisan Appeal to Resolve the Budget Crisis, a business group, which called for slower growth in defense spending, in a letter to William C. Clark, 25 Mar. 1983, published as an ad in the *New York Times,* 6 April 1983.

37. As calculated by the Defense Budget Project, Center on Budget and Policy Priorities, Washington, D.C., 1983.

12

A Labor-Oriented Perspective on Immigration Policy

Colin Greer and Josh DeWind

THE IMMIGRATION PERIL

Over the past decade, the public has been repeatedly told by bureaucrats, politicians and academicians that immigration poses a grave threat to the American way of life. The perceived danger is intensified by illegal immigrants—immigrants who do not possess official documents authorizing their presence. Similar fears of foreigners have been expressed throughout the history of the United States. The current wave of apprehension over illegal immigrants was first shaped for public debate in the mid-1970s when then-Commissioner of the Immigration and Naturalization Service (INS), General Leonard F. Chapman, in a *Reader's Digest* article, called the nation to battle claiming a "vast and silent invasion of illegal immigrants across our borders is reaching the proportions of a national disaster."[1] Not long afterward William Colby, ex-director of the CIA, claimed, "The swelling population of Mexico, driving millions of illegal aliens over the border is a greater threat to the future of the United States than the Soviet Union."[2]

Fears for the cultural stability of the nation, for its language and for its democratic traditions have been part of the hue and cry taken up by numerous other officials and organizations. Groups such as FAIR (Federation for American Immigration Reform), Zero Population Growth, and the Environmental Fund have regularly claimed that illegal immigration is the major source of the nation's population explosion and the subsequent depletion of its resources. Most re-

Colin Greer is vice president of the New World Foundation. *Josh DeWind* is director of the Immigration Research Program at the Center for the Social Sciences of Columbia University.

cently, Senator Alan K. Simpson (R-Wyo.) told the Senate that "although population and job market impacts are of great significance, I think most would agree with me that the national interest of the American people also includes certain even more important and fundamental aspects—such as preservation of freedom, personal safety, and political stability, as well as the public—and I emphasize the word 'public'—cultural qualities and the political institutions which are their foundation."[3]

The most serious problems that illegal immigrants or undocumented workers are said to cause are economic: citizen unemployment, decreases in wages, deterioration of working conditions, and union-busting. Even the AFL-CIO, standard-bearer of labor's interests, has blamed undocumented workers. The federation's executive council declared in 1977 that "the massive flow of illegal aliens into the United States is a serious problem. Illegal alien workers—estimated at 6 to 12 million—take jobs from Americans and undermine U.S. wages and working conditions." The reason why workers have such an adverse effect, says the union, is because "their status puts them at the mercy of unscrupulous employers who rely on their fear of deportation to keep them from protesting low wages and intolerable working conditions. Businesses which comply with the law suffer from the unfair advantage taken by competitors who exploit illegal alien workers."[4]

Although not all sectors of the society are equally concerned, the urgency of the situation has been increased by claims that illegal immigrants most affect already disadvantaged minority groups. A frequently cited article in *Ebony* magazine, for example, told its readers that "data about the vast numbers of these 'undocumented workers' and their impact on the U.S. labor force are scant, but the siphoning of jobs by them is a major reason for the employment crises among Blacks and especially young Black men."[5]

This view of the labor market has been strongly supported by labor economist and former secretary of labor Ray Marshall, who has publicly argued that "it is false to say American workers cannot be found for all the jobs filled by undocumented workers . . . no matter how undesirable the jobs may be. . . ."[6]

This general vision of the labor market and the impact of illegal workers upon it is shared by an influential group of academicians whose views have been influential in developing a restrictionist immigration policy for the United States. Notable among this group has been Vernon M. Briggs, who has collaborated with Marshall. They share the conviction that undocumented workers, because of their large numbers and disadvantaged legal status, compete unfairly with Americans for jobs. "No U.S. worker," writes Briggs, "can compete with an illegal alien when the competition depends upon who will work for the lowest pay and the longest hours and accept the most arbitrary working conditions."[7]

Because the unfair competition of undocumented workers is seen by Briggs and Marshall as the cause of declining employment and working conditions for poor Americans seeking the same jobs, their solution to the problem is "to reduce the unfair addition of millions of illegal aliens into this selected sector of the economy."[8] Likewise, the solution proposed by successive presidential commissions, congressional committees and numerous public organizations has been the obvious one: more-effective restriction of illegal immigration.

Each of the past three administrations—under Ford, Carter and now Reagan—has attempted to formulate a bill enabling us to "regain control over our borders," but controversy and conflict about the provisions of each proposed bill have paralyzed all attempts to reform the immigration laws. The most recent proposal to fail to pass the Congress was the Immigration Reform and Control Act introduced by Senator Simpson of Wyoming and Congressman Romano L. Mazzoli of Kentucky—notably, both states that are little affected by immigration. According to newspaper accounts, the bill has not yet been put before the House of Representatives because no strong constituency supports it. The strongest opposition comes from Hispanic groups, but the Chamber of Commerce of the United States, civil-rights groups, labor, and state and local governments have all objected to key parts of the legislation. Nevertheless, the bill's sponsors expect it will be voted on by the House in 1984. By then Congressman Edward R. Roybal of California and other members of the Hispanic Caucus intend to introduce a less restrictionist alternative.

Over the past five years of blocked immigration reform, legislative proposals designed to offset the supposed negative impact of illegal immigrants have sought to include reductions in legal immigration with a "temporary guest workers" program, sanctions against employers who hire illegal immigrants, and legalization of the status of some portion of illegal immigrants who have already settled in the

United States. The problem with trying to limit the total number of people granted access to American citizenship has been that the various groups cannot agree on what that number should be in order to reduce adverse affects, nor can they agree as to whom should be given priority for entrance and whom excluded. A second problem is that the proposed expansion of the temporary workers program, which now brings in 30,000 foreign contract workers a year, would negate employment benefits to American workers resulting from a reduction of legal immigration. The bill is an attempt to block further immigration. But that won't happen. It is going to bring in great numbers of foreign workers who will form a pool of marginal labor.

Employer sanctions are intended to stop the flow of illegal immigrants by depriving them of jobs, presumably their motive for coming here. Hispanic groups predict that in trying to avoid fines, employers would also deny employment to legal immigrants, Hispanic Americans and others entitled to work. The proposal to supply all American citizens and legal residents with nonforgeable identification cards has been deemed impractical (they will be obtainable with forged documents), and civil-rights organizations have also termed such proposals a threat to privacy and to freedom of movement.

Granting legal status to illegal immigrants already in the country has been proposed in order to let them emerge from their underground lives of misery and frequent exploitation by unscrupulous employers, landlords, immigration attorneys and others who take advantage of their vulnerable legal status. Which and how many illegal immigrants should be given what legalized status cannot be agreed upon. State and local governments oppose legal status for families who might seek public relief. Law-and-order groups want to avoid appearing to reward illegal immigrants while law-abiding applicants patiently await visas abroad. Labor is afraid that, once legalized, millions of undocumented workers will compete with citizens for better jobs. Proposals to limit legalization, however, have been criticized as costly, difficult to administer, and inhumane for those left in the shadows of illegality.

If nothing else, these controversies about immigration reform reveal that addressing unemployment and other problems of the labor market by way of immigration policy is enormously complex. The contradictions between the need to admit immigrants to work and the desire to protect citizens' jobs have ultimately, as with previous efforts, led to the flourishing of restrictionist sentiment, coupled with loopholes that would allow the stream of immigrant labor, legal and illegal, to continue as before.

Although sharp disagreement over various aspects of immigration bills may have for some time paralyzed reforms, the basic assumption that reforms in immigration laws are essential for resolving employment problems has not been called into serious question. Even if illegal immigration were brought under control by new legislation, it is not at all clear that any benefits would result in the job market for workers. Legal or illegal, there is little convincing evidence that immigrants are likely to be controlled by way of legislative action designed to limit their entry.

The history of attitudes toward foreign workers and of legislation to control their entry into the United States puts the current hysteria over the supposed effects of illegal immigrants into a more familiar and less threatening perspective, which could temper the current assumptions about the style of immigration reform to be sought. Above all, this history shows that restrictionist legislation, pioneered in the late nineteenth century, has never provided the controls on immigration its supporters claimed it would.

THE FAMILIAR HISTORY OF IMMIGRATION REFORM

The history of nineteenth- and early-twentieth-century immigration is also, of course, the history at once of the composition of U.S. labor on the basis of wide national and racial diversity and the exploitation of that diversity to set immigrant "strikebreakers" at odds with previously settled immigrant workers. The Chinese were frequently used as strikebreakers in emerging industrial and urban sectors, as were, for example, Italians, blacks and Mexicans in succeeding decades. In this context, "new immigrants"—defined either by virtue of recency of emigration from a particular source and/or recency of emigration of a "racially" distinguishable group—were popularly seen as vehicles of employer exploitation. And, of course, they were. In self-defense, victim blamed victim. Immigrants of one era were threatened by immigrants of another.

By the end of the nineteenth century, immigration already was seen as both the historic core of American strength and the prospective cause of the erosion of that strength. Arguments against more and easy immigration could be quite diverse: For some, the goal was to protect labor and to undo exploitative conditions; for others, racial purity and national security were the imperatives. But whatever the diversity of opinion, historic immigration was a benchmark of valued heritage, and current immigration a cause for worry and even despair.

From 1924 to 1965, a period commonly taken as one of effective restriction, a constant flow of illegal newcomers continued to fill American agricultural, manufacturing and service-industry needs for cheap labor. The process continues still. In the twenty years before 1982, about 7 million legal immigrants entered the United States. By the most conservative estimates, at least that number have entered illegally since 1965. Throughout, these immigrants have been greeted with hostility by the descendants of immigrants.

The only time there had been effective reduction in immigration rates to proportions in any way satisfactory to restrictionists was in the war years, 1914–18 and 1943–45. In those years, with quota rates in effect, quotas remained unfilled. As the years to 1950 saw a relatively slow rise to quota limits once again, deportation of "illegal" entrants increased. Given current experience with illegal entry, it is likely that the undocumented arriving across U.S. borders with Mexico and Canada were more numerous than those actually deported— a pattern of evasion that, after all, had prevailed through U.S. efforts to effect shipping codes in the mid–nineteenth century to limit the entry of the unhealthy and to close the doors on Chinese immigrants entirely.

Throughout U.S. experience with restrictive immigration policies, loopholes for entry have remained. Through legal quotas, explicit exceptions, or inadequate policing, immigrants have remained a significant part of the U.S. labor force. It is quite clear that the periodic crises around immigration policy have represented two distinct sets of concerns: on one hand, patriotic, race and cultural-purity anxiety; on the other, labor-capital tensions. Without doubt the rabid rhetoric and bigoted myopia of the racial-superiority arguments—especially as they included worries for the health of democratic institutions at the hands of peoples with no historical experience of them—added fiery spirit to the material battle under way between worker and employer in the U.S.

Nevertheless, it was the disproportionate strength of the contenders (employers and workers) that produced the actual legislation passed over the years. There was, for example, no instance of restrictionist victory analogous to Prohibition in which a moral crusading spirit commandeered the decision-making processes. The pattern of restriction legislation was, increasingly, to maintain immigration as a source of labor and to restrict those to whom the promise of integration in U.S. society was made. Indeed, with each piece of restriction legislation, the most recent immigrants can be seen straddling the two sides of the restriction dilemma as they experienced it: On the one hand, they recognized that their position as U.S. workers made some degree of restriction necessary—the use of immigrants by employers was clear-cut and unequivocal; on the other hand, at the same time, these new Americans sought to include their own compatriots in a favored relation to American discriminatory processes by pushing for a larger aggregate inflow than strict restrictionists contemplated and the establishment of more recent bases (e.g., 1920 instead of 1890) for the construction of native-origin quotas.

The 1921 and 1924 quota restrictions were the first direct legislative restriction predicated on particular national-origin sources. Its terms limited the number of any nationality entering the United States to 3 percent of the foreign-born of that nationality living in the United States in 1910 as determined by the census. Numerous exceptions kept the doors open to those classes of people (ministers, professors, etc.) deemed likely to come from northern and western Europe. Under the quota, 358,000 aliens would be admitted per year—155,000 from southern and eastern Europe. Meanwhile, by World War I, immigration from that part of the world had been four times the number from northern and western Europe. The immediate impact was a drop in immigration from 865,228 in 1921 to 209,556 in the following year. By 1923, immigration rose a little (reaching at least a par with current 1980s legal immigration levels). Now 98.5 percent of quota immigrants were from southern and eastern Europe.

Between 1924 and 1952, there was no major change in immigration law. The national-origin plan ruled, discriminating against groups in order to preserve the Nordic cultural pattern and Anglo-Saxon dominance. As of 1952, while the basic outlines of the 1924 act remained intact, the immigration scene had changed drastically—most especially, to the great concern of restrictionists, in the heavy demand for entry from nonquota Western Hemisphere countries. Mexico was the largest producer of immigrants. In addition to legal entrants, numerous other Mexicans entered the U.S. illegally. More than half a million illegal entrants, for example, were rounded up for deportation in 1951. The pressure of illegal numbers raised public consciousness as U.S. labor once again associated the numbers with threat to their employment. The Senate of the Eightieth Congress initiated a major investigation of immigration in 1950 to review the general immigration context of the time—and to examine for the first time the question of illegal entry.

Following the Senate investigation came a new immigration law in 1952, popularly known as the McCarran-Walter Act. Standards of admissibility were reemphasized, determining at once who would get in and who was to be excluded. According to this new public law, the annual quota for any quota area was fixed at one-sixth of 1 percent of the number of inhabitants in the continental United States in 1920 —the same used for computing national-origin quotas in 1924. With respect to Europe, the same Nordic preference ruled.

At the same time, the 1952 act broadened the provisions admitting nonquota immigrants. Among the nations excluded from quota restriction were Canada, Mexico, Cuba, Haiti and the Dominican Republic. Contract-labor restrictions were also removed at this time; now U.S. labor protection would reside in the Secretary of Labor's power to exclude newcomers on his determination that such entry would adversely affect wages and employment for U.S. workers.

The pattern had been developing for some time. Between 1925 and 1929, about 760,000 immigrants had entered under then-new quota laws. Some 630,000 nonquota immigrants were admitted, too. During the next decade, nonquota entrants, more than half of whom were admitted for temporary work, exceeded quota immigrants. A similar pattern prevailed soon after World War II; and until 1960, quota immigrants hovered around 300,000 per year, while nonquota entrants frequently reached the 1-million mark. Always, more than half the number admitted came to work in the U.S. Between 1951 and

1956, for example, nonquota entrants from Mexico exceeded 500,000 per year. Between 1956 and 1959, the nonquota entrants from Mexico were about 400,000 per year. In 1960 only half the aliens admitted for work were quota immigrants, almost 1 million were not. Congressional hearings in the 1950s confirmed that this alien-worker trend, grown unprecedentedly large by that time, had been recorded as a growing phenomenon concurrent with the advent of quota restrictions. Overall, the numbers of foreign workers had not changed greatly for more than a hundred years. The legal status of those workers, on the other hand, had changed a great deal.

In 1965, legislative action changed the basic immigration law so that hemisphere, rather than national origin, became the major factor in permitting entry into the United States. The Immigration Act abolished the national-origin system. Numerical restrictions were still imposed on the Eastern Hemisphere, subject to an overall limitation, with each European country given an equal limit. For the first time, in a kind of civil-rights declaration for southern and eastern Europeans, all European nations were given equal status in American pluralism.

Quotas among Western Hemisphere countries punctuated the quite different status of this continuing heavy source of immigration. The discriminatory force in this situation is subtle but clear since the question of differential demand is paramount. Emigrants from Western Hemisphere countries have far outnumbered quota allowances, as is confirmed by deportation and undocumented residence as well as applications for entry and consequent waiting lists. The rough quota equivalence given Western and Eastern Hemispheres actually draws two critical lines of exclusion. One is predicated on an even balance between hemispheres in the makeup of total legal immigrant numbers, as if, regardless of demand, certain groups would be undesirable in greater numbers. A second determines a preference system for entry that amounts to a class discrimination system, tacked onto the national-origin discrimination system; it allows worldwide privileged entry to professional and skilled immigrants, thus restricting the poorest and least skilled to illegal entry. Taken together, these measures produce an immigration rate that remains close to the rates in the historic immigration era before World War I.

Indeed, the current scenario is a replay of the more than eighty years of official and semiofficial agreements Mark Riesler examines in

By the Sweat of Their Brow. Through those agreements, the U.S.-Mexican border was wide open and Mexicans enjoyed special unnotice by U.S. immigration authorities, not even requiring a visa until 1929, and entering as nonquota immigrants until 1975.

By the mid-1970s the conflicting interests around this scenario set the U.S. Congress once again on the track of a basic reorganization of immigration policy. The tone of this legislative effort has been, above all, to restrict the flood of Mexicans and other Hispanics across the U.S. border. More recently, according to proponents of such restrictive legislation, the current joblessness among Americans in the face of new levels of economic recession makes a coalition workable that joins black groups, organized labor, and race and language purists.

Throughout the history of restrictive immigration laws, some groups have been favored over others. The criteria for entry have changed, but the underlying issues have remained, and employment competition has been central in this. Along with legal immigration, illegal immigration by disfavored groups has been a constant. What has changed is not the basic role of new legal or illegal immigrants as a source of cheap labor but rather the particular nationalities and racial groups that have served these functions. Restrictionist assumptions have not simply provided a game plan for the perpetual exploitation and persecution of immigrants, they have done so in lieu of directly addressing the conditions that demand and guarantee their service.

For restrictionists, the labor market operates on the basis of supply and demand, with the key variable being the number of illegal workers entering the market. The greater the supply of labor, the more workers must compete for jobs and the lower the wages employers will have to pay. Those hired will be the ones who will accept the lowest wages —in this case immigrants, and undocumented immigrants in particular.

Two alternative approaches to this question cast useful light on it. Michael J. Piore's (Massachusetts Institute of Technology) work suggests that citizens resist taking jobs filled by undocumented workers; displacement, if it occurs at all, is more complex than simple market expectations have suggested. Rejecting the abstract notion of our open labor market in which immigrant and domestic workers compete for the same jobs according to principles of supply and demand, Piore describes a segmented market, with social factors such as prestige, age and generational status determining what jobs workers are willing to take within those parts of the market that are open to them.

Following from this view that the bottom segment of the labor market requires the newest wave of illegal immigrant workers, Piore is not as worried about illegal immigration as are the restrictionists. He argues that "existing policy is nowhere near the failure it is presumed to be; in fact, it is a more rational approach to the problem than any protagonists in the debate are willing to admit." INS enforcement policy, he says, gives priority to apprehending illegal workers holding the best jobs—the jobs Americans want—and thus tends to maintain illegal workers as a "labor force that complements native workers."[9]

If it is true that illegal immigrants are employed in a niche of the labor market where citizens are loath to work, then the effect of restrictionist legislation upon citizen employment will depend on the capacity of native-born workers to force employers to make the jobs more attractive to Americans. Without such force, Piore predicts, "social pressures will tend to create a labor force by restricting the upward mobility of native workers or immigrants of a previous wave (Blacks, Mexican-Americans, etc). The extreme limit of this process would be the reimposition of the kind of racial caste system that once prevailed in the South."[10]

Or as Bill Jordan in his *Automatic Poverty* shows, the rush toward automation will compete with pauperization of the work force and with job export as mechanisms for keeping the costs of production low. These options are especially likely in the climate of massive reduction in the social wage, which has supported the improvement in native-born labor conditions since World War II.

Another point of view, not inconsistent with the view above, highlights the positive effects of immigrants, including undocumented immigrants, on the employment of American workers. Noting the potential of displacement as both historically and currently recorded by some observers, it is argued that displacement occurs in low-paying jobs that would otherwise be lost to job export. In this way, immigrants are both the mainstay of the low pay base line in U.S. employment and the protectors of the multitude of spin-off jobs made possible when established businesses stay at home and new businesses are established.[11]

The economy's assumption of this equation is reinforced by the incapacity of recent administrations to enforce other laws applying to work conditions in places of employment attractive to immigrants. Most recently, instead of beefing up the fight against wage and working-condition violations in sweatshops that exploit legal and illegal workers, as Labor Department Secretary Donovan promised, such investigations have been cut back drastically. The ILGWU has reported that sweatshops are flourishing more than ever. Clearly, the clandestine supply of labor has continued to become trapped in nineteenth-century working and living conditions.

ALTERNATIVE POLICY FRAMEWORK

The economic traditions and priorities that determine the employment of illegal immigrants in the labor market have been largely ignored by historical and recent immigration-restriction proposals; rather, the view has predominated that illegal workers create unemployment and the deterioration of working conditions. With support from the AFL-CIO, restrictionists have pushed for legislation designed primarily to reduce and regulate the presence of illegal immigrants, with the purpose of excluding them from employment and creating categories of immigrants who will still be available to work at cheaper rates than U.S. citizens.

Labor's defense against employer preference for a more docile and cheap labor force is, as has long been the case, directed at other victims of the process. The danger is accurately perceived in that a large low-wage sector unprotected by hard-won labor-regulation laws is a threat to all workers since it reminds of the predictable outcome of the uncontrolled drive for profit.

The basic premise remains that illegal immigrants cause the problems in the labor market. If this notion predominates, then illegal immigrants will, like multitudes of immigrants before them, become the targets of restrictions, but at the same time they will become the reservoir of "guest workers," "undocumented aliens" and "unprocessed residents" who will continue to provide muscle power at the bottom of the socioeconomic ladder.

Beefed-up border patrols, universal I.D. card/work permits, and fines imposed on employers for hiring undocumented workers would serve little purpose because they would be aimed at illegal workers and miss the economic roots of the problems. What are needed instead are, on one hand, immigration policies that both recognize the victimization of illegal immigrants and introduce effective policies to secure decent conditions for them; and on the other hand, labor policies, not immigration policies—deriving from the Department of Labor, not the Department of Justice—to address the drives of employers to profit from immigrant exploitation.

Employment needs, despite high-tech euphoria in current economic prognosticating, will still include the historic need for immigrant labor. To whatever extent *sunset* accurately describes the reduced status in the economy of once dominant industries, the hunger for cheap industrial and service labor continues. Indeed, the reduced status of the industrial sector intensifies that need—it does not eliminate it. Organized labor will be strengthened by including these workers, but its refusal to recognize the mutuality of interests will further deplete membership and divert attention from the pressing causes of the current crisis of its membership. The focus on restrictionism does not really deal with the problem—in fact, it intensifies it, reducing the ranks of labor and undermining the integrity of its purposes.

A national immigration policy aimed at protecting immigrants, including undocumented workers, should first remove their illegal status, which makes them more vulnerable to abuse than are other workers. This minimal protection could be accomplished by granting amnesty to all undocumented immigrants now in the country and designing the administrative measures to guarantee it. In general, rather than isolating illegal workers from citizens, they should be joined together to fight for their common interests in full and fair employment.

This direction requires seeing immigration policy as a means of dealing with the conditions for the entry, life and work of immigrants in the U.S. labor market. It is not the means of making direct labor policy but rather of exercising responsible oversight of the immigrant stream that is flowing into the country. While the presence of and dependence on immigrants are certainly major characteristics of the U.S. economy, as the history and continuation of loopholes in immigration policy show, these are not the causal factors that maintain or remove prevailing conditions of labor insecurity.

On the labor-policy front, American labor would cease its effort to exclude foreign workers from U.S. labor markets, an effort that seems impractical given the high rate of illegal immigration today; instead, the goal would be to help foreign and domestic workers wield greater control over the conditions of employment. Americans typically will not take the sort of jobs that are available to immigrants, and will continue in that style unless corporate and government action leaves no alternative. For Americans to choose such work requires that pay at those levels be significantly above minimum wage. And, of course, in this perspective immigrants will be encouraged to enter as an alternative to job export.

Traditional immigration reform simply seeks to manage the situation, not at all to address its causal features. At present, however, the AFL-CIO opposes the presence of undocumented workers more than it opposes their exploitation. A truly protective policy to expand work opportunities for Americans would require organized labor's joining with immigrant workers to fight for their common interests in the strengthening and enforcement of labor regulations in the workplace. Major elements of such policy would probably have to include raising the minimum wage (which, as some argue, might even contribute to economic recovery) as well as strict enforcement of federal and state laws regulating working conditions.[12]

Sharing reserve-labor status with old and new unemployed and with working and nonworking housewives, immigrants—illegal immigrants in particular—are a condition of the United States labor market. They represent a key element in the supply of labor to the system, which has historically been structured toward excess supply and shifting demand. Even if immigration restriction were achievable via immigration policy, which it has long proved itself not to be, the detente between labor and capital effected with the New Deal would still have been basically undermined by the wide segments of marginal labor, of which immigrants are a part, and toward which numerous, once-protected American workers have recently felt themselves pushed.

No one would argue to preserve slavery today any more than they would defend the exploitation of undocumented workers. To abolish slavery, however, no one proposed waging a civil war against slaves instead of slaveholders. Similarly, leaving illegal immigrants unprotected in the marketplace of labor, housing, etc., hardly makes sense as a way to end their exploitation.

Throughout, restrictionist policy has come in the garb of successive acts, each known as "immigration policy"—in effect, a style of immigration, not the actual rejection of it. Never has restriction legislation meant the successful culmination of efforts to keep foreigners out. What has been the case, however, is that "new" immigrants have long been hailed by native Americans as the cause of their problems.

Through restriction, workers persistently looked to government to resolve their conflict with employers in search of cheaper labor. The New Deal and its aftermath in government expansion on behalf of citizens institutionalized and broadened that scenario. American workers, caught between their ideological tie to allegedly self-reliant immigrant heroes (on which they have so strongly pinned their identity) and government intervention (on which their very security in America has depended since the depression), turn more easily to and on government for its failure to protect them from upstart competition than they do to resisting the effective use of government by corporate interests, which perpetually demand immigration and other styles of labor conditions that perennially make insecurity the central feature of working life.

Notes

1. General Leonard F. Chapman, "Illegal Aliens: Time to Call a Halt," *Reader's Digest,* October 1976.
2. "Colby Calls Mexico Bigger Threat Than Russia," *The Los Angeles Times,* 6 June 1978.
3. Senator Alan K. Simpson, *Congressional Record,* 17 March 1982, p. S 22216.
4. AFL-CIO, "Statement of the AFL-CIO Executive Council on Illegal Aliens," Washington, D.C., 29 Aug. 1977.
5. Dr. Jacquelyn J. Jackson, "Illegal Aliens: Big Threat to Black Workers," *Ebony,* April 1979, p. 34.
6. "Interview of Secretary of Labor Ray Marshall on Illegal Immigration and Jobs," *The Los Angeles Times,* 2 December 1979.
7. Vernon M. Briggs, Jr., "The Impact of Undocumented Workers on the Labor Market," in Robert S. Landmann, ed., *The Problem of the Undocumented Worker* (Washington, D.C.: Community Service Administration), p. 34.
8. Ibid.
9. Michael J. Piore, "The 'Illegal Aliens' Debate Misses the Boat," *Working Papers,* vol. VI, no. 2, March-April 1978, p. 67.
10. Ibid.

11. Charles Keely, *Global Refugee Policy: The Case for a Development-Oriented Strategy* (Public Issues Paper Series, 1981), p. 45.
12. Samuel Bowles, David Gordon and Thomas Weisskopf, *Beyond the Wasteland: A Democratic Alternative to Economic Decline* (Garden City, N.Y.: Doubleday, 1983).

13

The Future of the Environmental Movement

Richard Kazis and Richard Grossman

Public activism on behalf of the environment has a long history. In the late 1800s, Americans began to fight to protect wilderness areas. Public-health activists and urban reformers worked to reduce industrial pollution and to improve workplace safety beginning in the early 1900s. Hunting and fishing enthusiasts began fighting to save wetlands and protect streams in the first two decades of the 1900s. After World War II, as the U.S. economy boomed and new technologies brought major changes in both production and political power relationships, serious new environmental problems emerged. As a result, more and more people responded at local, state and national levels to protect their communities and the nation's natural wealth.

The history of the environmental movement is, in fact, a history of the democratization of activism. Early wilderness preservationists were predominantly wealthy and male. But as environmental damage —such as contaminated drinking water; overdevelopment; flooding due to strip mining and clear-cutting; foul air; toxic-waste dumps; highways charted through poor urban neighborhoods; and nuclear power plants—directly touched more and more lives, people of every age, race, sex and class have reacted. Many of these people may not consider themselves "environmentalists." They might say they are hunters, or union members worried about their health, or farmers worried about water supplies, or people who like to go to the mountains for their vacation, or parents worried about their children's futures. But in each case, health, safety and resource concerns have energized them to political action. And as new issues have emerged,

Richard Kazis and Richard Grossman are co-authors of *Fear at Work: Job Blackmail, Labor and the Environment.* Richard Grossman is coordinator of Environmentalists for Full Employment.

the shape of the environmental movement has changed.

The environmental movement is rapidly coming of age. Emerging from explosions of outrage and activism in the 1960s and early 1970s, the environmental movement is playing a leading political role in the 1980s. Environmental organizations—from the National Wildlife Federation, National Audubon Society and Friends of the Earth at the national level to local groups fighting against toxic-waste dumping or for safe energy, wilderness protection or clean air—have multiplied and expanded. The movement has been able to increase public support for pollution control, wise resource use, and protection of the natural environment, despite the current economic crisis.

Environmentalists have become more politically and analytically sophisticated. They are questioning the impacts of national tax, budget and investment priorities on present and future environmental quality. They are challenging public and private investment strategies that ignore ecological limits or that fail to provide for sufficient public participation. And while expanding the definition of what constitutes "environmental issues," the movement has been building impressive structures for locally based but nationally oriented political action.

These trends were in motion before the election of Ronald Reagan, but the onslaught against environmental and public health protections since Reagan took office has accelerated the process. In 1984, as we work to build progressive political coalitions, environmental issues are clealy a major focus. Now, the key question is whether the environmental movement will take a leading role in moblizing other constituencies around sane economic and ecological alternatives.

Ronald Reagan ran for president pledging to "get the government off the backs" of the American people. Environmentalists had gone too far, he claimed. Building on a decade-long campaign by business leaders to convince the public that the nation could not afford and did not need strict environmental and occupational health and safety protections, Reagan hammered away on the false claim that regulation was bad for the economy and bad for jobs. Once elected, the Reagan administration systematically attacked the role of government as social protector—an attack that hit hardest at workers, the poor and the environment. While all three came under heavy fire, resistance has been most vigorous and effective from the environmental community.

It is not surprising that environmental protection became one of the most hotly contested public conflicts after 1980. The stakes are high. On one side stands corporate America, which currently spends over $30 billion each year to comply with environmental laws, and which sees such forced spending as a challenge both to profits and to management's right to manage. On the other stands a very diverse cross section of the American public fearful of environment-related health problems and concerned for the integrity and diversity of the nation's public resources. While corporate leaders claim that social priorities are best met via the profit motive, many Americans are demanding a greater public role in—and greater use of non-market criteria for—decisions that effect environmental quality and human lives.

The economic crises of the past two decades and the accompanying decline in corporate profits exacerbated this deep conflict. The business community reacted to economic decline and to the new wave of environmental laws by resisting added costs and controls and by trying to make government into a cooperative, quiescent partner for business. The environmentally concerned public—some more aware than others of the implications of their actions—responded by trying to extend the boundaries of political and economic democracy.

THE ATTACK ON COMMUNITY AND WORKPLACE ENVIRONMENTS

The business community may well have understood the significance of the environmental threat to "business as usual" before many environmentalists did. As soon as the first national environmental and occupational health and safety laws were proposed in 1969 and 1970, industry groups organized in opposition. The Business Roundtable, founded by Fortune 500 firms in 1972, put environment, energy and "regulatory reform" among its top policy priorities. Former Florida congressmember Paul Rogers noted in 1978 that American industry had "fought every inch of the way against every environmental health requirement." After the 1980 election, opposition to environmental regulation—from business and government—received a boost in the person of Ronald Reagan. Behind an ideological campaign that focused on exaggerating the costs of government regulation, and using "job blackmail" to try to scare people into accepting anti-environmental policies, the administration attacked pollution-control laws and initiated private giveaways of public energy and other natural resources. Political appointees at the Environmental Protection Agency, the Department of Interior and the Occupational Safety and Health Administration, many of whom had previously worked for major timber, mining and energy corporations, became vigorous advocates for their former employers' interests. Using a mix of executive orders, legislative initiatives, administrative rulings, staffing changes and budget cuts, they were able to undermine existing pollution-control and health protections.*

THE PUBLIC RESPONSE

Public awareness of squandered resources, contaminated drinking water, toxic chemicals, acid rain, cancer, nuclear power, nuclear weapons and other environmental threats has grown significantly since 1980. Despite several years of double-digit unemployment and economic chaos, people became more angry about environmental abuse and more adamant that the government has the responsibility to protect their health and environment. Public support for a stricter clean-air act rose from 29 to 47 percent between 1980 and 1982, and for a stronger clean-water law from 52 to 61 percent. Between 78 and 88 percent of those polled in January 1982 by Louis Harris and Associates opposed any relaxation of air-pollution, hazardous-waste and toxic-substance-control protections. Among the most adamant in their support for existing environmental laws have been union members, skilled workers and minorities. In the West, where the Sagebrush Rebellion was alleged to be so dynamic in 1980, threats to national parks and public lands have enraged even many rock-ribbed conservative Republicans. And new grass-roots groups—like the direct-action-oriented EarthFirst! and local anti-MX-missile coalitions—began to emerge.

* At OSHA, for example, enforcement citations have dropped precipitously: Inspections in response to complaints fell 58 percent between 1980 and 1982, and inspectors issued 50 percent fewer serious citations in 1982 than in 1980. There have been delays in needed standards for formaldehyde, benzene and the fumigant ethyl dibromide, and the agency adopted what it called a more "cooperative" relationship between business and government.

The environmental movement has worked carefully to transform public concern into political clout. Beginning in 1980, environmental groups at the national and state levels entered electoral politics—with impressive results. In 1982, five national and thirty state environmental Political Action Committees (PACs) raised $3 million for proenvironment candidates. Of the 125 federal candidates supported by some or all of these PACs (most of whom, it should be noted, were also the favored candidates of labor, minority and women's groups), 70 to 75 percent won their elections. Perhaps even more significant than the funds raised was the volunteer labor recruited. In Jeff Bingaman's successful race for the Senate in New Mexico, over 700 environmentalists volunteered their time for phone calls, door-knocking and other campaign activities. Environmental PACs plan to raise more money in 1984, recruit more volunteers and perhaps run "green" delegates for the Republican and Democratic conventions.

This visible electoral impact, combined with continuing environmental education, lobbying, litigation and direct action campaigns, has impressed—and chastened—many elected officials. Public reaction to attempted rollbacks of environmental protections has been strong enough to keep Congress from significantly changing any major environmental laws, particularly the Clean Air Act, through the legislative process. At the height of Reagan's antiregulatory rhetoric, Congress even quickly renewed the Endangered Species Act, an environmental law without the public-health aspect that usually rallies support outside the environmental community, and an act that the administration had initially targeted for ridicule and weakening.

Public pressure also slowed the giveaway of public timber and oil and gas resources. Increased funding for national-park management, action on some Superfund toxic-waste sites, and the forcing out of Anne Burford, Rita Lavelle, James Watt and more than a dozen other Reagan appointees are all the result of public opposition to antienvironmental policies. In fact, many of the environmental protection and sound resource strategies that the Reagan administration claimed as its own were forced on an unwilling government by an angry public. That does not mean that the past three years have been good for environmental protection. According to Bill Drayton, President Carter's assistant administrator for planning and management at EPA, "Even assuming a new president is elected in 1984 who is deeply dedicated to the environment and gives it top priority, it will be 1990 before we get it back to where we were." But the determination, organization and resistance of environmentally concerned citizens have created a broad-based political force.

Consider, for example, the current environmental threats posed by acid rain, nuclear power/weapons, and toxic chemical wastes. When the Clean Air Act passed in 1970, there were no specific provisions to address environmental and health damage from acid rain. Yet, acid rain is now recognized as a major threat to aquatic life, trees, ground-water and human health. In the northeastern states and Canada, citizens are furious at the lack of adequate strategies for reducing sulfur-dioxide emissions, particularly from midwest U.S. power plants. In New Hampshire's 1983 town meetings, 197 of 199 towns passed resolutions in support of Clean Air Act amendments that would cut current sulfur-dioxide emissions at least 50 percent. In January 1984 a national conference on acid rain held in New Hampshire attracted hundreds of local activists—and every major Democratic presidential candidate. Many people have become involved in the environmental movement for the first time because of their concerns about the damage caused by acid rain.

In the early years of the Reagan presidency, millions of people mobilized against increased military spending and for the nuclear freeze. Many of these people had not been politically active before, but now consider themselves a vigorous part of the peace and environmental movements—two movements that were linked as early as the fight for the Limited Nuclear Test Ban Treaty in 1962 and that have often worked together against nuclear energy. A number of today's "freeze" organizers have their roots in the safe-energy movement of the 1970s, and now most environmental groups have come to believe they cannot defend the earth and its creatures if they are silent about nuclear war, the arms policies of our government and the powerful nuclear industry. The anti-nuclear-weapons activism spurred by the Reagan administration has brought environmentalists into new areas, such as the fight against the MX, enabling environmental organizations to recruit new members and forcing environmentalists to take a hard look at national investment priorities—something that would have seemed inappropriate to some of the more traditional conservation groups a decade ago.

The third specific environmental challenge that has had a profound impact on environmental organizing in recent years has been the almost daily revelations of unsafe landfills, abandoned chemical wastes, and illegal dumping of toxic chemicals with their attendant health hazards and cancer risks to workers and community residents. From Love Canal to Times Beach to Rocky Flats and the agricultural valleys of California, toxic chemicals have become a grave threat to people's daily lives. Because toxic-waste sites are more often than not located in poor and working-class neighborhoods and rural areas, this issue has accelerated the breaking down of traditional class lines that have often separated "middle-class" environmental groups from largely "blue-collar" groups. Labor unions have taken some initiative in this area, as shown by the labor-led Silicon Valley Toxics Coalition in California. Civil-rights organizations, such as the Commission on Racial Justice of the United Church of Christ, have also made toxics a priority. Citizen action and community organizing efforts such as the Clean Water Action Project are focusing on disposal and effective cleanup at the local, state and national levels. In some cases, established national environmental groups have been pushed to play catch-up on this issue, pressured by ad hoc grass-roots groups and activism by people outside the environmental movement. In February 1984, a new national coalition of local anti-toxics groups kicked off the National Campaign Against Toxic Hazards at a day-long meeting that attracted 800 people.

ENVIRONMENTALISTS, ECONOMICS AND POWER

The current economic crisis and the growing sophistication of the environmental movement have led many environmental groups to place new emphasis on economics. More and more frequently, these organizations are demanding that environmental protection and wise resource use be integrated into any response to the nation's economic problems. According to Janet Brown, a scientist who is president of the Environmental Defense Fund, "There are major environmental issues embedded in everything else—jobs, housing, community development, land use, health, everything. And it is becoming increasingly clear that a sustainable economic policy is not possible unless it begins from a sustainable environmental policy."

Given the current persistent high level of joblessness and the real possibility of a decade of "jobless growth," environmentalists have had to examine the relationship between their goals and other priorities such as jobs, economic recovery, a more equitable distribution of income and public participation in decision-making. Moreover, they have been forced to confront these questions by intense industry and government campaigns aimed at isolating environmentalists as antijob and antiprogress and portraying environmental laws as too costly.

Our own studies—published in 1982 in our book, *Fear at Work: Job Blackmail, Labor and the Environment*—demonstrate the positive correlation between a clean environment and a healthy economy. We found that hardly any jobs have been lost due to environmental laws, thousands have been saved, and hundreds of thousands created. Charges that environmental laws have lowered productivity, sent inflation soaring and forced businesses and taxpayers to spend billions of needless dollars are false, as we document in detail. In spite of these facts, however, many business and government leaders have worked hard to persuade the public they must choose between jobs and environmental quality, and have often succeeded. It would not be surprising to see the promise of new jobs—via either "reindustrialization" or "high tech"—used to rationalize antienvironmental policies in the future.

Environmentalists are eager to avoid unnecessary conflict with other pro-job, pro-health and pro-people constituencies. Indeed, these fragile political coalitions have become somewhat easier to form in recent years as environmentalists have been lumped together by the Reagan administration with labor, civil rights groups and other "special interests." In addition, the economic collapse in many "smokestack" communities has been so massive that industrial-union members no longer buy the line (if they ever did) that environmental laws have anything to do with their plight. Steelworkers, for example, know that the companies' failure to modernize and their decision to abandon basic steel is to blame for layoffs, not the Clean Air Act. Similarly, the United Auto Workers, which sided with the Big Three auto makers in 1977 in support of weaker auto-emission standards, has stayed out of the current Clean Air Act reauthorization fight.

This evolution of the environmental movement parallels similar developments in the German Green Party and other European ecological movements. It reflects a recognition that major industrial and economic changes are occurring in the Western world and that these changes will have a direct effect on environmental quality and re-source use. The fight over which interests will guide U.S. economic policy—which people will benefit and which will suffer—is taking place right now. That is what the antilabor, antienvironmental on-slaught of recent years is about. And that is what the "industrial policy" debate is about. Environmentalists, many of whom might have thought ten years ago that questions of industrial policy were outside their area of concern, are now forcing their way into this debate, for they understand that to stay out is to lose the opportunity to shape environmentally sound economic and industrial policies, conserve resources and protect public health.

There are, of course, potentially serious problems that could slow environmental momentum. One is the business community's antienvi-ronmental rhetoric. In January 1983, for example, in an editorial entitled "Where the Environmentalists Go Wrong," *Business Week* chided environmental organizations for taking on "unrelated areas of public policy" and "causes far afield of environmental concerns." There will undoubtedly be more attacks along these lines.

The use of "job blackmail" in a high-unemployment economy could also prevent environmentalists from joining with labor, minor-ity, farmer and other constituencies. In the 1982 elections, four of five state bottle-bill initiatives were defeated, in part because of business's job threats. In Massachusetts, the opponents of a nuclear-waste initia-tive tried to convince voters that over 200,000 jobs in health care would be lost if the initiative won. In Congress's 1982 lame-duck session, the administration posed an either/or choice between in-creased appropriations for EPA or for a HUD construction-jobs pack-age.

In addition to job threats, industry and government can step up the use of job promises to play one constituency off against another. The highway-gas-tax bill that steamed through Congress in late 1982 was not a jobs bill and was bad for the environment, yet environmentalists found themselves in the position of either supporting the legislation or appearing to be against jobs and recovery. If environmental organi-zations decide to use their new political strength to oppose certain environmentally destructive job-creation schemes without proposing viable alternatives, they may quickly find themselves in a very public and damaging showdown with organized labor.

Finally, a public perception of economic recovery could also slow the environmental movement's development of economic alternatives and political alliances. Many of the traditional sources of tension between environmental groups and organized labor have not been major issues in recent years: nuclear power, uncontrolled development, energy use, land use. A quick, uncontrolled growth spurt could force these back into the public eye, and once again pit environmentalists against unions and minorities. A sense of economic improvement could have another negative effect: It might diminish the interest of some environmental constituencies in tackling difficult—but, in terms of coalition-building, critical—issues of employment, development and public participation.

As always, political coalitions are fragile. But as we move through and beyond 1984, environmental activism provides both an opportunity and a challenge to progressive coalition building. The environmental movement has demonstrated that any progressive coalition can benefit from the growing strength and sophistication of environmental organizations and activists. At the same time, the movement has also demonstrated the importance of integrating the environmental ethic into a programmatic agenda for change. How well this opportunity and challenge will be addressed is one of the critical political questions of the 1980's.

PART IV

POLITICAL PARTICIPATION

Editors' Introduction

Democracy is not only the most humane form of government, it is also the most fragile. It depends on the involvement of the governed not only for its legitimacy but also for its health and well-being.

Government agencies spend millions of dollars every year making sure that wage earners register with taxing bodies, young men register for the draft, and car owners register their automobiles. Yet when it comes to the constitutional right to vote, government spends little to make sure people are registered, although the threshold to democracy is the right to vote and the secure knowledge that one's vote will count for as much as anyone else's.

For more than 200 years, that has not been the case in the United States for many black Americans. After the civil-rights movement, we saw massive voter-registration campaigns sometimes obstructed and impeded by people who had not yet fully accepted the abolishment of slavery and the full citizenship of black Americans. Since those days of the early 1960s, there have been almost two decades of comparative calm, and some of the grossest racial injustices have been overcome. Still, many citizens remain unregistered.

Something of the potential of the as yet unregistered black voters can be seen in comparing them to President Reagan's 1980 victory margins: Alabama, 287,720 unregistered black voters in 1980 and 17,462 President Reagan's margin; Arkansas, 86,858 and 5,123; South Carolina, 327,722 and 11,456; Tennessee, 171,268 and 4,710; and New York, 915,320 and 165,459. In the section that follows, Hulbert James et al. describe one effort to mobilize that potential, while Curt Gans offers cautions as to the prospects of increased voter registration without more-fundamental changes.

Hungry and destitute people can best be fed and can best fulfill their human potential if they have the opportunity to determine their own future and play a significant role in their own society. It will take the empowerment of poor people who have been waiting a long time for justice to secure the foundations of that justice for them.

In this perspective, participation in the society means voting. And it is a great failure of our democracy that so few citizens vote. It is worth remembering that the electoral process has been used as a primary avenue for making democracy a reality. That view reached its height with the Populist movement of the late nineteenth century, a movement whose origins and strength lay in the South. White and black farmers formed an alliance that controlled the governments of several states and deeply influenced both major parties nationally. In the last decade of the nineteenth century, the power of that alliance was forcefully crushed and black voters were disenfranchised. The view that electoral politics could be a vehicle for positive change rose again with the New Deal and became a focal point for the southern civil-rights movement.

Following the victories of the Civil Rights and Voting Rights Acts, a general split occurred within the progressive community. One trend, centered mainly in the black community, focused on building strength by using the tools of voter registration, the Voting Rights Act, and electing blacks to public office. The other trend, centered more among white-led activists, used protest strategies, media attention and public exposé to challenge specific areas of the system's foreign and domestic policy. The two trends are not isolated, and lately women's and environmental organizations have especially merged the approaches of agitation and grass-roots issue organizing with lobbying and electing sympathetic public officials.

Gittell and Naples assess the developments in the women's movement, while Aronowitz points to labor's key role in coalition, for it is in coalitions that progressives can marshal the forces to challenge the power of the new and old Right. Nader points to the consumer movement as cutting across old fracture lines, while Boyte calls our attention to often excluded potential allies, invoking the traditional and yet powerful concept of a commonwealth. All this is an effort to build a sane, viable progressive movement.

Since the U.S. is the only advanced industrial country without a labor or social democratic party with a mass electoral base, building a viable progressive movement means pulling together a progressive coalition or, rather, coalitions that must operate both inside and outside electoral politics. Atlas, Dreier and Stephens offer one set of proposals to address this inside-and-outside conundrum.

While we do have a great number of active issue groups—probably more than in other advanced industrial societies—forming coalitions of these groups has repeatedly proved extremely difficult. As Bogdan Denitch has pointed out, one major reason behind this has been single-group "sectarianism," the position taken by many single-group organizations that unless their issue is the basis of the coalition, they will not participate. Until the progressive community deals with this problem, our politics and programs will continue to be marginal to the real world of political mobilization and decision-making, and we will remain mere witnesses to our faith.

Every coalition need not extend over the whole range of issues, and we have to be willing to think through the minimal basis for each specific mobilization. Further, a coalition is based on people who have differing agendas, and what we now need is to continue working for our individual issues while also building the ties of mutual trust with groups that have other priorities. The question of trust and mutual respect becomes fundamental.

Issues of race and class provide the best basis at present for coalition. Why the stress on blacks and economic issues? There are many reasons, but the major one is that these two issues have an overwhelming advantage in coalition-building as they are broader in range and more general (i.e., affect more people) than most other issues. A dramatic illustration of this is captured by Ernie Chambers, a black state senator from Oklahoma, who spoke at the Kansas rally mentioned in the introduction to part 1. He said, "You know, you farmers have a lot of land but few members. Us blacks have no land but a lot of members. We really ought to get together, don't you think?"

The best symbol of coalition built around a black and economic agenda is the Black Congressional Caucus budget. No other group has produced as fundamental a set of alternate priorities as the BCC. This budget did more for more groups than any set of demands raised in or out of Congress in the last few years. However, the tragic fact is that the progressive and liberal organizations have all but ignored it. We ought not let it happen again.

The idea and character of citizen participation are much more broadly conceived than an emphasis on the electoral process might imply. The emphasis in this section on direct political processes is guided by Rousseau's argument that in a democracy—especially a modern-day democracy, we might add—while a vote may represent only a very small share of the polity's sovereignty, it is important because it symbolizes membership and gives it concrete meaning. Michael Walzer, in *Spheres of Justice*, argues that the vote is the equivalent of and a mechanism for contributing to the rule against exclusion in the sphere of welfare, of the principle of equal consideration in the sphere of opportunity and office, and of the guaranty of access to school in the sphere of education and preparation. The vote, then, is at the heart of all distributive measures, and the framework of participation that it represents challenges the traditions of special influence, power and wealth. In place of privilege, it promises the imperative need—debate and organization in the local, regional and national exercise of government.

14

The New Voter-Registration Strategy

*Hulbert James, Maxine Phillips
and Don Hazen*

The prospect that new voters and old ones who are reenergized can provide a constituency for progressive politics in the 1980s is lending a fervor to voter-registration drives unmatched since the crusading days of the civil-rights movement. On the one hand, there are groups concerned with equity in society and the large number of low-income and minority people who don't participate in the system. In addition, infuriated by defeats of liberal members of Congress who had been targeted by the right wing and reeling from the impact of Reagan administration policies, a broad array of issue-oriented groups have launched voter-registration and -education campaigns to reverse what has been billed as a mandate for the Right. Together, these efforts are providing an unprecedented focus on voter registration and education.

Leading the charge to register voters and urge them to the polls are major national and regional nonpartisan voter-registration organizations, such as the Voter Education Project in Atlanta and the Southwest Voter Registration and Education Project in San Antonio, Texas. These efforts, supplemented by traditional civil rights groups, such as the NAACP, are focusing their work in the South, Southwest, and the urban East and Midwest, where the highest concentration of unregistered voters—minorities, low-income, women, and young adults (18–24)—are located.

When you add to this base a proliferation of other voter registration efforts—Citizen Action, the women's movement, peace groups like SANE, environmental groups, tenant organizations and other low-

Hulbert James is president and director of the Human SERVE Fund, a national voter registration campaign. *Maxine Phillips* is executive director of Democratic Socialists of America. *Don Hazen* is a New York-based consultant on citizen participation issues.

income advocates such as the Human SERVE Fund and ACORN, unions, students, and a number of state and local coalitions—the potential to register 6 million or more new voters is evident.

On the surface it might seem that this renewed voter interest is simply a product of the anger of many Americans disgusted with Reagan administration policies. What is more likely, however, is that electoral efforts by minorities, women, and citizen groups have set in motion forces that will carry far beyond the 1984 election and may truly alter the landscape of American politics for years to come.

Even in 1980, many observers pointed out that a president elected by 27 percent of the eligible voters couldn't really claim to have a mandate to dismantle fifty years of legislation begun in the New Deal era. The 1980 election marked a low point in voter turnout. Since 1960, voter participation overall had declined by 10 percent, down to 53.95 percent in 1980. This figure was only a couple of percentage points higher than the turnout when Herbert Hoover was elected. Once again in the case of Reagan a candidate chosen by a predominantly white male electorate backed policies harmful to the poor and working classes, minorities and women. After the 1928 election came the New Deal coalition and rising voter-participation rates. From the election of 1980 may come a new coalition nourished by a variety of movements that gained strength in the Seventies and are now aided by conditions that will spark large-scale voter participation.

The first indication that a major change was under way in the electorate was revealed in 1982 when, for the first time in twenty years, voter participation actually increased. On paper it doesn't look like much: According to the U.S. Census Bureau, some 48.5 percent of the adult population said they had voted in this off-year election —just 2.6 percent more than the percentage that claimed to have voted in 1978. What was striking were the increases in certain categories. Blacks reported an increase of 5.8 percent, blue-collar workers an increase of 4.5 percent. The jump of 6.7 percent in the turnout rate of the unemployed, a group that usually doesn't vote, was explained by some as being due to the fact that many newly unemployed people had a history of voting and were not as likely to stop. But even those no longer even seeking work reported a 2.5-percent increase. Compared to past elections, the percentage of women who said they voted increased and was not significantly different from that of men.

The upturn were felt in such places as New York State, where they started turning into major cracks when liberal Mario Cuomo beat millionaire conservative Lewis Lehrman; and in an extremely close gubernatorial race in Illinois, where massive voter-registration drives set the stage for the 1983 Chicago mayoral victory of Harold Washington. The Chicago story illustrates the crusading quality of the voter-registration drives.

"In fifty years I've never seen anything like it in electoral activity," recalls Milt Cohen, who worked in the campaign that added more than 100,000 blacks and Hispanics to the rolls and provided the incentive for Washington to challenge Jane Byrne and the Chicago machine. The original voter-registration drives started after People Organized for Welfare and Employment Rights (POWER), a coalition of low-income people, lost a legislative battle against welfare cuts and decided to focus on the electoral process. In addition, Adlai Stevenson III, trailing governor James Thompson by 20 percent in the opinion polls, pumped money into voter registration, as did the unions backing him. All of the groups came together to form the People's Movement for Voter Registration, which later received financial and staff support from a national coalition, Project VOTE, and financial help from the Midwest Voter Registration Education Project, which concentrates on registering Hispanics.

The effort was impressive. A hundred volunteers a day were stationed in thirty unemployment and public-aid offices. Because Illinois law requires that registration be conducted indoors and the campaign was refused access to the buildings, vans were rented at a cost of $30,000 a month and parked in front of the offices in order to put a roof over the registration process. During August and September, almost 100,000 people were registered. All stops were pulled out as the last day for registration approached. "Come Alive October 5" was the message played on black radio stations and displayed on billboards. The black business community funded a slick advertising campaign. Enthusiasm built up so that on October 5 an additional 100,000 people were registered. Challenges cut the 200,000 total in half. Still, the number of new voters made the Thompson-Stevenson race in November so close that the result remained in doubt for days after the election. More significant, it made Harold Washington amenable to a draft. "Register fifty thousand more and I'll run" was one of the conditions Washington laid down to his supporters, who launched drives that winter to meet this goal. The mayoral primary was decided by 32,000 votes, and the general election in April by 40,000.

Throughout 1982 and 1983, in other areas with lower minority populations than Chicago, voter-registration drives and astute coalition-building put minority liberals like Frederico Pena and W. Wilson Goode into City Hall in Denver and Philadelphia, and Tony Anaya into the statehouse in New Mexico. An alliance of minorities, women and progressives came close to making black socialist Mel King the mayor of Boston; he lost to a populist who appealed to many of the same people who might otherwise have voted for King.

The successes and near-misses have inspired activists to plunge into the electoral arena. They believe that registering potential voters who are suffering under present government policies could have a major influence in redirecting the Democratic party and putting together a coalition to replace the shattered New Deal alliance.

The figures are convincing. Most close congressional races are decided by fewer than 7,000 votes. In 1982, thirteen congressional races were decided by margins of fewer than 1,500 votes. A shift of 44,000 votes in 1982 would have changed the results in five Senate races and in twenty House races won by Republicans. Some 90 million eligible adults did not vote in 1980. The largest number of people who don't vote and the largest number of people adversely affected by Reagan's policies are poor people. Thirty-four million people have incomes under $10,000 per year, but surveys taken after midterm elections over the past ten years show that only 25 to 35 percent of the eligible voters in that population claim to have voted, as against 70 to 75 percent of those making more than $25,000 a year.

Blacks, although only 11 percent of the population, are strategically located and largely unregistered or uninvolved in electoral politics. Since blacks vote Democratic by about 90 percent, their participation could be crucial in defeating Reagan. The number of unregistered blacks in six southern states—Alabama, Arkansas, Mississippi, North Carolina, South Carolina and Tennessee—so far exceeds the plurality by which Reagan won in 1980 that even a 5-percent upward shift in the number of blacks voting could give Democrats the edge. New York, with only 40.4 percent of its black population voting, gave Reagan a plurality of 165,459 votes. If even 20 percent of the unregistered 893,773 were to register and vote, the Democrats would gain thirty-six electoral votes.

POLITICAL REALIGNMENT

Large numbers of nonvoters are not new in this century. Neither are voter-registration campaigns. Neither is the swing in American politics as conservatives and liberals are voted out while the pendulum seeks the center. What is new about the situation today is that the circumstances now exist to involve very large numbers of nonvoters in forcing the realignment of the political parties to create a progressive electorate that will fight for social change. Four factors combine to make this possible.

Ronald Reagan

The most obvious factor is the antipathy that Ronald Reagan inspires even among those who have long despaired of the benefits of electoral politics. Almost everyone who used to shrug off elections with an "All politicians are the same" attitude now takes an "Anybody but Reagan" posture.

Since the New Deal, there has been an expectation that government will be involved in people's lives. The Right may have struck some responsive chords with its diatribes against government intervention, but the influence of beneficial programs—jobs, school lunches, student aid, federally financed mortgages, occupational-safety and health programs, Medicaid, welfare programs, day care and many more—has created a constituency that could react strongly to cuts or elimination. The victims of the cutbacks understand more clearly than in the past that their condition has to do with what is happening in Washington. The issues of entitlement to food, shelter, work, education, health care, and education are ones around which registration and education can focus. Political action has become a form of self-defense, bringing together groups that have not made common cause before.

One of the striking features of American politics in recent years has been the rise of special-interest groups, many of which fought each other in competition for government resources. The right-wing special-interest groups were able to coalesce around the goal of electing a president, and have been bickering ever since because he has not satisfied them all. Because the effects of the administration's programs have been so devastating across the board, more and more groups are coming to have one common purpose—getting Ronald Reagan out of the White House.

Lowered Barriers

At the same time that it is easier for people to understand why they should register, it is easier for them to register. Many of the barriers to participation—such as literacy tests, poll taxes and complex residency requirements—no longer exist. Sixteen states still require voters to report to a local courthouse or board of elections office to register, but 49 percent of the population lives in states that allow registration by mail.

As activists have become involved in campaigns, however, they have discovered that many barriers still exist. The problem of registering voters in Illinois, where registrars often refused to deputize volunteers, and where access was denied to the voter-registration campaigns, led to a recent legislative-reform victory spearheaded by Project VOTE and the Illinois AFL-CIO.

A case in Florida shows the obstacles activists face. Florida IM-PACT's Voter Registration Project concentrated on two congressional districts with many poor people and low turnout rates. Since Florida has a thirty-day cutoff period prior to Election Day, the registration campaign was timed as close to the election as possible. A list of people to be deputized as registrars and of registration sites was given to the supervisor of elections, who, after the campaign began door-to-door canvassing, refused to deputize the volunteers, mostly black and Hispanic, or approve the sites. Volunteers rushed to place notices on the previously identified registration sites and to transport registrants to the approved new sites. The coalition rented a car-to-public address system and on the last day of registration urged people to sign up. There was a large response, and on Election Day both districts showed large increases in voter turnout. After the election, the coalition, determined to eliminate some of the barriers, moved the battle into the state legislature, where it waged a strong effort to institute mail registration. In June the bill was defeated by five votes in the House, after having lost by two votes in the Senate.

When there are overt attempts to intimidate voters, volunteers and reform coalitions often need legal help on Election Day. Such help is scarce and stretched to the limits. Much of the protection southern voters have had since the Sixties has dwindled; the burden of enforcement now falls upon private "watchdogs" rather than the federal government. Since the Voting Rights Act was extended and strengthened in 1982, the Justice Department has filed only three lawsuits to enforce the act's protections.

Thus, groups working on registration find themselves involved in reform efforts as well. Such reforms center around procedural barriers such as personal registration rather than mail registration; purge laws; and registration deadlines. They advocate mail registration and Election Day registration as well as efforts to increase student registration. In Mississippi, voters have to register twice before they can vote, while in Minnesota and Wisconsin they can register on Election Day. (On Election Day the voter places the ballot in a sealed envelope, which is placed in another envelope that the voter fills out with qualifying information and signs. After the voter's qualifications have been verified, the sealed inner envelope is taken out and placed with other "challenged" ballots to be counted.)

Despite the barriers, reforms begun by the civil-rights movement have enfranchised many blacks in the South, and voter-registration drives by black organizations have led to an increase in the number of black elected officials from 1,469 in 1970 to 5,160 in 1982. Still, there is only one black congressional representative from the Deep South.

Hispanics, too, have been active in voter registration, even though language barriers and outright discrimination still exist. Between 1976 and 1980, the Southwest Voter Registration Project (SVREP) helped raise Hispanic voter registration by 44 percent in Texas, California, Arizona, Utah, Colorado and New Mexico. The result was that between 1975 and 1980, the number of Mexican Americans elected to office rose by more than 30 percent.

These groups have learned a lot about how to register voters, how to educate them and how to protect their rights. Says Ronald Walters, a Howard University political scientist, "The old-time religion was to register at all costs, turn out at all costs." Now, "the new religion, the new methodologies, the new emphasis on strategy . . . is to count more on the question of motivation and education."

Research, research, and more research should be the first step of a voter-registration campaign, according to SVREP head Willie Velasquez. "Find out what is bugging the electorate," then gear a campaign toward those issues. Every four years, he notes, money was spent to "herd Mexicans to vote Democratic," but registration in Texas stayed stable at about half a million until 1976. Then the San Antonio-based SVREP polled Hispanics and discovered that they didn't care much about remote presidential elections, but were incensed about unpaved streets and poor schools. Registration of Mexican Americans has risen to 832,398 in Texas, and, laughs Velasquez, "after we did the survey, everybody who ran for office in San Antonio said, 'You elect me, I'm gonna pave the streets.' "

Other research led SVREP to concentrate its efforts among middle-aged rather than young voters because they found that older people, having experienced more discrimination, are more highly motivated in wanting to change conditions. SVREP conducts its publicity campaigns in the Spanish-language media only, both because research showed that Hispanics had confidence in such media and read and listened to them, and because Anglos, who might mount countercampaigns, don't pay attention to them.

But even research may not be the first step in some districts. No amount of research and registration activity could have been successful in the sixty-six rural counties in Texas that SVREP found to be gerrymandered against Mexican Americans. Successful court battles for redistricting had to come first.

The expertise and experience gained as groups fight in court and in legislatures will be valuable as the current campaigns expand and encounter more resistance.

Cost-Effective Registration

The sophistication and experience gained by activists in the past twenty years can now be used to even greater advantage because of another condition of the times: the accessibility of large numbers of nonvoters in public places. Every day thousands of people victimized by Reagan's policies stand in line for unemployment checks, surplus food, welfare appointments, or food stamps. As they wait, they are receptive to the message "Fight the cuts. Fight for more jobs. Register to vote!" In the past, many voter-registration drives foundered because they could not field the large numbers of volunteers needed to go door to door.

In eight days of activity in 1981 at a food-stamp distribution site in New Jersey, 11,500 voters were registered. Twelve social-work students in New York spent four hours with six church members registering 1,800 of the 7,500 people waiting in line for surplus cheese in front of a Baptist church. In contrast, one house-to-house canvasser in a low-income housing project can register six to eight people an hour.

Now, say Frances Fox Piven and Richard Cloward, theoreticians of the welfare-rights movement of the late Sixties and early Seventies, the conditions of the welfare state make its clients ready and able to be mobilized to vote. Piven and Cloward are among the conceptualizers and spokespeople for the Human SERVE Fund, one of the newest and most ambitious of the nonpartisan voter registration projects. Human SERVE believes that the power for reforming society lies in coalitions of the underclass in alliance with the hundreds of thousands of human-service workers who provide services to the millions of government-assistance recipients. This alliance is in part forged by Reagan's wholesale attacks on the entire welfare-state system. Human SERVE is working to mobilize human-service workers and social work students to register their clients at the point of service, either during their spare time or as part of their regular job.

A problem with cost-effective voter registration is the potential lack of organizational back-up to get out the vote, an important ingredient in any effective citizen participation strategy. Without follow-up, as few as 20 percent of new voters may go to the polls. Research conducted by Project VOTE, however, shows that with mailings and follow-up phone calls and reminders participation figures can go well over 60 percent.

Some argue, and probably rightly so, that get-out-the-vote efforts will not be as crucial in 1984, because of the Reagan phenomenon and the unprecedented amount of resources and attention focused on voting. Nevertheless, the most savvy organizers never stop emphasizing the importance, not only of voter education, but the necessity of working closely with community-based groups to help hold candidates accountable when they are elected. Project VOTE, Human SERVE, and others have moved to make this aspect a staple of their operations.

New registrants can make quite a difference in close races. In New Haven, Connecticut, more than fifty agencies, community organizations and labor unions joined together in the spring of 1982 to encourage voter registration, education and participation. Funding came from three church groups. The project registered 1,800 new voters, most of them black, Hispanic or low-income. The seventy-five volunteers found them in housing projects, health clinics, cheese lines, and unemployment and welfare offices. City registrars tried to deny the coalition permission to continue registering people and backed down only when a temporary restraining order was issued. A postelection survey of voting records showed that 75 percent of the new registrants voted, compared with 69 percent of already registered people. There's no way of knowing how the newly registered group voted, but since the winning congressional candidate's margin of victory was 1,500 votes and he campaigned on issues of importance to poor people, coalition members believe that poor people in New Haven have gained leverage in Washington.

NEW NETWORKS

Another condition that can help provide the people to conduct registration drives as well as to run education and get-out-the-vote operations is the existence of movements that are already in regular contact with hundreds of thousands of people.

Many of these networks grew directly from the activism of the Sixties and early Seventies and involvement in the McGovern campaign. Despite the popular assumption that the Seventies were somnabulant, several movements were growing at the grass-roots level and now in the Eighties, having pushed pressure politics to its limits, are ready to claim a place in the electoral arena.

The women's movement, the citizen action network, the peace movement, mainstream churches, the labor movement, students, and the environmental movement have varying degrees of strength and different agendas, but they form the basis for the "rainbow coalition" that gathered on August 27, 1983, to recapture Martin Luther King's dream. The potential of these groups, coupled with the strategic importance of blacks and Hispanics, could add up to a powerful movement.

Gender-Gap Politics

The women's movement is one of the keys to the new voter-registration movement. The term *gender gap* is now one of the political catch-phrases that signifies major changes in voting patterns. It used to mean that women didn't vote in the same proportions as men. The squiggle in 1980 was that women showed up at the polls in the same proportion as men. Since there are more voting-age women than men, politicians started worrying about the gap in voting preferences.

They noticed that Jimmy Carter got 50 percent of female blue-collar workers' votes, compared to 43 percent for Reagan. Carter got 53 percent of unionized women's votes, versus 39 percent for Reagan. Sixty-two percent of Hispanic women voted for Carter. Public-opinion polls have often shown women to have different opinions from men on questions of foreign policy, militarization, equality and social programs, and this trend continues. Exit polls conducted after the 1982 elections showed women voting Democratic more frequently (by a margin of 5 percent) and disagreeing with men in their opinion of Reagan's handling of the economy, Social Security, inflation and unemployment by 7 to 14 percent. Twelve percent more women than men approved of the nuclear freeze, which won in eight of the nine states where it appeared on the ballot, plus the District of Columbia, and in some thirty cities and counties.

Election results confirmed the importance of the gap. Women had determined not to be beaten as badly as in the Equal Rights Amendment battle. When the ERA lost in the Florida State Senate by 22 to 16, one state representative vowed to give up her seat in the pro-ERA house and run for the Senate. Others also entered races, and Florida now has nine women in the Senate instead of four, one of whom is black. If the ERA were to be reconsidered, it would now win. Similarly, enough seats changed in the Illinois legislature so that the ERA could probably get the necessary three-fifths for ratification.

Women want political power. Only 10 percent of all officeholders are women and only 4 percent of all federal officials. There is a lot of room for expansion.

Because women have opinions different from men's on many issues, the basis exists for coalition-building that can cut across party, class and race lines. This concept was the motivating factor in the creation of the Women's Vote Project, a collaboration of more than 50 women's organizations geared to increse significantly the number of women registered and voting. The project membership ranges from the League of Women Voters to coalitions of minority, working, and religious women to the National Association of Social Workers. Utilizing the slogan, "It's a man's world unless women vote," the project is particularly concerned about the large numbers of low-income, single heads-of-households, young working women, many of whom are minorities, who are traditionally under-registered. At the same time that registration and education campaigns were mounted, political action committees from the National Organization for Women, the National Women's Political Caucus, and special-interest groups such as the National Abortion Rights Action League and Friends of Family Planning targeted state legislators who had stopped the ERA and congressional representatives most likely to oppose Reagan's policies.

Not everyone believes that the women's vote is necessarily progressive—witness right-wing women's opposition to the ERA and many other "women's issues." However, in the 1982 election, New Jersey women supported liberal Frank Lautenberg over pro-ERA but economically and socially conservative Millicent Fenwick. Massachusetts women voted for Barney Frank for Congress against pro-ERA conservative Margaret Heckler.

Influencing the cast of the votes by women is the fact that more and more women now live in poverty; thus, voter-registration drives aimed at the poor are also likely to register many women who will have an interest in economic and social programs of benefit to them. Preliminary research on voting patterns of black women shows that the gap is even wider on social and economic issues than it is with white women.

The overlaps of race, class and gender are extremely important in close races. When Mario Cuomo faced stiff opposition in an expensive campaign against Lewis Lehrman, men preferred Lehrman by 3 percent, while women preferred Cuomo by 19 percent. ABC reported that women were 51 percent of the vote. At the same time, voter-registration drives in black and Hispanic communities are also credited with having helped Cuomo squeak through. Down in Texas, where only 49 percent of the turnout was female, 58 percent of the women voted against the Republican incumbent governor to elect the Democratic candidate.

Citizen Groups

Another movement that developed during the Seventies and is now entering the electoral fray is that of the citizen action networks. Many activists of the Sixties went to work in local communities on a variety of issues, from utility rates to toxic wastes to tax reform. Veterans of the civil-rights and antiwar movements, they never lost their idealism, but channeled their desire for social and economic justice into pressure politics that could unite people who might not have been able to unite easily on issues of race or foreign policy. Taking their cues from community organizer Saul Alinsky, they avoided electoral politics as divisive. After all, everyone in a neighborhood could probably agree to pressure a legislator on tax reform, but not all could unite behind a candidate who favored or opposed school busing. They continue to take their issue-oriented politics into electoral contests, focusing on what can unite people across class and race lines.

Citizen Action, a coalition of twenty community networks, from Massachusetts Fair Share to Illinois Public Action Coalition, claims to have more than 2 million members and to send several thousand canvassers a night out to more than 40,000 people's homes to raise money and talk to citizens about economic issues. These canvassers, argues Citizen Action head Heather Booth, are a natural registration force. First they enter the homes with registration forms. On return trips they can educate voters about issues. On Election Day they can help pull out the vote.

The Midwest Academy, a training school begun by Booth for community organizers, has established the Citizens' Leadership Foundation to provide the electoral training arm for citizen action organizations and other issue groups like the Freeze. CLF provides strictly nonpartisan training in both voter registration efforts and local coalition-building. In addition, training is given in how to mount campaigns that help candidates project issues important to citizen groups and hold them accountable long after election day. CLF has made strides in helping to build interracial "Rainbow Coalitions" in Philadelphia and in Charlotte, North Carolina, where the addition of several thousand new voters presumably assisted Harvey Gant, a liberal Black, to win the mayoralty in a city with a minority population of 30 percent.

The citizen action network tries to build its own leadership as well, and many of the leaders and activists in the network are now campaigning for public office. Some, like Doreen Del Bianco, have already won. Del Bianco joined the Connecticut Citizen Action Group in 1979 when she signed a petition for lower utility rates. She described herself to a reporter as "just a housewife" who "blamed all my troubles on blacks, Puerto Ricans and other victims." Now, she says, "I know it's the corporations that are keeping people down in the workplace and in the community." She is now a state representative, having won by 137 votes out of 8,200 cast.

In the South and Southeast, the Association of Community Organizations for Reform Now (ACORN), which in 1980 staged a counter-convention to the Democratic National Convention in order to draw attention to the needs of the poor, is now actively engaged in voter-registration drives and plans to have many of its members in San Francisco for the 1984 Democratic National Convention—this time as delegates.

The new peace movement that has grown up around the nuclear freeze has tasted success on the freeze referendum and is now involved in voter registration and education. Randall Forsberg, the defense analyst who thought of the idea for the freeze, tells audiences that the freeze campaign's goal is to have a president and Congress that will support the freeze. She reminds them that the battle won't end in 1984, but must be carried on to 1986 and beyond. In 1984 the movement plans to sign up a million people pledged to work for candidates who support the freeze. Next steps will be the more controversial agenda of decreasing the military budget and eliminating nuclear weapons.

In the Sixties the peace movement was not able to forge alliances with blue-collar workers or minority groups. The verdict is still out on the Eighties, although the peace groups were a large contingent in the rainbow coalition that gathered in Washington, D.C., in August 1983.

Other forces that carry great potential for the new coalition are students, many of them threatened and hurt by cutbacks in education and their parents' unemployment; the growing tenants' movement; and environmental groups. Recalling the dedication of the Mississippi Freedom Summer of 1964, the United States Student Association and Human SERVE will launch a summer 1984 registration and education drive to bring in hundreds of thousands of new voters.

In addition, Public Interest Research Groups (PIRGs), a Nader-inspired effort that is an activist presence on and off campuses in a number of states, is mounting a major national student campaign to reach the 14 million Americans between the ages of 18 and 24 who are not registered. They state that young people are the most nonvoting group in America and the trend is acceleration. Working with Human SERVE and the U.S. Student Association, the PIRGs intend to support the many voter registration efforts around the country to increase registration, particularly among minority young people, emphasizing efforts on campuses in the fall.

Churches, as they did during the civil-rights struggle, will play an important role in the new coalition. The U.S. Catholic Bishops statement on nuclear arms propels the American church not only into activism but into alliances with groups that might have avoided coalitions with them in the past because of disagreements over other issues. The influence of liberation theology coming from Latin America has radicalized many church people and made them amenable to political action in coalition with the poor. Mainstream Protestantism, which has seen right-wing churches succeed with many of their political agendas, are becoming more political. Twenty-one representatives from denominations and ecumenical groups have joined to form the Churches Committee for Voter Registration (CCVR). Focusing on parts of the country where the organizers believe there are churches capable of carrying out campaigns and where large numbers of poor people are underrepresented at the polls, CCVR has selected thirty-three areas in which it will conduct research, train staff, support legislative changes in voter-registration laws, run voter-registration and -education campaigns, and try to build secular support for its voter-participation activities.

Whether labor as a federated force will be in the coalition is still in question. Certainly the public-sector unions and those with many women in them will be, and labor unions are conducting aggressive registration drives. For the first time in its history, the AFL-CIO endorsed a candidate well before the primaries and bound all its members to support him. However, the the Federation's ability to deliver its members' votes (50 percent of union members voted for Reagan) may depend less on its skill than on Reagan's actions. The president's consistent antiunion stance and disastrous economic policies have made him unpopular with many segments of the work force. However, his undisguised patriotic appeals and ability to appear as a "regular guy," combined with veiled attacks on minorities and some improvements in the economy, may keep many voters on his side.

ELECTING BLACK CANDIDATES

The lack of enthusiasm for the slew of democratic presidential candidates, including Walter Mondale, highlights the problem of the voter who is "all dressed up with nowhere to go." In this context, the candidacy of the Reverend Jesse Jackson adds another element to the fervor of the voter-registration campaigns.

No one expects that Jackson will win, but the figures of potential black voters alone show that he could well act as a power broker at the Democratic convention or a spoiler in the general election, especially on the heels of the success of his Syrian initiative and his positive performance as a presidential candidate. There is no doubt that the national publicity he receives and his electrifying oratory inspire people to register. Local black political hopefuls, regardless of what they think of Jackson, see coattails that can aid them on Election Day. Many black politicians who are emerging as leaders in the Democratic party support the idea of a Jackson candidacy as a way to bring more blacks into the party and give them more leverage in turning it into a party responsive to a progressive agenda.

The Congressional Black Caucus in Congress has been consistently progressive on issues affecting all of the movements now involved in these voter-registration campaigns. Studies of black mayors show that they consistently support social programs for health, housing, education and welfare—items that benefit more than blacks.

If Jackson's campaign can bring more blacks into office and gain more bargaining power for blacks within the party, the Democratic party will begin to change, becoming more responsive to issues of economic and social equity as well as to a noninterventionist foreign policy. Such a change would depend on the ability of whites in the various movements to work with such officials rather than against them.

"Why is it that when a white defeats a black, it's always assumed that blacks will support the white person; but when it's the other way around, whites don't automatically assume they'll support the black?" asks a longtime activist. Harold Washington's bitter fight with deserters from his own party is but one example of the long way that whites have to go in coalition-building.

Even though the experience of black elected officials has been one of harassment and distrust once in office, they are forging strong networks with each other and their constituents and reaching out to broaden their bases.

Can increased public participation and the momentum that is building for progressive politics be sustained after 1984? Some think not. But the activists in New York are already contemplating the 1985 mayoral campaign and a possible 1988 statewide race by a black candidate; the people in Quitman County, Mississippi, who this year came to within a handful of votes of electing black county supervisors after years of intimidation and vote-stealing, aren't giving up; the women keep tallying the number of statehouses still hostile to the ERA; the peace activists are determined to avert nuclear holocaust.

It seems safe to say that if Reagan is defeated in 1984, many people will relax, having made the country safe for democracy for at least another four years. Those for whom the country has never been safe can be counted on to continue the battles. The taste of power, however limited, is addictive. Disenfranchised groups won't be willing to return to the status quo ante.

If Reagan wins, we could see another period of seeming inactivity like the Seventies, when many in the vanquished McGovern coalition returned to local activity and built bases in their communities. The movement for voter registration may seem to be a new one, but the people in it have been seasoned in other struggles. They know that they are in for the long haul.

One such veteran is Herman Lodge, a bulky, slow-talking man, now a county commissioner in Burke County, Georgia. He remembers graduating from high school in 1947 when only sixteen other black youths in the county made it all the way through. The civil-rights movement made its way slowly to that rural area. With thoughtful understatement, he remembers, "We wanted to sit-in, but there was nothing to sit-in. We wanted to boycott, but you can't boycott farmers." He traces the twenty-five-year-old struggle for integrated schools, for blacks to get on the grand jury that appointed the school board, and for change in the at-large elections system that put his name on one part of a Supreme Court case. Today the struggle is paying/off as black elected officials win seats that allow them to respond to the formerly disenfranchised. Lodge lets himself chuckle at the irony that now, as an elected official, he has to negotiate the court costs incurred by the county in fighting him up to the Supreme Court. The newly elected officials face harassment—arriving at meetings to find agendas already set and parliamentary procedures used to deny them a voice—but they are learning the ropes. When they started the fight two and a half decades ago, says Lodge, they learned fast that "God don't pave roads, politicians do." It took longer to discover that the people who really ran the county were "not elected officials but people in clubs." They're still learning, and still fighting.

Others in this old movement with new players are also ready to learn. They know that they need grass-roots activism, broad-based coalitions, well-run organizations and efficient use of the new technology the Right has used so well. They know that they need articulate spokespeople to use the media effectively and to provide effective analysis and fresh ideas. No one movement has all these yet, but together they present a formidable power in this decade. The Eighties will be the time of coming of political age for blacks, Hispanics, women, peace activists and community activists. The tremors have started and American politics will never be the same again.

15

The Gender Gap: Coalescing for Power

Marilyn Gittell and Nancy Naples

In the 1980s, two major historical landmarks were reached: Women for the first time comprised almost half the labor force and almost half voters. Differential political attitudes and voting behavior of women as compared to men, strongly evident in the 1980s, have been characterized as a "gender gap."[1] In fact, however, the "gender gap" is not a new phenomenon. For as long as gender has been distinguished in opinion research, social scientists have identified significant differences in political attitudes between men and women. Women are more antiwar and less likely to support an aggressive foreign policy. Women are less prejudiced, more sensitive to racism, more concerned with social and environmental issues and more supportive of social-service programs. Women have depended on government to resolve social problems, which they are more likely to view as socially caused. In 1982 polls, women consistently disapproved of the president's conduct of domestic and foreign affairs more than men did. The major thrust of the Reagan administration—a reduction in the role of government, elimination of social programs, and an emphasis on military buildup—is antithetical to the historical political orientation of women. The president and his advisers seem not to understand that women are particularly concerned with these issues.

It is argued that the increased number of women in the labor force —now 44 percent of workers as compared to 35.3 percent in 1960— will result in even greater differences between men and women in social goals and values. In fact, young women just starting college show distinctive differences from men of the same age in their political

Marilyn Gittell is professor of political science at the Graduate School and University Center, City University of New York. *Nancy Naples* is in the doctoral program in sociology at the City University of New York.

and social attitudes and in their social consciousness. Strikingly, the political gap between males and females is strongest in the 18–24 age group. This raises some question regarding the thesis that it is because more women are working that they have changed their attitudes and the gender gap has increased. The results of a survey of college freshmen in January 1983 demonstrated the extent of the gap at an early age. Significantly, there is almost no difference in male and female attitudes toward traditional feminist issues—i.e., body issues, abortion, ERA. This confirms other survey research of older populations. There was, however, at least a 10-percent differential in attitudes on social and political issues; young women were more concerned with social and environmental issues and more likely to want the government to act on behalf of the public on these issues. Interestingly, there is a 15-percent differential in the response of young men and women on the issue of the importance of helping others who are in difficulty.[2]

These attitudinal differences reflect the contrast in the socialization of women in American society. In the last two decades, the women's movement has further influenced attitudes and behavior, encouraging women to assert their differences, thus explaining an increasing gender gap.

Differences in women's values were not translated into electoral politics in the past, at least in part because women did not vote in large numbers. In most elections political parties and candidates were not clearly distinguishable from each other, and differences in values could not be registered in elections. The 1980 and 1982 elections provide more obvious distinctions in party policies and candidates' positions, and the turnout of women voters has increased substantially. Campaigns to register women voters have also been especially successful.[3]

If history provides instruction for movement politics and strategy, the move by women's organizations and activist women to capitalize on gender-gap publicity as a means of projecting their political goals is a wise political strategy. The social feminists of the 1920s and 1930s were the most accomplished wielders of political power and successfully influenced public policies. They gained passage of the Sheppard-Towner Federal Maternal and Infancy Act in 1921, which funded maternity and pediatric clinics for instruction in the health care of mothers and babies. They forced the adoption of child-labor laws and the creation of the Women's and Children's Bureau in the federal government. Historians agree that these policy responses by those in power were a reaction by elected officials to their concern that women, having been granted suffrage rights, might vote as a bloc. When that fear was dispelled by election results showing that women did not vote differently from men, women's political power was undermined. They failed, for instance, to gain renewal of the Sheppard-Towner Act in 1929. Contemporary concerns about the women's vote have proven real and can be an effective tool in electoral politics and, more important, in shaping responsive public policies for the next several decades.

Among the current responses to the awareness that women can play a major role in the electoral arena is the creation of the Women's Roundtable, a coalition representing many of the key women's organizations such as NOW, the League of Women Voters (LWV), the National Women's Political Caucus (NWPC), the American Association of University Women (AAUW), the Women's Equity Action League (WEAL) and Business and Professional Women (BPW). On the national level, the Women's Roundtable—chaired by Joyce Miller, president of the Coalition of Labor Union Women (CLUW) —has developed a campaign entitled "It's a Man's World—Unless Women Vote!" On the state level, the California Commission on the Status of Women successfully worked with the state legislature, the lieutenant governor's office, and women's and community groups to obtain testimony on the feminization of poverty in California. They brought the issue together with the "gender gap," noting that "two out of three of those living in poverty are women. What if we were all to go to the polls?"

In the city of Chicago, after the primary, women came together in a coalition to elect Harold Washington. Following the mayoral election, this coalition remained intact as Women's Network for Chicago to press for city-level attention to women's needs. Women activists from a cross section of groups we interviewed two years ago, and then again in the summer of 1983, indicated their growing communication and strong mutual support to defeat Reagan and promote social programs and policies.

Two main questions arise: (1) What will be the influence of organized women's action on the American political system in the next decade, and (2) how will the character of American politics and the state of the economy influence the evolution of the women's movement?

It is inescapable that the most immediate impact of women's political behavior will be a response to the Reagan policies. The Reagan ideology has stressed the importance of marriage and family as a norm, encouraging the continued dependent role of women on the family. The facts belie that ideology. The increased number of women forced into the labor market as independent wage earners, the growth in the number of women who are single parents, and the large percentage of single older women have in fact reduced the dependence of women as a group on the family and increased their reliance on government and social policies to replace the family as a support. Day-care centers, education, job training, medical care, environmental controls, and maintenance of a vital economy are increasingly important programs to women. This gap between women's needs and social conditions and the Reagan policies that undermine these programs will be a direct stimulant to increase women's political activism, and perhaps provides the best explanation of why women see President Reagan, in particular, as so much more unacceptable than do men. The major cuts in social- and human-service programs have had a dramatic impact on women in all age groups, since women are often the major recipients of benefits under each of these programs.

Some political analysts prefer to interpret the distinctive character of women's political behavior in the narrowest terms possible. Women are described as reacting to Reagan on a personal basis. This analysis underestimates the historical political differences between men and women. In the 1952 election, women's deferential support of Eisenhower was also interpreted as reflecting his personal appeal, his "father image." Those analysts failed to see that Eisenhower was a peace candidate, and that this fact probably better explains his support by women, just as Reagan's aggressive military attitude makes him less attractive to women as a candidate.

A sexist interpretation of women's political behavior is evidenced in much of the research on participation. Social-science research has stressed that women are less participatory as voters and less politically sophisticated. These data not only disregard the exclusion of women from traditional avenues of politics, they eschew important aspects of women's political involvement, particularly in voluntary and community organizations. More recent studies by feminist scholars have provided new information and interpretations of these circumstances.

Barbara Berg's in-depth portrayal of the role women played as members of voluntary associations in the nineteenth century characterizes the distinctive quality of women's political activity.[4] She concluded that women who were active in those organizations were less likely to blame the victims of poverty and more likely to seek social solutions to problems. Other evidence identifies women as social reformers in America. As a result of contemporary historical research, evidence of women's significant role in the abolitionist movement has been identified.[5] An increasing body of research illustrates the distinctive role of women in the progressive and settlement-house movement and in civic reform at the turn of the century. The legislative success of the women reformers of the 1920s and the special reform role of women in the New Deal are described in a 1981 study by Ware.[6]

Women historically have invested their energies at the local and community level—the areas they knew best and saw as most relevant to their own and their families' needs. Traditionally, local government and voluntary and community organizations have been the major political arena for women. However, women encouraged the federal government's redistributive and equity role as essential to the resolution of local problems, while continuing their own concentrated interest in the neighborhood and community.

The role of voluntary associations and community organizations is a history of women's political participation. The women in these organizations used their numbers, status and knowledge to press for social reform. Although political analysts have periodically stressed the importance of interest groups in American politics, they generally minimize the power of most of these organizations, whose membership happens to be comprised largely of women! Labeled "volunteers," women were denied their role and status as political activists. In practical political terms, women often failed to act as a cohesive force for certain common goals, and thus it was easy for those in power to ignore them as an important force for social change in American politics.

Not surprisingly, women's lack of access to, if not blatant exclusion from, traditional political institutions has also been ignored in the professional literature. As barriers have been removed from these institutions—for example, in the case of the party conventions in the 1970s—women's participation has expanded significantly.

Alice Kessler Harris considers that women's activism has been strongly influenced by the larger political arena and that their significant role at the turn of the century and in the New Deal period was eclipsed by the "campaign for Motherhood" of the 1950s, which drove women temporarily out of politics.[7] Because of economic and political changes in the status of women, she foresees an ever more active role for women in the 1980s to address their pressing need for social programs.

In 1965, only 39 percent of women were in the labor force; in 1982, 52 percent were working, and the Labor Department estimates that 65 percent will be working by 1995. One-third of the 15 million women who entered the labor force since 1970 are in traditionally male-dominated fields. These working women have already asserted themselves as consumers. As the *Wall Street Journal* recently noted, "it's clear that the working woman trend has complicated marketing of consumer products and squelched some outmoded assumptions. Marketing of household products for instance now should emphasize thrift, convenience and speed. . . ." This recognition of the more rational response of women as consumers will certainly spill over into the political arena.

Given the historical role of women's activism, plus the contemporary impact of the women's movement and the backdrop of the immediate environment of the Reagan policies, a number of issues arise and several scenarios can be imagined. There can be little doubt that women's activism will increase and expand to new areas. As Women USA has reported as a result of five pilot projects, women are anxious to register to vote and to pressure for major policy changes encouraging the adoption of government programs to answer their social needs. All of the evidence also points to a narrowing of the gap of interests by class and race among women. Their common needs as members of the work force and as single parents should negate differences in emphasis and style so evident in the 1970s. The Reagan policies have fostered a closer identification of common problems by these groups. The Reagan disavowal of the value of social programs of the last fifty years, denial of a constructive role of government in achieving equity and social justice for formerly excluded groups, undermining of participation in the policy process, and discounting of the need to redistribute power and wealth have all served as a stimulus to greater coalition-building among women. More important, these policies have activated women politically, in electoral politics, in community organizations and in women's organizations. As a local president of

NOW summarized it, "We now know that key legislators prevented us from getting our bills through, and we had to plan to get them out of office—electoral politics was a necessity."

The women's movement has matured sufficiently to encourage the engagement of many groups in electoral politics at all levels. The effort to remove Reagan is a national rallying point. The limits and constraints of the economic system and the indifference of political leaders necessitate that reaction. The maturity of the movement and the wider acceptance of its ideology make that thrust more possible. Class and race differences among organizations in the 1970s are blurred by broader economic and political issues. This is not to suggest that differences will disappear, but merely that the Reagan ideology and program have provided the impetus for coalition-building and recognition of common interests among women, because his policies challenge the most fundamental needs of a large majority of American women. Reagan politics denies the basic concerns of women and their reliance on government to deal with the problems of society, problems that disproportionately affect women's lives.

In 1981 we found that women active in women's organizations and women in community organizations had conflicting priorities and political strategies.[8] These conflicts appear to have been mitigated somewhat by the recognition of common pressures and concerns. We observed in that study that leaders of community organizations perceived their constituency as the entire community. They saw their primary issues as education, employment, housing, and child care. Some also emphasized health care as a major concern. They framed their concerns in terms of the needs of the men, women and children in their community. Leaders of women-specific organizations, on the other hand, had primary and often exclusive identification with women as their constituency, virtually ignoring class differences. They focused on legislative and institutional changes that would counter sex discrimination.

The community or neighborhood-based-organization women resented the fact that women-specific-organization women did not identify sufficiently with the problems faced by low-income, working-class and minority women. Women-specific-organization women, however, defined their issues from within their own experience. Issues of abortion rights, sexual harassment and equal pay were seen as priorities for these women; while the low-income and minority community-organization women emphasized increases in public assistance and "more jobs, period." These differences resulted in a diversity of political strategies, a lack of coalition politics, and often overt antagonism. This tension reminds us of the earlier period of the women's movement, when suffragists, working women and professional women could not find a common meeting ground. Perhaps the failure of the ERA and the backtracking on women's issues in recent years are at least partially explained by these diverse, if not conflicting, interests and agendas. However, when women activists in the early part of the twentieth century joined forces with women of diverse experiences and backgrounds, and framed issues as questions of power and influence, they were able to influence public policy and to effect fundamental changes in the political system that benefited women (and men) across class lines. The achievement of equity goals was far-reaching.

In more recent interviews with activist women, we find significant change from our 1981 findings. There is greater interest in common goals—saving social programs, defeating Reagan, electing supportive officials. These different groups clearly have important resources worthy of exchange. Together, these activist women can exercise influence and power in areas of common concern, particularly in response to the regressive policies of the Reagan administration.

Reagan's policies will provide the basis for coalition-building in the women's movement in the 1980s. Class, racial and ethnic differences can be addressed if these different women come together to discuss barriers to mutually supportive coalition politics and policies that are mutually beneficial. In this way, each group can begin to understand the other's perspectives and to explore jointly the intersection between poverty, racism and women's oppression. By entering into issue-oriented political coalitions, these divergent groups of women will broaden each other's political and economic analysis. What at first seemed to be diverse issues are now being explored as directly related to economic and social inequities. Important efforts have begun to develop a "feminist economic program" as Stallard, Ehrenreich and Sklar advise.[9] For example, the State Communities Aid Association (SCAA) and the Coalition of the Concerned for Older Americans (COCOA) in New York State are cosponsoring a forum to bring a feminist perspective to issues of concern to the aging. They are bringing together women's groups, senior advocacy groups and local councils on the aging to develop a legislative agenda.

Women have traditionally been more active at the local level, eschewing national politics as participants or excluded from national politics by sexist policies. Women, however, benefit from expansion of the public sector and a strong central government. As reformers, therefore, they have been important participants in the movements for social justice and equity, and have supported a strong redistributive role for the national government. In societies with a limited state, women are less likely to participate and benefit and are more unlikely to get the kinds of programs necessary to support their independence as wage earners. Large public-sector societies offer women more job opportunities and more support services.[10]

Women have favored decentralization and responsive institutions at the same time that they have pressured for strong central human-service programs, expanded education, family services and health care. Women's organizations and community organizations originally provided the services that were later taken on by the welfare state. Those organizations continue to work with the state and/or confront it to ensure an adequate level of service. Through these organizations, women have historically expressed their political activism and continue to do so. Organizations that were in an earlier era humanitarian voluntary organizations are now political and interest-group organizations—in some cases delivering services for the state, in others challenging and pressuring the state to resolve social problems. Some analysts suggest this organizational activity has kept women out of the mainstream of politics because these are outside the organizational power structure of society. In fact, the tie between women's organizations and the welfare state is a strong one and is one of the major reasons for the political activism of women and their support for a redistributive role for the welfare state; they recognize that it serves their and society's needs.

The political role of the women's movement and its response to the Reagan policies has two major facets: one in electoral politics, which is widely publicized and characterized by the "gender gap"; and a second in the development of strong organization and coalition politics on policy issues. The history of political activism of women suggests that they are not likely to confine themselves to electoral politics. They are more likely to address issues, to want to solve problems and to build institutions that empower them. They are likely to register a strong protest vote against Reagan policies and, judging by the polls, also register a strong anti-Reagan vote. Equally important or perhaps more important, women are likely to expand protest and movement actions to change those policies to recapture the ideology of social justice and equity. Women already comprise a major portion of the antinuclear movement,[11] and if education does become a major campaign issue, they will likely emerge as important participants in that effort.

In *Poverty in the American Dream,* Stallard, Ehrenreich and Sklar call for the development of a "feminist economic program for *immediate* action to include guaranteed adequate income; full employment; an end to employment discrimination; child care; reproductive rights; and the provision of other basic human needs and services. They conclude:

> Women have a long history of fighting for economic and social justice. Today the stakes are higher than ever. The challenge of the 1980s is to build multi-racial coalitions which bring together women's organizations with welfare rights, civil rights, labor, antiwar and other groups. Women can and will continue to play a decisive role in constructing a society centered not on greed and war, but on human needs and aspirations.[12]

CONCLUSION

As women are perceived by political leaders as a distinctive political group, acting in their own interest, leaders will be increasingly responsive to their needs. The characterization of a "gender gap" and its verification in electoral politics serves that function. Leaders in the women's movement and community organizations recognize the value of the gender gap as an organizing tool. In addition, over the last several years there has been a demonstrated change in the willingness of women's groups to communicate with each other, meet together, seek joint strategies on important issues, create coalitions and address broader social concerns. This more cohesive identification of the political concerns of organized women is a potential electoral threat capable of extracting support for legislation. The gender gap has been further enhanced by the Reagan policies, which are perceived as antithetical to the interests and sensibilities of a large segment of women voters. Also enhanced are the organizing efforts of women leaders, who recognize the importance of group identity and cohesion as a form of political power. This in turn closes the gap among different groups of women, blurring class and race lines that were so evident in the early years of the women's movement. Consolidation of women's concerns across the spectrum of types of organizations can propel a significant stage of the women's movement concentrated on economic and political action. Drawing on the tradition of generations of women activists and reformers, this new thrust can be a major force in returning American society to goals of social justice and equality.

There is ever-increasing evidence that women's groups and women in other organizations (e.g., NEA, unions) are joining forces to nominate and elect candidates at all levels of government. Major efforts are being made to register women voters and train them to engage in electoral politics and run for office. Alliances on political issues are also emerging on housing, day-care, health and welfare issues. Importantly, the 1982 election analysis showed a closing of the gender gap, with men moving closer to women's views on many issues. The 1982 elections were the first overt repudiation of Reagan's policies at the state and local levels. There is strong support for a wide-based coalition to displace Reagan in the 1984 elections. It is also evident that without a clear alternative candidate on the issues, the women's vote is likely to be less significant in determining the outcome. If the Democratic party nominates a candidate who is not distinctively different from Reagan in major policy areas, the gender gap will not defeat Reagan. If coalition-building around policy issues is expanded and continued, women will be an important political force to be contended with at the state and local levels. The shift in the structure of federalism under the Reagan administration, making the state policy-making arena more significant, presents a challenge to women's groups, many of which have neglected that arena. Their counterparts in community organizations can be important and knowledgeable allies in that effort, which is another advantage to be gained by broadening coalitions and developing an expanded policy-issue orientation.

The impact of the women's movement in the 1980s will be measured by its ability to develop a more cohesive, more inclusive movement addressing important political issues. Concentration on economic and public policy concerns can be an important organizing tool, encouraging coalitions to seek responsive action in legislation and the allocation of resources. Engagement in electoral politics is important but cannot be an exclusive endeavor. Many of the most activist women will not be drawn into those efforts; with good reason, these women recognize the limited value of total immersion in electoral politics as a means of achieving social change.

If the women's movement is to get a new head of steam—which it clearly appears to be working on—it will come from broadening its issues and approach in the political arena. What was identified as its failure in the ERA battle of the 1970s, its lack of understanding of the state political arena, should be an area of significant development in the 1980s. A national campaign against Reagan and his policies is an important rallying and organizing point, but it cannot be an exclusive effort. In a recent public statement to women leaders, Gary Hart said: "Women have the power to elect the next president of the United States." The temptation will be great to invest major resources in that campaign. Projecting the issues and values of concern to women on policies should, however, take precedence over party politics and partisanship. Women USA has set a constructive tone, asking all of the Democratic hopefuls to take public positions on particular policies in advance of announcing their support for a particular candidate.

The "gender gap" concerns issues, not candidates or parties. The women's movement must recognize and capitalize on that fact. The test will be in the ability of the women's movement to move both parties and a wide spectrum of candidates to take positions on issues that serve women's purposes. Their power lies in the movement politics, the flexibility to build and support issue and policy coalitions, the commitment to bridge class and race interests with gender issues, to respond to pervasive needs of a growing body of poor women, to counter the policies of an insensitive administration. No one can deny the importance of electoral politics in a democratic society, nor can we deny that it is only one means of exercising power. By itself, without organization and other pressures, it can easily undermine or misdirect energies of well-meaning reformers.

Notes

1. Kathleen A. Frankovic, "Sex and Politics—New Alignments, Old Issues," *Political Science* 15 (Summer 1982).
2. Alexander Astin, "The American Freshman: National Norms for Fall 1982," *Chronicle of Higher Education,* 26 Jan. 1983, 12.
3. Women USA, "The Women's Voter Registration Project" (New York: Women USA, 1983).
4. Barbara J. Berg, *The Remembered Gate: Origins of American Feminism—The Woman and the City, 1800–1860* (New York: Oxford University Press, 1978).
5. Willie Lee Rose, "Reform Women," *New York Review of Books,* 7 Oct. 1982, 45–48.
6. Susan Ware, *Beyond Suffrage: Women in the New Deal* (Cambridge, Mass: Harvard University Press, 1981).
7. Alice Kessler Harris, "The History of Women's Work," presented at the Feminization of Poverty Conference sponsored by the American Friends Service Committee, New York, 11 June 1983.
8. Marilyn Gittell and Nancy Naples, "Women Activists: Conflicting Ideologies," *Social Policy* (Summer 1982), 25–28.
9. Karin Stallard, Barbara Ehrenreich and Holly Sklar, *Poverty in the American Dream: Women and Children First* (New York: Institute for New Communications, 1983).
10. Helga Maria Hernes, "The Role of Women in Voluntary Associations," part 3 of the "Study of the Situation of Women in the Political Process." Preliminary study submitted to the Council of Europe, Steering Committee of Human Rights (CDDH), December 1982.
11. *Ms.* Gazette, "The Nation Mobilizes for Peace," *Ms.* magazine, Aug. 1983, 83–86.
12. Stallard, Ehrenreich, and Sklar, op. cit., p. 58.

16

Labor Is the Key

Stanley Aronowitz

Despite ample evidence that, on particular issues, the broad liberal consensus still prevails, conservatives have been able to set the agenda for American politics since 1968. For example, polls have revealed that on almost every issue concerning the provision of social welfare —schools, health, and Social Security are perhaps the major institutions—an overwhelming majority of those questioned favor substantial federal aid. Even on such hotly contested social issues as abortion rights, divorce and sexual preference, most of those questioned favored the right to choice or defended privacy rather than approving them as moral practices. With the major exception of the death penalty for capital crimes, which most citizens now support, the social and political "old-time liberal religion," when taken singly, still has a commanding lead over conservative policies such as massive federal cuts in social programs and repressive positions on gender and other sexual issues.

Unfortunately, although public-opinion polls are important for guiding candidates seeking public office and for business executives seeking customers, they do not guide public policy. Aggregating individual views on various issues may occasionally constrain unpopular policies, but it cannot make new policies or programs; otherwise, it would be difficult to explain how the Reagan administration has managed to dismantle some popular social programs, cut others to the bone, and freeze a third group when public support is overwhelming for their expansion.

Reagan's charisma is often used to explain the apparent paradox of Reaganism: the president's personal popularity; his uncommon mas-

Stanley Aronowitz is professor of sociology at the Graduate School and University Center, City University of New York.

tery over Congress; his exercise of political will, matched in recent years only by Franklin D. Roosevelt; and his ability to mobilize public support on specific issues through adroit use of the media. These points, while helping to explain how Reagan has succeeded in realizing more of the conservative program than his two Republican predecessors, do not tell us why Congress was so supine or why the progressive movements have not been able to mount a strong counterattack against the administration's domination of the political agenda, even when, as in the case of Social Security, they have slowed the conservative effort to dismantle.

Arguments that delve beneath conjunctural circumstances of personality rest on three points: first, the widespread economic perception that America is in trouble because it cannot compete in a sharply more competitive world market; second, the shift of population and industrial and commercial centers from the Northeast and the industrial heartland of the Middle West to the South, Southwest, and southern California; third, in consequence of the first two factors, the breakup of the political coalition that set the agenda for American politics from 1933 to 1966 even when the Democrats were not in power during the 1950s.

This essay will focus on the third point, not because the others are less important but because there has been more discussion of their dimensions. However, I will outline the effects of the economic and demographic changes since the late 1960s on the fate of that progressive coalition—for in the final accounting, it is not economic changes or personalities that immediately determine social, economic and other features of public policy; policy is shaped by the decisions of *the politically active* population—those who vote, work for various candidates, put up the money for electoral campaigns and otherwise possess social weight, measured by command over economic power, mass organizations or intellectual resources. At different times, these three aspects of modern social power have a different relationship to each other as well as to the legislative and, more broadly, political processes. Since 1970, when the fortunes of the national economy turned sharply downward, the major changes in American politics have been formed by the simultaneous weakening and partial breakup of the progressive coalition and the ability of the conservatives to dominate the *discourse*—that is, their account of the economic crisis and their proposed solutions became boundaries of debate; liberal and conservative alternatives had to speak the vocabulary of conservative ideology.

The progressives were forced to speak the language of budget-balancing, tax "relief" for the middle classes, cuts in social spending and, more globally, "getting the government off our backs." The progressives' response to Reagan was confined to disputation about *how much* to cut social spending, not *whether* to cut; *how much* to decrease taxes for the rich in order to encourage them to invest, not *whether* to cut taxes; and *how much* tighter they should permit money to get, through high interest rates, in order to reduce inflation. Reagan proposed a recession to control inflation, which inevitably entailed considerable unemployment. The congressional progressives were reduced to trying to moderate the recession's effects on the poor and the working people, and could not oppose the anti-inflation strategy itself.

A major reason for the progressives' inability to respond effectively to the conservative attack on the gains of the past forty-five years is that the coalition has lost its active base. The progressive program for increased government economic and social interventions gained widespread acceptance and succeeded because of two historical developments: First, Roosevelt brilliantly pinned the Great Depression and the mass suffering that accompanied it on Hoover's conservative policies, a political maneuver that contained, at best, a half-truth; second and more important, the Roosevelt coalition was sustained by the rise of the mass industrial-union movement that organized 10 million workers during the twelve years of his administration and constituted the backbone of the coalition long after his death.

From 1936 through Johnson's sound defeat of the first genuine Republican conservative since Hoover, Barry Goldwater, the trade-union movement provided a large chunk of campaign workers, financing and public support for Democratic presidential and congressional candidates. By 1944 the CIO's support was considered indispensable for a Democratic hopeful. When Roosevelt replaced Henry Wallace with Harry Truman as his vice-presidential running mate, labor had to be convinced. In the parlance of the period, the president had to "clear" his choice with CIO political-action director Sidney Hillman, the leader of the Amalgamated Clothing Workers. Hillman and his successors were more than talented political operatives for organized labor; they were key figures in the high councils of the party.

The coalition was formed out of the disenchanted middle class, including a large fraction of farmers and professionals, the overwhelming majority of blacks of all social classes, and the bulk of workers, especially the industrial and other blue-collar workers who constituted the key sections of the labor force. In addition, Roosevelt persuaded a portion of bankers and industrialists that his program could save capitalism. Among these were some traditional supporters of the Democratic party, but most of them were new recruits. The Harrimans, Lehmans, and Kuhn-Loeb among the investment bankers were joined by liberal industrialists such as Henry Kaiser, conservative corporations such as U.S. Steel and, among commercial groups, Marshall Field in Chicago and the Gimbel family in New York.

The course of organized labor held the fate of the coalition after World War II. At the war's end, unions claimed 30 percent of the wage-earning labor force. This figure was the highest labor ever achieved in American history.* In the 1950s, the long exodus of manufacturing from eastern and midwestern industrial centers began —at first with the migration of the shoe, textile and garment factories from New York and New England; then, toward the end of the decade, the furniture industry left New York and the Midwest for the Carolinas. Although the half-dozen unions in these industries became alarmed by the loss of shops and members, the labor movement and the liberal coalition still prospered in the late 1950s and 1960s. The coalition held together despite the deep fissures cut into the progressive camp by anticommunism, which, in the late Forties and early Fifties, nearly destroyed it on ideological grounds.† Even as low-

* It is even more impressive when one considers that a very low percentage of white-collar and service workers were union members in either the public or private sectors. Perhaps 60 percent of all production workers belonged to unions. In some industries, such as auto and steel, the figures were closer to 90 percent; in the basic rubber industry, all production and maintenance workers belonged to the union. Among men's clothing workers (as distinct from children's and sportswear, which were already migrating to the South and rural areas), the Clothing Workers Union organized practically the entire industry.

† Some historians and commentators have attributed the decline of the progressive coalition to the open-throated support given the Truman administration's pursuit of the cold war by the CIO's hierarchy and the majority of liberal and civil-rights organizations. Although the split between labor's center, led by CIO president Phillip Murray, and the Left led to a series of internecine battles within the industrial-union movement that occupied many unions for most of the 1950s, it cannot be said that, especially under conditions of economic expansion, American foreign policy produced the defeats progressives sustained on virtually all of their domestic programs. The reasons for the atrophy of the welfare state until the late 1950s go deeper; labor retreated from political combat during this period of conservative

technology, mass-production industries were migrating to nonunion areas, labor's losses seemed minor because a new wave of organizing was taking place among public employees.

The upsurge began in New York in the late Fifties when a revitalized State, County and Municipal Employees Union (AFSCME) successfully won bargaining rights among a large number of New York City's municipal workers, paralleled by similar organizing gains by the Teamsters and uniformed services such as police, fire and sanitation. In the Sixties, impelled by the entrance of millions of blacks and women into the public-sector labor force and President Kennedy's executive order permitting collective bargaining among federal employees, the campaign gained national momentum. Although most of the early public-employees unions were composed mainly of clerical and blue-collar workers, the early 1960s Teachers Union drive in New York showed the potential for organizing professionals. By the early 1970s, nearly 4 million new union members had been recruited in the public sector and another million and a half brought into organized labor in the private services, especially food retailing, hospital and communications workers.

In retrospect, we can better understand the Johnson administration's amazing innovations in social policy during the Vietnam War if we take into account that this period witnessed the rise of four important social movements that, despite their frequent mutual antagonisms, constituted together a dynamic force in American politics. The trade-union movement was helped by the growth of feminism, by the student movement that helped radicalize a section of professionals (again), and above all by the black freedom movement that mobilized ideologically and politically the vast majority of blacks and other minorities for the progressives. An analysis of the composition of the new unions that developed in the 1960s reveals the extent of their dependence on the other social movements.

Take the case of hospital organizing. The most aggressive efforts began in 1959 in New York among mainly black dietary, housekeeping and patient-care workers in voluntary nonprofit hospitals. Coincidentally, this was the precise moment of the rise of the lunch-counter sit-ins, the voter-registration drives and the emergence of the Rever-

---

control in Congress and reproduced the welfare state within the labor contract (see Stanley Aronowitz, *Working Class Hero,* chapter 3, Pilgrim Press, 1983).

end Martin Luther King, Jr., as the undisputed tribune of the civil-rights movement. Local 1199, the union conducting the organizing drive, identified its efforts with the civil-rights movement and particularly with King, who frequently joined picket lines and rallies. Similarly, the teachers' and municipal-workers' unions were closely identified during the first half of the Sixties with civil-rights issues. Later, AFSCME was a leading war opponent, linking its organizing efforts —particularly among social workers, planners and other professional categories—to its generally progressive policies.

When combined with the traditional progressivism of the auto workers, electrical workers and a dozen other mass-production and service unions, the public employees helped create a political environment that consolidated the left wing of the traditional coalition and provided significant support for the new movements, even though there were frequent altercations with them because the feminists and the antiwar movement wanted labor to be more forthcoming and the black-power phase of the freedom movement produced veritable confrontations with some progressive unions, particularly the auto workers and the steelworkers.

In the 1970s the new international division of labor generated a second wave of plant migration, not primarily within the U.S. but overseas. Another difference from the earlier postwar runaway shop was that now intermediate-technology industries such as auto assembly, steel and electronics were leaving. For example, Wayne County (Detroit and suburbs), Michigan, once produced 70 percent of all cars in the U.S. Even after some decentralization to the East and South after the war, it still retained 50 percent of auto production. In the 1970s its share was reduced to 30 percent as a significant fraction of Chrysler, Ford and GM parts production shifted overseas and new major assembly operations were established by the big three companies in Mexico and other Latin-American countries as well as Spain and elsewhere in southern Europe. Steel plants that had once supplied the world were closed in Buffalo, Youngstown and the Pittsburgh area because foreign producers were more efficient and could produce steel more cheaply. As U.S. and world markets shrank for American-made machine tools, U.S. capital went abroad seeking cheaper labor and more-advanced technologies.

With the exodus of major production to the Southwest and overseas, urban centers in the Northeast and Midwest began to suffer a shrinking tax base, creating an uncertain climate for investment in municipal and state bonds. Even before Reagan, local governments were experiencing budget deficits as federal funds were cut or failed to match inflationary costs. Local governments increasingly turned to property and excise taxes to pay for services. By the mid-Seventies, the crunch on services was threatening public-employees' jobs, which were by now fairly well paying because of union-led gains. After the fateful New York City fiscal crisis—when thousands were laid off, pay raises were deferred and union pension funds were lent to the city to ward off bankruptcy—the forward march of public-employee unionism was stopped cold.

Taken together, severe membership losses in mass-production industries and the long series of concessions in the public sector have held unions to a defensive posture for the past decade. Even during a union-backed, but conservative, Democratic administration in the late Seventies, unions could do no more than hold on to the traditional social programs. The AFL-CIO's campaign to improve the National Labor Relations Act to make organizing easier in antiunion strongholds such as the South failed despite an overwhelmingly Democratic Congress. The Kennedy bill for national health insurance did not even get to the floor of either house. Clearly, by 1980, labor and its allies were on the defensive.

Pressured by conservative calls for budget-balancing, lower taxes and spending cuts, and by the nearly runaway inflation afflicting the economy, the Carter administration tried to head off its opponents by adopting their posture, if not all of their remedies. Under these conditions, the many mistakes of the administration, such as the so-called hostage crisis, can be blamed only for having provided the most obvious attributes of the losing 1980 election campaign. Reagan rode to power because the progressives had already accepted his terms for the debate and the conservatives' general outline of the cure.

Of course, the new adminsitration's cure for inflation entailed mass unemployment through cutting federal intervention in the public sector, imposing high interest rates that reduced small investment and durable-goods purchases, and reducing taxes for the rich, all of which combined to produce layoffs in both the public and private sectors. These policies were initiated as the international economy was plunging into a major recession, which U.S. policies helped deepen. At the same time, Reagan has instituted a new arms race that has exacerbated budget deficits without dramatically improving the employment picture because much the new military technology is labor-saving.

As the world recession lingered, employers began to intensify efforts to cut labor costs. Computerization became a major technological innovation for American industry. It took three principal forms: Robots replaced many assembly-line workers; numerical controls reduced the size of the machinists' trade and affected many other fabricating operations; memory chips replaced the intellectual part of manual labor, eliminating the function of thinking involved in setting up machines and diagnosing needed repairs. The computerization of the office threatens to wipe out the traditional secretary, replacing her/him with video display terminals (VTDs) and word processors. The automatic office and the automatic factory are by no means a *fait accompli,* but they are advanced tendencies in the way most Americans work.

Recession, government policies and technological change have combined to weaken the strength of American unions and the progressive coalition to which they have been the key. Here are some membership figures: Since 1981, the UAW has lost about a quarter of its 1.5 million members; the Teamsters, afflicted not only by recession and automation but also by trucking deregulation, have lost 700,000 members since 1979, or about one-third; the Steelworkers are 40-percent smaller than they were at the beginning of the Seventies; the Garment Workers have been reduced by nearly 50 percent; and the Shoe and Hat Workers have all but disappeared since the late 1960s. Of the major unions, only the Communications Workers, the Food and Commercial Workers, and the Service Employees grew during this period. Perhaps the most dramatic loss was among the building trades, which once claimed 3.5 million AFL-CIO members and now have been reduced to half that size. Today the labor movement represents about 20 percent of the work force, a reduction of a third since 1946, a period when the wage-labor force increased from about 55 million to more than 100 million. Clearly, the declining social weight of the unions has a great deal to do with the victory of conservative politics and ideology in American life.

Equally important, traditional centers of labor's political strength such as New York, Detroit, New Jersey, eastern Ohio and western Pennsylvania can no longer be counted on to deliver for the progressives. To be sure, Democratic elected officials in these cities and regions are still preponderant, but with few exceptions they are not genuinely representative of labor's interests or those of its historic allies, particularly the minorities. "Representative" legislators and executives would see themselves as genuinely beholden to workers, blacks and other social movements, unlike those who "vote right" on progressive issues as they reach the floor of Congress or state legislatures.

To take some historical examples: New York's Senator Robert Wagner actively shaped labor legislation precisely during the period of the upsurge of the Thirties. Similarly, James Murray, senator from the strong labor state of Montana, was cosponsor of national health insurance legislation in the Forties. Rhode Island's Representative Aimie Forand introduced Medicare legislation in the late Fifties; and during the following decade, the package of antipoverty legislation emanated from the House Education and Labor Committee, whose chairman, Adam Clayton Powell of New York, and the senior Democrats were closely aligned with labor and the civil-rights movements. During these three decades, labor and the progressives not only enjoyed considerable congressional support for their programs but formed a bloc of active sympathizers who acted as floor leaders for various parts of the coalition program.

Today, the congressional progressives have been reduced in numbers not only due to population and industrial migrations from their old strongholds but also because the strength of organized labor has declined. In this connection, I wish to make two points: First, labor has not organized among the new workers in the large cities where, in some instances, employment gains in such industries as financial services, communications and administration have matched the losses in manufacturing; second, with the notable exception of public employees, labor has lost touch with its own members.

If labor is the key to the size and strength of the progressive coalition in American politics, having provided not only the major segment of votes but also finances and political roganization for important national and local election campaigns and legislative struggles, the key to its social and political influence is the degree to which it is able to recruit among the most dynamic sections of the labor force. Today, those involved in high-technology production, many of whom are in technical and professional occupations, and those engaged in services linked to the international economy, such as finances, communications and information, constitute the basis of the American labor movement of tomorrow.

Another important group consists of those in the most exploited production industries, many of which recruit labor from among immigrants or migrants from agricultural regions in this country. Labor cannot identify itself with those at the cutting edge alone; it must also champion the interests of the Latin, Caribbean, Asian and southern U.S. migrants who are paid low wages, often below legal minimums, and suffer working conditions that resemble those of peonage. Both groups are growing and their expansion in the labor force corresponds to changes in the structure of the world economy. The advanced sectors respond to the competition from Japan, Germany and other European countries and the new markets for capital and goods in the Third World; the recent rise of low-paid production industries feeds on the displaced illegal immigrants from those very Third World countries, who have become subject to employers who operate beyond the law. Furthermore, labor still has unfinished business organizing among low-wage southern textile, lumber and garment workers, as well as hundreds of thousands of production workers in intermediate-technology industries that are traditional union strongholds in the North and the West.

Like the upsurges of the Thirties and the Sixties, labor must become a social movement rather than merely an institution of collective bargaining. Unions never organize effectively by presenting themselves as business representatives; they must represent social justice and be perceived by workers as alternatives to the unjust system of the open shop at the workplace and the uncaring state in legislative arenas.

Today, union conventions still routinely approve the resolutions of the progressive agenda, but unions are not widely perceived as resolute champions of it. To their memberships as much as to unorganized workers and the public, unions present themselves as interest groups that exclude everyone except their own members. Now, to some extent this political perception is produced by unremitting antiunion propaganda perpetrated by right-wing and business groups. Sometimes labor's image is tarnished by misunderstandings with other progressive social movements, which expect unions to be more than they are prepared to be. However, despite the hostility of labor's opponents on the right and their deliberate misrepresentations of labor's programs, the contemporary ills of American unions are not entirely produced by enemies or by adverse economic conditions. Two further problems plague labor, and unions have been slow to recognize them.

The first is that union leaders are more removed from the rank and file politically and ideologically than at any time since the early 1930s. Members are both to the right and to the left of their leaders—to the left on issues of union democracy and corruption, which are not so much caused by outright dishonesty at the top (although this remains a problem in some unions), as by the fact that the leaders at the bargaining table are prone to take the point of view of management, especially in hard times when higher wages and benefits are difficult to win.

The second problem is that union leaders often tend to regard democracy as an obstacle to effective unionism; they have implicitly taken the view that the union is not a town meeting so much as an army dedicated to a single goal—better wage and benefit standards— which is best achieved when the rank and file mutes its criticisms and unites behind a single program. The leader believes that "too much" democracy tends to be disruptive of this objective, apart from being threatening to his or her tenure of office. While there are important exceptions to this general attitude, notably some industrial and public-employees unions, democracy is by no means an approved part of the practice of contemporary unionism. Although the rank and file is asked regularly to support labor's political, legislative and, above all, collective-bargaining program, it is not asked to participate in making decisions. Many members have become increasingly distanced from the everyday life of their unions except at contract time. The union is regarded as little more than an insurance company dispensing benefits for which the member pays a premium (dues). When the union fails to deliver these benefits, members may become involved to change leaders, reject a soft contract or get rid of the union itself, but they rarely understand that they can "own" the union through their participation.

Therefore, when leaders ask members to vote or write letters supporting a candidate or issue, they increasingly face an indifferent or hostile response: indifferent because members pay attention to their unions only on economic matters, and hostile because the members have moved away from union goals and ideologies—to the right. We

cannot focus here on the factors responsible for this state of affairs—
be they the mass media, effective conservative appeals that have
weaned workers away from class self-definitions, racism and sexism
or other factors. What matters here is that unions rarely make sustained efforts to get members involved in union work beyond contract
ratification and grievances. In recent years, some unions have improved their educational programs aimed at training stewards, local
union officials and other unpaid leaders. However, many union leaders are either suspicious of education as a potential factional threat or
regard it as an expensive luxury program that at best is valuable for
helping to train bargaining committees, but not for broad political and
ideological education.

In sum, unions are not weak simply because of the new ideological
and economic environment that has reduced their membership and
political power. Union power is diminished because its still formidable
battalions are not being brought into the broad processes of leadership, education and social action. Organizing is left to specialists
rather than the rank and file; full-time officials handle most grievances; and lobbying becomes an expert function rather than a mass
activity.

Even if the Democrats replace the conservative Reagan administration, there is little chance that a new politics will be born in the process
of their victory until labor becomes a "movement" again. That is, the
chance for reconstituting the progressive coalition depends on
whether millions of workers can be brought into unions from the new,
growing sectors and, having been unionized, are subject to a coherent
progressive ideology and program that, at least, provides an alternative to the dominant conservative economic and social discourse. No
other force in society can provide the counterweight to the finances,
the command over media and the sheer economic and ideological
power of giant corporations and neoconservative institutions. The
illusion of the Sixties that strong feminist, minority and antiwar coalitions could displace the "labor bureaucracy" as the core of a new
politics has been definitively shattered in the wake of the progressive
defeats of the last decade. Even with an important and strong environ-
mentalist movement that in the Seventies was able to impose many
restrictions on corporate and individual polluters, the centrality of
organized labor is by no means diminished—for social movements
confined to particular, albeit crucial, struggles have been unable to

match the global character of the conservative appeal.

In sum, the labor movement, despite its many shortcomings, remains the only effective global contestant to capital, in part because it embraces class, race, gender and broader economic interests, and is almost by definition the largest movement of this cross section in any industrial country. Further, unions possess vast resources, at least when measured by the size of other movements. National and congressional Democratic campaigns receive about a third of their campaign contributions from unions; and even considering losses, unions have still provided thousands of campaign workers for Democratic candidates in many states. A recent example, Mario Cuomo's victorious primary and general-election victory for New York governor, illustrates the point. The AFSME, CWA and other unions provided more than 10,000 telephone canvassers in the 1982 elections, constituting, in these close races, more than the margin of victory.

The Cuomo victory points up an important problem beyond labor's capacity for mobilization. As the candidate of labor and other members of the progressive coalition, Cuomo could have been expected to initiate a new, broad policy and economic program corresponding to the interests of working people, minorities, women and the middle classes. Although Cuomo has taken some decisions that were urged upon him by unions (elimination of a regressive pension system for public employees is one small achievement thus far), the new governor lost little time announcing austerity measures that resulted in some layoffs for state employees and virtually froze the education and health budgets. Cuomo has initiated no significant economic measures designed to provide jobs and training for the unemployed. Perhaps the only clear-cut victory for labor has been a modest increase in unemployment compensation, which was made possible, in part, by the fact that New York lagged behind many other comparable industrial states. Cuomo is plainly not the governor of the same coalition that elected him. At best, labor and its allies can prevent him from drifting too far right, but they lack an alternative program or the political will to impose their own policies on what experts agree is an administration that owes its political life to the progressives, especially unions.

Cuomo has paid attention to patronage demands among his constituents and has responded to interest-group issues, but remains a fiscal conservative dominated by the priorities of banks and other private investors. These seem to be the terms of the new liberal contract: business-trades patronage (in a Democratic administration) and some politically visible state benefits, for almost complete control over the budget. It is not only Cuomo who observes this contract, but all wings of the Democratic party, including organized labor. And there's the rub. Until unions and their allies develop a new economic and social program that departs from the major assumptions of neo-conservative/liberal policy, even a revived labor movement, a strengthened feminism and a new surge in black organization will not succeed in turning American politics leftward, however, important these advances would be. For we are caught, both here and abroad, in the stranglehold of social austerity, with its concomitant programs of fiscal conservatism and social repression. Since there is little prospect in the near future for a major economic revival that would open vistas for new struggles for social justice without redistribution, labor is faced with a hard choice: It must oppose the main drift of U.S. foreign policy that posits rearmament as the basis of national security in order to free resources for job creation and massive transfer payments such as health care and education, and simultaneously declare the formation of a "party within the Democratic party" to challenge the rightward drift of its congressional and national leadership.

The alternative is implicit in its current course: Labor would be brought into a junior partnership with the so-called neoliberals who combine fiscal conservatism with the idea of a new social contract in which labor plays a subordinate role to a revived "high-tech" capital. In return, unions will be offered a place in the national planning mechanisms to coordinate economic revival. This alternative is attractive to a weakened labor movement, but would be unacceptable in the event of a new upsurge that was grounded in class rather than collaborative assumptions. Although unions, like most liberals, feel they have no choice but to go along, the price appears, to many leaders and members, already too high. After initial concessions to management, Chrysler UAW members are already demanding a payback of the $400-million concession they granted in 1979.

University employees at Columbia and California joined unions in large numbers in 1983, after having identified with management for decades. And the AFL-CIO is taking a direct hand in the Democratic primary rather than waiting for the outcome of the convention before making an endorsement. Similarly, New York labor played an aggressive primary role in the 1982 elections, as did the Massachusetts

AFL-CIO. These moves do not prefigure a change of political direction for labor and the progressives unless they are accompanied by a new ideological politics. For even if labor is still powerful enough to elect its preferred candidates, only if it sharply departs from its current compromises can its potential power to change public policy be realized.

The progressive alternative is a program of democratic planning and trade-union growth on the basis of labor's firm commitment to help constitute a new coalition in which the interests of the poor, minorities, women and middle classes are embraced as labor's own. For if unions are to escape the fate of all subordinates—that is, escape extinction or permanent servitude—they must build their *independent power*, which, in the earlier upsurges, was based on identifying themselves with the dynamic movements of political opposition as well as those elements in the ruling elites prepared to bargain on an equal footing. Democratic planning differs from neoliberal planning because it entails bringing workers, consumers, communities and professionals together at the base of society to control economic, social and political institutions within the framework of negotiated goals.

This alternative, which would place popular need above military or corporate demands, requires a strong, militant and democratic labor movement. This kind of formation can only emerge if labor declares itself on the side of the aggrieved and refuses to join partnerships of privilege. It remains to be seen which road labor will travel. In the near future, we can expect only a minority of unions to embrace the democratic alternative until the rank and file and an important portion of union leaders recognize that the neoliberal alliance results in further decline.

Given the depth of labor's slide, one can hope that the shock of recognition occurs sooner rather than later.

17

The Consumer Movement Looks Ahead

Ralph Nader

In their own way, the self-styled Republican conservatives and the Democratic liberals have difficulty providing an affirmative role and horizon for consumers. Politically there is a distinction between the comparative sensitivities to consumer rights by these Republicans and Democrats. The former are more averse than the latter to the process of government regulating for greater consumer safety and less consumer abuse. In practice, however, the liberals are not so keen on making a real difference out of that distinction when they come up against determined corporate pressures. This narrowing of the differences between the two parties—especially in a period when recessions paradoxically give corporations more power over government—became deplorably apparent during the last two years of the Carter regime and the present Reagan administration. The transition from one president to another on deregulatory policy was quite smooth due to Carter's paving the way.

But then, how new was all this movement away from using the laws of the democracy to police the marketplace? Historically there had been a moving away during many cycles of the periodic emergence of regulatory agencies designed to defend consumers. Where such a mission is explicit, as with the Food and Drug Administration (1907), the drift is toward industry co-optation, meek leadership appointments and obsolete legal authorities. Where the regulatory mission is less consumer-explicit, as with the Interstate Commerce Commission (1887) and the Civil Aeronautics Board (1938), the agencies become instruments of private cartels who do what they could not otherwise do legally under the antitrust laws.

Conservative and liberal enforcement of the antitrust laws have

---

Ralph Nader is director of the Center for the Study of Responsive Law.

reflected common tolerances toward obsolescence, as with their inadequacies toward conglomerate mergers and new-technology suppression (product-fixing), their emphasis on behavioral violations (price-fixing) and their neglect of structural market distortions. Some Republican regimes were stronger than Democratic regimes and vice versa during these statutes' ninety-four-year tenure.

Both the regulatory and antitrust approaches to consumer protection were more ministerial than empowering for consumers. The level of activity behind these two mechanisms depended on who was in government office. Apart from Election Day and its often narrow political choices, there was little in these laws that empowered consumers to initiate or challenge any of the numerous economic and safety rules regarding food, drugs, transportation, communications, housing, banking, insurance, energy, health and other services. Consequently, the administration of these laws was subject to instabilities, to ebbs and flows that were not only debilitating to agency staff morale but also invited public cynicism that lowers those public expectation levels that keep agencies on their toes.[1]

The absence of consumer-empowerment laws (about which more later) is, of course, a reflection of the dominant and adversarial power of corporations over both markets and politics. This secular imbalance is more than a predominance of organized economic might; it also is rooted in a predominance of production-side economic theory that embraces the production orientation of both Marx and Ricardo. It is this "cultural bias," which analyzes economic dynamics and criticality as coming from the production side of the market—from capital and labor and selling—that has shaped the historic view of economies by both the Left and the Right.

When the consumption and production functions ceased being lodged in the same family units and began, with the onset of mechanization and specialization, to be more and more separate, it was only natural for scholars to focus on these new agents of change—the capitalist entrepreneur, factory proletariat, capital markets, mass-production systems and the like. The complex exchange economy, replacing barter and consumers producing their own meager food, shelter and clothing, naturally attracted the economic theorists and public philosophers. Then it was only a short step to the widely shared belief that what is most studied is what is most important. Such a belief became a self-fulfilling prophecy that massively excluded empirical acquisitions and imaginative disquisitions regarding neglected social and normative phenomena on the buying side. By contrast, when Marx developed his dialectical materialism and labor theory of value, he set in motion a heightened attention to the labor factor.

Although Adam Smith did write that the end of production is consumption, most economists during the eighteenth and nineteenth centuries focused their observations on the mostly unabated trend from an economy of scarcity to an economy of greater productive abundance. Production was king; production made consumption possible; production put people to work so that they could be more liquid consumers. The measure of economic progress was quantity and those goods and services that could be measured in money terms. There were, to be sure, some successful reform efforts to more equitably distribute income and wealth and to reduce the harshest edges in the workplace and the urban environments. But the preeminent yardstick, as it is to the present, was the monetary and numerical values symbolized by today's gross national product accounts. *It is the number of cars and drugs sold that is the measure, not what the auto and drug industries add and subtract from the transportation usage and health of people.*

In the Eighties, both liberals and conservatives believe that production is the engine of consumption (supply-side thinking), although they differ in their commitment of social transfer payments to add extra assurance that poorer consumers will possess some dollars to spend. There are also differences in their concern with health and safety consequences of production—though more in their rhetoric than in their practice. But these distinctions, while important, fall far short of the requisites for a just economy, which a consumer-side economic dynamic and agenda can provide.

The present seller-sovereign economy is quite different from the classical market model where consumer sovereignty is supposed to reign supreme. In this idealized system, "everything" that is sold is, by definition, proof that buyers want that "everything." A seller-sovereign economy includes sellers who are monopolistic or oligopolistic without being confronted by ultimate consumers who are organized in monopsonistic or oligopsonistic modes. It is an economy where enormous skill, artifice and resources are used in getting consumers to buy what the sellers want to sell, notwithstanding the availability of more efficient, safe, economical, durable and effective alternatives, including that of buying nothing at all. Over the past twenty decades, congressional, state, judicial and media inquiries have documented this appraisal. Let a short mnemonic list do for many: widespread price-fixed products and services; product-fixing to thwart innovation; deceptive packaging and false advertisements; wholly ineffective or hazardous drugs; product obsolescence; energy-wasting vehicles, appliances and other products; unsafely designed cars; junk food; serious product side effects such as pollution and poor land use; adulterated products; overselling of credit, insurance and alleged health care.[2]

Allied with this systemic ability to sell such harm and deception are media driven by similar mercantile values and commercial motivation.[3] As a business feeding off other businesses, the media have narrowed the accessibility of consumer-side communications, although when bland, modest consumer messages have been transmitted, reader appeal and viewer/listener ratings have been high. Media that live off advertisements urging people *to buy* are not about to give much time to announcements or programs urging people *not to buy*.

After many years of economic imbalance between sellers and buyers, little-studied corporate practices started putting down roots. Companies began paying more attention to skimming the cream off the top of the market and subjecting the remainder to discriminatory pricing or exclusion. Companies began paying attention more to peoples' wants than to peoples' needs. There are shortages for millions of Americans in housing, food and health care, while there are ample supplies of cosmetics, video games, soft drinks and entertainment.

An expendable subeconomy takes a clearer form. Its millions of members are thrown on the state for sustenance while they are mercilessly exploited by business for their addictions (cigarettes, drugs, alcohol). There appear to be more innovations for wants than there are for needs—perhaps most graphically exemplified over the past generation by the automobile industry. Stagnation for years was the fate of safety, fuel-efficiency and pollution-control needs, in comparison with the creative merchandising of style, power and psychosexual appeals. Increasingly, private capital investment flows from needs to wants and on to speculation such as stock-market-index futures. Forced condominium conversions, empire-building mergers and acquisitions, and other unproductive uses of capital expand, as compared with uses that meet recognized necessities of a population and generate employment. Financial institutions use "other peoples' money" (savings-bank deposits, pension moneys, mutual insurance assets) to service the short-range preferences of economic elites while the economic masses are deprived of the reinvestment benefits from funds that they own but do not control. The separation of ownership from control is a rampant form of centralized manipulation over the economy.

All along the companies perfect the art of flattering consumers while keeping them in the dark about what is being sold. Supermarket chains praise the homemaker as a "human computer" who is "razor-sharp," and then expose her to a stream of supermarket traps. Companies work artfully to induce consumer dependence on them (Texaco was "earning your trust" while fleecing huge sums from consumers during the energy shortfalls of the Seventies). Dependence, not critical capability, is what the firms seek from consumers.

Mainstream economic theorists have been legitimizing for decades this conceptualization of corporate behavior. Thorstein Veblen, in his essay titled "Why Is Economics Not an Evolutionary Science," wrote about this consumer stereotype earlier in this century:

> In all the received formulations of economic theory, whether at the hands of English economists or those of the Continent, the human material with which the inquiry is concerned is conceived in hedonistic terms; that is to say, in terms of a passive and substantially inert and immutably given human nature. . . . The hedonistic conception of man is that of a lightning calculator of pleasures and pains, who oscillates like a homogeneous globule of desire of happiness under the impulse of stimuli that shift him about the area, but leave him intact. He has neither antecedent nor consequent. He is an isolated, definitive human datum, in stable equilibrium except for the buffets of the impinging forces that displace him in one direction or another.[4]

With the applied social science known as modern advertising, coupled with electronic media, the large sellers' skill in obscuring, diverting and deceiving adult buyers, while conditioning with shameless persistence the minds of young children, is awesome of itself. When such mercantile bombardment continues daily without countervailing responses, the impact is all the greater. Televised ads, conveying to grown-ups and youngsters alike the lure of false tastiness (chemical additives) over genuine nutrition and flavor, reach into their health as well as into their pocketbooks.

Shaping a widespread consumer perspective among buyers when they go shopping has been the objective of a myriad of books, pamphlets and now videotapes. "How to buy" guides for this and that are legion. Yet they seem little read and less used. The culture is averse. Students grow up being taught by their courses the selling trade, not how to buy—home economics excepted. Schools are filled with free, colorful materials, slide shows and video, compliments of the oil, auto, drug, meat, coal, fashion and other industries.[5] Nearly a decade ago, a Random House teachers' kit titled "To Buy or Not to Buy," for which we advised, generated unease and controversy. Teachers and curricula were not prepared for its adoption. To some local businesses, such a course was tantamount to teaching subversion. Unlike bland consumer-education courses, this kit encouraged students and their instructors to study or survey, for example, local supermarkets, auto dealers and banks. It was learning by experiencing various buying roles equipped with a refined consumer perspective.

There is a major differential benefit to themselves and to the larger political economy when buyers bring a consumer's perspective instead of a seller's perspective to the market transaction. The energy-consumer value would press for energy efficiency; renewable, self-reliant energy; safer and competitively priced energy. The energy-seller value presses for more centralized energy, supplied by often interlocked sellers whose technologies foster waste, environmental damage, disease and political corruption. If in the last fifty years the consumer value had the power to prevail, our nation would be humming along on one-third of the energy now used, with highly advanced passive and active solar energy using direct sunshine, biomass, hydro, wind, solar cells and solarized architecture. We would not be dependent on risky global supply lines; we would not be so indentured to the menace of atomic power, nor the silent violence of acid rain, nor the looming greenhouse effect over our climate, nor the lung-corroding consequences of fossil-fuel combustion; and the misallocation of economic resources, unemployment and geopolitical conflict would have been substantially diminished.

The selling of pharmaceutical products and automobiles also reflects the power of the sellers' image rather than the informed preferences of the buyers. An organized consumer perspective on cars long ago would have achieved the safety, efficiency and pollution reductions so ignored by manufacturers who sold stylistic pornography over engineering integrity. That there have been advances in these areas is testimony to a partial reassertion of consumer-perspective power through regulatory programs and sporadic bursts of public exposure. But the interwoven adversities and risks that arise from the vastly expanded influence of global corporations deploying new chemical, computer and genetic technologies can no longer be expected to be contained by the regulatory state of whatever vintage. Public justice in our country is basically nourished from private-sector activities; it cannot be grafted very well onto a private economy concentrated in the hands of the few over the many. This thesis is historically evident. Regions with one-crop economies or company towns have less responsive governmental structures. Regions where workers are organized obtain better treatment from their factories and mines. Where industrial power is less unilateral, elected political representatives tend to be more sensitive to human needs.

The next logical extension of private-sector economic democracy moves to the consumer arena. Unlike workers wanting a greater piece of the economic pie, consumers have it in their interest to reshape the pie and its quality for broader-based well-being for all.

The range of potential consumer demand for any set of products and services is very wide. Buyers can purchase medical services that embody quackery, malpractice, mediocrity or competence. These purchases can sustain fee-for-service medicine or cooperative, prepaid health clinics. These dollars can also lend themselves to understanding the need for greater self–health care (exercise, nutrition, ceasing smoking), which displaces sizable demand for health services. Consumer dues with organizational involvement can generate public policies and law enforcement that take hazardous drugs and devices off the market, prevent waste, reduce disease-producing pollutants in the workplace and community, and facilitate the rights of patients and injured persons in pursuing their individual grievances.

If the documentation of the past quarter-century has taught us anything about consumer abuse, it is that there are readily available ways to dramatically squeeze such waste, fraud, crime, peril and anticompetitiveness out of one industry and commerce line after another. Likewise, there is a popular literature of economic self-reliance, right down to the drawing boards, especially in the areas of housing, food, energy and health care. The large circulations of Rodale publications and *Mother Earth News* are beginning to suggest the emergence of an alternative economy embracing billions of dollars of displaced demand out of the conventional marketplace. Rediscovering old knowledge and applying new do-it-yourself technologies join to expand what consumers are producing and saving for themselves.

The progressive challenge is how to accelerate this process in a more integrated, empirical and conceptional fashion. Since everyone is a consumer, it is difficult to develop a class consciousness; for some consumers see themselves first as workers; other consumers view themselves as part of the poverty class. Moreover, many consumers, when financially strapped, see moonlighting or putting another family member to work as the way out. Few consumers think of broad reductions in their expenditures as a way out, even when they can afford to do so. The supreme ethic is not in that direction; "Thrift is out, growth is in" represents the thrust and ideology of the corporate economy.

However, in the past decade have come warnings of basic shortages and shrinkages—of conventional energy, water, reasonable credit terms—and more scarcities on the way. Sporadic shortages from cartel-prone behavior, such as the natural-gas shortfall in the late Seventies, are sending alerts to consumers, who are organizing door-to-door canvasses. Refusal-to-sell shortfalls, as in bank and insurance redlining, are fueling neighborhood solidarity among homeowners and tenants. The compulsory consumption of toxic pollutants and the erosion of the nation's resources are raising serious concerns about seller-sovereign economies, concerns that the Reaganites found they politically could not ignore. Nonetheless, the politicians and media do not view the consumer as a heavyweight economic issue. It would be too tumultuous to do so. Though the recovery and prosperity of an economy rely on consumer confidence and consumer dollars, the players on the primal media stage are still business, government and organized labor. It is not surprising that the burden of many decisions made by these parties is transferred onto the shoulders of consumers. And those most burdened tend to be most ignored.

In one of the more grotesque illustrations of this endemic practice, the federal government, under a 1979 law, is subsidizing high-cost synthetic-fuel production. Then, when that energy moves to market, the government is authorized to subsidize a price-support program. While this corporate welfare program is going on, the Reagan administration has virtually destroyed the Energy Department's conservation programs and standards.

Contempt for consumer justice is seen in many ways, such as legislators' reluctance to back energy-efficiency rules for fear of reducing certain employment or reducing profits; waste here becomes an employment policy as well as a way to increase sales. Or when the Food and Drug Administration proscribes a drug or food product but lets companies sell off their remaining inventory. Or when the Congress and Mr. Reagan enacted a law requiring consumers to bear the full risk of a $40-billion Alaskan pipeline even if it was never finished and no gas flowed to their homes. Or when congressional Democrats and Republicans teamed up in 1982 to pass legislation to pay up to $50 million to manufacturers of tris-treated children's pajamas; it was deemed more advisable to spend this amount of money to save the manufacturers the trouble of taking their chemical suppliers to court than to use such a sum to establish an ongoing program of diagnosis for the children exposed to this carcinogen, or some comparable program of deterrence.

These developments represent the more extreme frontiers of the corporate state's "transfer economy." Using extramarket powers of government, these companies transfer their risks, failures, waste and corruption onto the ultimate consumers with increasing ease. This provocation against the market competition model is driving more conservative and liberal civic groups into active alliances. Such coalitions came forth in the struggles against the Alaska gas pipeline, the breeder-reactor subsidy and the bailout bills for the large banks' foreign loans. It will not be long before more conservatives begin to view the megacorporations as principal subverters of the market enterprise system.

All these currents and crosscurrents are starting to provoke organized consumer response—not simply to demand regulation but to initiate direct private action for negotiating the conditions of buying. These actions revolve around consumers banding together in the following categories:

Banding Together for Group Buying
This format is different from consumer cooperatives, which buy and then resell to their members in an institutionalized context of build-

ings, inventory, capital investment and other features of an established retailer.

Over the past decade, thousands of informal wholesale buying clubs for fruits and vegetables were organized on a neighborhood basis. Households take turns going to produce wholesalers to purchase, at a discount of 20 percent or so, the pooled order, which then is distributed at a convenient place in the neighborhood. Since 1980 about sixty home fuel-oil cooperatives have started in the Northeast. These co-ops obtain discounts from local fuel dealers, who benefit from larger volume sales. One such co-op, the Citizens Alliance Fuel Buyers Group, with 8,000 members in New York City, saved its members about 20 cents per gallon last year. Individual members place their order directly with the dealers, who provide the fuel under the overall co-op/dealer contract.

On an entirely different scale is the American Association of Retired Persons (AARP), which claims a membership of 14 million composed of anyone age fifty-five or older who pays $5 in annual dues. In 1969 AARP was 1 million strong; now, 100,000 new memberships are coming in each month, according to James Sullivan, director of AARP's member services. AARP's appeal is diverse—members receive a variety of periodicals, support AARP lobbyists on issues before Congress concerning the elderly, and benefit from a variety of other educational and advisory services. But the major attractions are discounts—on prescription medicines and other health-care items, and on group health insurance. Since it broke away from its founder, Colonial Penn. Insurance Company, in 1981, AARP invites bids from insurance companies for its group policy and negotiates the terms for its members.

Banding Together for Group Complaint Handling

With mass production of identical products, like car models and drugs, it was only a matter of time before the victims began to find each other for common action. Class-action litigation and publicity about defective and recalled products helped lay the groundwork for this rise in common consciousness. What follows is refining the instruments for organizing such networks.

Diane Halferty, owner of a GM diesel lemon in Seattle, has organized Consumers Against GM (CAGM) with chapters around the country of similarly indignant GM diesel owners. CAGM has technical, fund-raising, communications and other committees. A newsletter is exchanged. When group negotiations with General Motors, which sent four officials to Seattle, came to naught because GM would not negotiate with its customers *as a group,* lawsuits were filed against the company.

With the coming of two-way, interactive cable TV, there is the likelihood of a quantum leap in such group-complaint associations. Imagine a program that parades a series of such groups across the tube, followed by an address or telephone number for viewers to call if they've been the victims of similar corporate lemons or abuses. Viewers would have to possess certain rights (discussed shortly) for such media freedom to be practiced.

Banding Together for Group Negotiating

Though largely ignored by national media, there is a growing proficiency in neighborhood or community negotiations with banks to reduce their redlining, and with potential cable-company franchisees to provide more access and facilities. Trade-union negotiations for prepaid legal services have reached fruition in some 5,000 plans. The likely next stage of development is for consumer associations to negotiate changes in preprinted contracts covering installment loans, insurance policies, leases and warranties. These contracts are drafted by sellers and are very one-sided—"contracts of adhesion," as the lawyers call them. The unilateral corporate process should become more bilateral with consumers before another decade passes.

The new technologies of home computers, telecommunications and cable (and related methods of transmission) make this projection more than a hope. And the proposed consumer checkoff groups can provide the public policy muscle to make these technologies work for many people and not just for a few corporations. Although there is an abundance of available communications technologies, it will take a public-access drive to make them usable by the American people.

For starters, we have suggested to Congress an idea called "Audience Network."[6] Based on the public airwaves belonging to the public, Congress would charter a viewer and listener group and revert back to this organization (open to membership for $5-per-year dues) one hour of prime or drive time each day on each television and radio station. This audience network, through its full-time producers, programmers and reporters, would use that time both locally and nationally for the vast variety of subjects—scientific, political, cultural, civic, corporate, etc.—that are largely ignored or restrictively treated by contemporary media monopolies. Controlling a little portion of what the audience owns can quickly raise the alert and response levels of citizens to problems and solutions.

The new information technologies will breed a new kind of commercial, consumer-side business. Computerized information services that, for a subscription fee, can inform people about the up-to-date best auto-insurance policies in their cities or towns, or the best savings interest rates or loan rates at banks, or the repair services with the best records. Until now computers have been overwhelmingly deployed for sellers and underwhelmingly used by consumers for their market transactions. While it is too early to assess the "community sociology" that widespread home computer use will generate, consumer networking is likely to increase significantly.

In some U.S. and Canadian cities, there are homeowner repair associations whose staffs prepare lists of approved contractors and handle homeowner complaints. Once households band together, the potential for other cooperative activities—from monitoring City Hall to reshaping the cable franchise—is limitless. One of the signal marks of twentieth-century America has been the drastic shift from neighborhoods to the corporate employment site as the all-embracing societal focus. Lately, the tide is turning modestly against this community atomization. Linkages between households on concrete matters within and outside the neighborhood can produce seismic changes in the distribution of power throughout the nation's political economy.

Before that shift occurs, collaborative consumer associations need to be more equal participants in public policy-making with corporations. Decades of legislation have built barrier after barrier and inequity after inequity between consumers and corporations. Most states, for example, prohibit neighbors from joining together to buy group homeowners and auto insurance policies. Also prohibited is bargaining with insurance agents for a reduction of their commission. Long ago, the insurance lobby saw to it that these market-restrictive laws were passed. At the federal level, vast assortments of corporate subsidies, unchallengeable licenses, regulatory abdications and campaign-fund influence serve up large dollops of consumer injustice.

Procedural and economic obstacles—such as the lack of standing to sue, or the absence of intervenor funding—present additional hurdles confronting people who wish to petition their government.

Here is where the consumer checkoff insert can revolutionize the consumer movement into voluntary, mass-based policy organizations with professional staff backed at the grass roots by active members.[7] Citizens in Wisconsin find that periodically a small postage-paid envelope comes with their electric, gas and telephone bills. The envelope contains a stimulating headline and several paragraphs explaining why consumers should band together as part of the Citizens Utility Board (CUB) to represent themselves with technical skills, public information and political power before all branches of government on utility matters affecting them. Minimum dues are $3 a year, and about 80,000 residential consumers have chosen to join.

The structure is in place for advocacy in many areas. Similar structures can emerge from similar state or national laws that would simply charter these consumer groups and give them the right to insert their solicitation message in the billing envelopes or on printed contracts (warranties) of legal monopolies (e.g., utilities) or regulated industries (banks, insurance companies, auto companies, etc.). In the future, other mechanisms will be developed to help consumers find one another in order to band together. In the electronic media, for instance, time on the screen can be allocated for both viewer programming and solicitation.

These consumer-empowerment systems have attracted both liberals and conservatives in the states where they have been seriously proposed.

The CUB bill passed four years ago in Wisconsin with a Democrat-controlled legislature and a very conservative governor. The same sequence has just repeated itself in Illinois. In Washington, D.C., the Reagan administration opposed legislation to establish a Postal Service consumer group, based on twice-yearly delivery of solicitations to all household patrons. It is also opposed to pending legislation to create a residential-telephone-customer CUB to cope with the forthcoming, staggering increases in monthly local telephone bills.[8] For all their cries for new ideas, the congressional liberals, with few exceptions, have not responded actively on behalf of these empowerment ideas—none of which either cost the taxpayer anything or create another government agency. The bipartisan sway of corporatism over the U.S. Congress is so profound and PAC-ridden that it will take strenuous popular advocacy to snap many liberals out of their now cozy, industry-indentured status. But then there will be strenuous corporate provocations to fuel such advocacy.

Whether private- and public-sector consumer collaboration will rise to these challenges depends on the perception that there will flow benefits commensurate with this unusual allocation of consumer energy and time. It is necessary for consumers, therefore, to think of their role in broad terms, beyond their pocketbooks and immediate purchases, if they are to be pleased by the consequences for their pocketbooks and purchases. If motorists had thought big and organized together in the Twenties to shape the many facets of the automobile economy, motorists today would be getting to their destinations more safely, more healthfully, more economically and more efficiently.

But then, the reader might reply, what about the AAA and its 40 million members? What about the mutual savings and loans associations, and the mutual insurance companies? History does have its lessons. One of them is that any economic organization that presumes to be directed and/or owned by the consumers it is designed to serve will gravitate toward managerial domination and corporatist behavior if consumers are passive owners or members. While the aforementioned institutions did make unique contributions and did engender deterrences of some value in their early years, as they matured they moved toward the corporate model and enfeebled their original purpose of expanding the consumer-sovereign sector of the economy.

A new stage of consumer history is presently unfolding. To succeed, both by the standards of a respectful prosperity and in terms of a sensitivity to reducing the domination of economic concerns over other basic human values, this new movement must be grounded in philosophy and a mass commitment to working at and perfecting the consumption function as a shaper of political economies.

The seller-sovereign economy is delivering less quality and less employment while its failures and greed are implicating our nation in worldwide crises. As long as millions of consumers find themselves, for example, spending hundreds of hours a year to earn enough money to buy food or energy while spending virtually no time learning how to buy food or obtain energy, the deterioration will continue. Banding together as buyers can broaden and metabolize the community quest for economic justice and liberate both political and economic thinkers from their invisible chains of thought.

Notes

1. Morton Mintz and Jerry S. Cohen, *Power, Inc.* (New York, NY: Viking Press, 1976).
2. Mark Green and Robert Massie, *Big Business Day Reader: Essays on Corporate America* (New York, N.Y.: Pilgrim Press, 1980).
3. Ben Bagdikian, *Media Monopoly* (Boston, Mass.: Beacon Press, 1983).
4. Thorstein Veblen, "Why Is Economics an Evolutionary Science," *Quarterly Journal of Economics* 12 (July 1898).
5. Sheila Harty, *Hucksters in the Classroom* (Washington, DC: Center for Study of Responsive Law, 1979).
6. U.S. Congress, House, Committee on Interstate and Foreign Commerce, Subcommittee on Communications, *Hearings on the Communications Act of 1979: H.R. 3333*, 96th Cong., 1st sess., 5 June 1979.
7. Andrew Sharpless and Sarah Gallup, *"Banding Together: How Check-offs Will Revolutionize the Consumer Movement"* (Washington, D.C.: Center for Study of Responsive Law, 1981); and Arthur Best and Bernard L. Brown, "Government Facilitation of Consumerism: A Proposal for Consumer Action Groups" 50 *Temple Law Quarterly* 253 (1977).
8. Joe Waz, *Reverse the Charges: How to Save $$ on Your Phone Bill* (Washington, D.C.: National Citizens Committee for Broadcasting, 1980).

18

Democratic Planning: The Bottom-Sideways Approach*

Bertram Gross and Kusum Singh

In most planning—public or private, civilian or military, local or national—a few powerholders and experts try to control the lives of many more people. Obvious examples are Reagan-Thatcher-style plans for huge military buildups and other handouts to the powerful and wealthy at the expense of middle- and lower-income people.

Yet even with people-oriented plans, participation by the people planned for (or at) is usually ceremonial, or else it focuses on minor details, sidetracking attention from decision-making at "higher" levels. "Maximum feasible participation" is too often a ritualistic minimum involving only illusory changes in the structure of power.

As a result, many progressives throughout the world are disillusioned with planning. Experience tells them that even well-designed plans to meet human needs are too often transformed into autocratic, bureaucratic or corporate-state controls.

But what about "democratic" planning?

This question reminds us of Mohandas Gandhi's response to a

Bertram Gross, emeritus distinguished professor at Hunter College of the City University of New York, is visiting professor-at-large at Saint Mary's College. *Kusum Singh* is associate professor of communications at Saint Mary's College of California.

* This essay has been developed as an outgrowth of work by members of the Democratic Planning Project, a modest national network of activists and scholars concerned with community communication and participatory legislative initiatives on behalf of democratic planning. After starting in the urban-affairs department of Hunter College, City University of New York, with the help of David Hunter of the Stern family fund, its nationwide activities are now based at Saint Mary's College of California in Moraga (east of Berkeley and Oakland). The authors express their gratitude for the help received from scores of other associates throughout the country, and, above all, from Frank Riessman and other editors of *Social Policy.*

reporter who asked what he thought of Western civilization: "It would be a good idea . . . "

If democratic planning were less of a rhetorical slogan, it would be more than a good idea—it would be a powerful tool in building more civilized societies in East and West, South and North. Unfortunately, many of those most interested in democratic planning think of it in technocratic terms divorced from the realities of a country's power structure and interest conflicts. Any realistic model, however, recognizes that *planning is an effort to affect the future by mobilizing, keeping and using power.* We call this the "power theory of planning."

Autocratic planners build concentrated power by developing goals and policies to compromise conflicting interests among top power-holders and to keep most of the population impotent. To accomplish this, they do everything possible to divorce planning from human rights and from the democratic processes of electoral and legislative politics. For them, private planning is something done by big business alone, as distinguished from small business, nonprofit enterprises, labor, cooperatives, voluntary associations and other nongovernmental sectors of civil society. Public planning, in turn, is seen in segmental terms that deny a comprehensive approach to either local or national planners, subordinate both to the short-term interests of the rich and the powerful, and reserve transnational planning as the privileged domain of transnational corporations.

In the hands of autocratic planners, management is an exercise in hierarchy, command and manipulation. Budgeting is an esoteric device for obscuring not only social costs but even the activities on which money is spent. When reforms are needed, autocrats seek solutions through technical reorganizations isolated from broader values and pressures. They see communication as an exercise in top-down indoctrination and top-top networking among the powerful, the wealthy and their far-flung research agencies. For them, leadership is the province of faceless powerholders operating behind the scenes and on-stage actors who project charismatic images of superiority and machismo. As for democracy, they contend that enough of that, perhaps even too much, is provided by the formal machinery of representative government.

In truly democratic planning, however, *the majority of the population is empowered to articulate their common interests and guide their collective future.* This might be called the "empowerment theory of democratic planning."

Corporate leaders never doubt the power of planning. For them, planning is much more than an exercise in analyzing trends and alternatives; it is an integral part of all the managerial processes: decision-making, communicating, organizing, evaluating, developing staff, handling external relations, and mobilizing and utilizing resources. Strategic, tactical and operational planning—both short- and long-range—are ways to get results. Among the hierarchy of desired results, the most important are usually more money and power for corporate leaders and their organizations.

Progressive leaders often fail to focus on management. Unwittingly, they pick up autocratic managerial styles. Many of our best friends think that specialized technical knowledge, intuition and a feeling for human relations and politics are all one needs to help guide a complex undertaking. Some think that a large corporation can be democratized merely by putting a few labor, consumer or government people on its board of directors. While most of these things are essential, they are not enough. In our judgment, *democratic planning cannot come to fruition without democratic management.* This is as true for nonprofit and voluntary organizations as for profit-seeking corporations and government agencies.

Although democratic management is still in its infancy, a few concepts are becoming clear. To combat autocratic management, it is desirable to reduce unnecessary hierarchy, increase multilevel participation at all decision-making stages, encourage the free flow of information and have independent labor unions.

Some degree of hierarchy is necessary in any organization, particularly in a complex system. Yet any amount of hierarchy can foster delusions of grandeur among the "higher-ups." These delusions can best be combated by lateral relations of shared responsibility (sometimes referred to in organization theory as "heterarchy" or "polyarchy"),[1] the encouragement of counterbalancing hierarchies, and by geographical decentralization of authority. It is also necessary to uproot the myth of a single, central planning agency. No representative panel, chief executive, budget agency, accounting office or advisory or research staff could, by itself, carry out all the many functions of central planning. Nor can a chief executive or governing council simply impose on subordinate agencies the coordination of their plans. Rather, the functions of each are necessary parts of "central guidance clusters."[2] As Mary Parker Follett proposed over half a century ago, coordination should be "a process of auto-governed activity—the reciprocal relating of all factors."[3]

A popular form of fool's-gold democracy is for managers to encourage participation by the managed *after* the broad decisions have already been made at the top; others are then encouraged to fight about small details. While helping to polish the managers' self-images, this kind of manipulation cannot fool all the nonmanagers all the time. Nor can it bring the managers themselves into contact with the many realities best understood by their subordinates. This is one of the reasons why Mary Parker Follett urged participation from the very beginning. "The process of the interpenetration of policies," she wrote, "must begin before they are completed, while they are still in the formative stage." When this approach is attempted, it can broaden the vision and unleash the cognitive powers of the managed. This educational process may take time, and it will invariably undermine traditional managerial prerogatives. But over the long run, it can add to an organization's effectiveness and efficiency.

Since information is always a source of power, it rarely flows freely through an organization. Bureaucrats cling tightly to privileged information. Technicians use specialized jargon to keep others from "interfering" with whatever they are doing. The rules needed by any formal organization indirectly foster the falsification of records by those engaged in rule-breaking. Information systems, as Russell Ackoff pointed out in his classic "Management Misinformation Systems," may produce huge amounts of garbage.[4] The annual reports of corporations and government agencies mix objective information with slanted data and outright disinformation. Budgeting and accounting, the most important of their information systems, tend to be still more deceptive. Thus the highest priority in the invention of democratic management is to democratize budgeting and accounting.

The best place to start is government. Program budgeting should be used more widely, but with clear descriptions rather than rhetoric to identify programs. Like most local and state governments, the federal government should be required to have both a capital budget and an operating budget, rather than be allowed to continue lumping all outlays together. All government agencies should be obliged to set up capital accounts that bring into the open the basic facts on the land, facilities and inventories under their control. Each should be required to develop *total* impact statements estimating—qualitatively as well as quantitatively—the direct and indirect costs and benefits of each capital and operating program. No agency can do this by itself, however. Good result area information—whether on the environment, inflation, unemployment, health, education, crime or social structure —can be properly collected only by general statistical agencies like the Census Bureau or the Bureau of Labor Statistics. The social-indicator movement of the mid-1960s, energized by people who saw improved quality-of-life data as an aid in rational planning, tried to promote this kind of collection. Although a little progress has since been made, old-line economists and statisticians have taken command of the movement and steered it toward fixation on traditional definitions and monetary measurement.[5]

A reconstructed social-indicator movement is sorely needed—one rooted in popular politics and oriented toward the replacement of obsolete concepts and the invention of a progressive "social calculus" or "social accounting." An important part of this effort would be a great leap forward in providing improved "input-output" data, as pioneered by Wassily Leontiev, on the changing relations among economic sectors. And as Jay Gould has pointed out (with strong support from Si Kahn, the activist/expert on community organizing), "The test of any true commitment to national planning would be the encouragement of regional [input-output] studies for all areas" of the country.[6]

Labor unions are strange intruders in any formal organization. As representatives of nonmanagerial employees, they offer a profound challenge to autocratic management. The slow and reluctant acceptance of collective bargaining—that is, industrial democracy—has been an integral part of the historic transformation of earlier capitalism's "dark Satanic mills" into the modern workplace. It has brought employees from many different organizations together into labor and political movements that have helped strengthen and protect political democracy.

Today, however, the processes of industrial democracy are being reversed. Corporations have learned how to entice some union leaders into helping management "keep workers in line." They are replacing employees with machines, conducting sophisticated union-busting drives or moving to areas where labor unions are not tolerated.

Some unions, unfortunately, are themselves afflicted by autocratic styles of union management. Their officials sometimes prefer weak unions made up of docile locals in contrast with stronger and expanding unions whose new members might threaten to replace the present leadership. These weaknesses are compounded when union leaders accept bribes from management or cooperate with racketeers. The situation becomes still more critical when leaders and members allow racism, sexism or both to undermine the solidarity needed for successful unionism.

Democratic management, therefore, means that unions must free themselves from the iron grip of prejudice and oligarchic management. They should take the offensive in organizing the unorganized. Instead of concentrating entirely on wages, hours and working conditions, they should broaden the collective-bargaining agenda to include the quality of work, employee training, management development, plans for expansion or contraction and workplace democracy as a whole.

Our empowerment theory is based on concepts that have emerged from this practice, both in our own countries (the United States and India) and in others that we have often visited or carefully studied. Among the major elements in this practice are (1) a growing commitment to human rights and needs as guiding values for democratic planning; (2) the effort to build a popular political party able to unite people behind plans that express this commitment; (3) active participation by all private sectors, not big business alone; (4) public planning that is locally rooted, has national scope and can take part in transnational decision-making; and (5) the nurturing of management and budgeting approaches that break with established traditions of hierarchy and bureaucracy. Last but not least are new styles of (6) educating hierarchs and bureaucrats, (7) horizontal communication among society's lower and middle strata and (8) working toward more responsible and accountable leadership.

COMMITMENT TO HUMAN RIGHTS

For most planners, particularly those concentrating on economics or land use, "human rights is another subject." But without an overriding commitment to human rights, planning is destined to be technocratic and bureaucratic at best—and at worst dehumanized.

Fortunately, the idea of rights as a guide to planning is slowly beginning to mature. In 1980 the Progressive Alliance, with the help of the Institute of Policy Studies, revived the eight-point Economic Bill of Rights used by Franklin Roosevelt in 1944 as preparation for his fourth-term election victory. More recently, as part of its excellent "rebuilding America program," the International Association of Machinists has articulated a bill of technological rights. In *Beyond the Wasteland,* Samuel Bowles, David Gordon and Thomas Weisskopf have published a miscellaneous set of twenty-four economic rights.[7] In *A New Social Contract,* Martin Carnoy, Derek Shearer and Russell Rumberger expand, with some updating, FDR's version into a ten-point Economic Bill of Rights resolution to be brought before legislative bodies and the public through city and state initiatives.[8] The new economic program of Democratic Socialists of America concentrates on the right to earn a living. The new Conyers planning legislation articulates this concept as "the right to earn a living at real earnings high enough to provide the purchasing power required for sustainable recovery and a full employment society." It also establishes a supplementary right for all Americans unable to work for pay: "the right to an adequate standard of living that rises with the rising productivity of the society as a whole."

These two basic rights branch out to other economic rights—and to the broader (and less economistic) principles embodied in the U.N. covenants on economic and social rights and civil and political rights. An effort to get ratification of these covenants by the U.S. Senate, even if unsuccessful in the short run, could help us escape the simplistic fallacy of stressing economic rights at the expense of the political, or political rights at the expense of the economic.

The human-rights approach to planning has many advantages. It can (a) help transcend localism and parochialism, (b) place specialties and single issues in their broader context, (c) appeal to the basic moral values on which more-civilized societies would have to be based, and (d) help escape the indignity of the means tests and bottom-up pleadings for compassionate crumbs from top powerholders.

Rights, of course, cannot be *given* through legislation. "Laws and systems of polity," wrote John Stuart Mill more than a century ago in an unprecedented attack on the subjection of women, "always begin by recognizing the relations they find already existing between in- dividuals. They convert what was a mere physical fact into a legal right."[9]

If Mill were alive today, he would be the first to recognize as *physical facts* political movements on behalf of rights not yet estab- lished under law. He would also recognize that proposed laws can be educational instruments in mobilizing people to win, and keep, such protection. That is the way women won many of the rights Mill advocated. That is the way for progress to be made in establishing the right to learn a living.

PRIVATE PLANNING: NOT BY BIG BUSINESS ALONE

"Instead of relying on government, we should provide more incentives for the private sector!"

This is one of the slogans repeated ad nauseam by corporate ideo- logues and neoliberal academics eager to give business more subsidies, usually through federal, state and local government tax deductions (more properly referred to as "tax expenditures"). By "private sec- tor," of course, they mean profit-seeking enterprise.

But the alternatives to government action go far beyond profit- seeking business. They include the full range of all the many sectors outside the formal structure of the state: labor unions, professional and trade associations, cooperatives, voluntary associations (includ- ing political parties), most private schools and hospitals, and all churches and foundations. Thus we have no hesitation in advocating "more incentives for the private sectors of society."

This is the view embodied in a special title of the "Recovery and Full Employment Planning" bill being prepared under the guidance of Congressman John Conyers, a founding member of the Congressio- nal Black Caucus and one of the country's most dedicated and imagi- native proponents of full-employment planning. In this pending pro- posal, recipients of federal incentives are defined to include "not only profit seeking enterprises but also associations or other organizations representing both employees and the unemployed, non-profit enter- prises, cooperatives and other voluntary associations."

Accordingly, incentives are provided for all the private sectors other than profit-seeking companies. Provision is made for promoting the organization of the unemployed, the expansion of cooperatives and self-help groups, and greater involvement by voluntary and non-profit organizations in various aspects of planning for sustainable recovery and full employment. Above all, a special role is defined for organized labor in redressing the balance between highly developed planning by corporations and government and planning by other private groups. Incentives are mandated to promote such actions by organized labor as

- employee purchase, operation or management of plants or other facilities closed down or abandoned by profit-seeking enterprises;
- the extension of workplace democracy (including experiments in joint management and self-management, as well as management-labor consultation) based on collective-bargaining agreements; and
- more union involvement in housing, education, employee and management training, and the organization of the unemployed and underemployed.

All of these nongovernmental groups are to be eligible for the same broad array of federal incentives now available to business—namely, "contracts, subcontracts, loans, guaranteed loans, tax expenditures, grants and technical and informational assistance provided by any agency established under federal law."

Business, in turn, cannot be neglected. Participation by large companies and transnational corporations is inevitable, and should be brought into the open. The situation is different, however, in the case of small companies and the self-employed, who, comprising the largest number of profit-seeking enterprises, are systematically squeezed by big business and the banks and are constantly living on the brink of foreclosure, bankruptcy, liquidation or take-over. A mandate is therefore given for special plans to provide them with improved access to equity capital, credit, public contracts and subcontracts, and technical and informational assistance.

One of the most obvious principles of democratic planning is that any recipient of public funds should be held accountable for their use. In public contracts, this principle is formally observed by detailed specifications of the work to be done and administrative follow-up by contract managers. With tax deductions, in contrast, this principle is formally overturned: The billions given away through tax shelters become legal entitlements. Sheltered from any form of accountability, the recipients of these entitlements then launch powerful campaigns against Social Security and welfare entitlements for middle- and lower-income people.

The remedy, in our judgment, is to make tax incentives conditional upon certificates of necessity. Thus the billions of tax giveaways for additional investment in productive capacity would be conditioned upon actual performance. This could mean expanded incentives for companies that distinguish themselves by contributing to sustainable recovery and full employment. It would also mean the reduction or take-back of incentives in the case of companies that, like U.S. Steel, use the funds for take-overs and higher executive salaries instead of productive investment.

Another condition for all government incentives—no matter who the recipients may be—should aim at preventing the use of government aid to foster lawbreaking or law evasion. One approach is to require (as in the new "Recovery and Full Employment Planning" bill) law compliance or honesty oaths from the top officers of any organization seeking a government contract, loan or subsidy.

PUBLIC PLANNING:
LOCAL, NATIONAL, TRANSNATIONAL

With a "layer cake" model in their heads, some people see local government as the bottom layer, state government in the middle, and national government at the top.

The only trouble with this imagery, as Morton Grodzins of the University of Chicago pointed out almost 20 years ago, is that it is nonsense. Village, town, city, county, regional, state and national governmental agencies are commingled or intertwined in remarkably complex mazes. Grodzins, a pioneering analyst of American federalism, suggested that we take the layer cake out of our heads and instead think of government as a "marble cake."[10] If federal government is the chocolate in the batter, we can find large strands or small traces throughout. Thus there is little basis for allocating, let us say, education or public assistance to local governments and equal rights or civil rights to the states. There is even less basis (other than demagogic obfuscation) for reserving general scanning of the economy for the federal government.

One of the best ways to avoid undue concentration of federal power is to continue the historical process of strengthening the 15,000 city, county and state planning agencies now in existence. When first established, these agencies concentrated on land-use, zoning and building controls. Over the years, other functions were added: public-facility planning, capital budgeting, highways, social services, environmental protection, promotion of private developments, community involvement, etc. Most of these functions became increasingly dependent on state and federal aid. Yet few local governments or their planning advisers have ever attempted to parallel even the limited economic planning carried on by the Office of Management and Budget and the Council of Economic Advisers.

Some old-time planning technicians think that, in the words from the song in *Oklahoma,* "we've gone about as far as we can go." We believe that the entire country has a long way to go—and that many hundreds of local governments are already seeking, even beginning, to lead the way. Hence the authors of *A New Social Contract* look forward to "a new positive role for local planning commissions that includes a creative use of zoning, but goes beyond it . . . and breaks the hold of the downtown business/Chamber of Commerce/real-estate interest over the city planning process."[11]

One tool to do this is the local development agreement. Some cities —like Santa Monica, where author Derek Shearer is a city planning commissioner—give private developers the right to build shopping centers, office buildings, industrial development parks or luxury housing only if they, in return, contract to provide middle-income housing, a public park or day-care center, or train a specified number of the locally unemployed for the construction jobs involved. Also, the authors suggest, "every large- and middle-sized city should have its own development bank and/or a public development corporation to engage in enterpreneurial activities."

For our part, we look forward to the time, well before the end of the century, when local governments and their planning staffs will scan the entire local economy and plan for its short- and long-term future. This will involve

1. initiating publicly debated assessments of unmet needs for additional employment, goods and services and real income;

2. conducting labor-availability surveys to find out how much unemployed or underemployed labor is being wasted;

3. setting local goals for whatever employment and output increases (by sectors) might be needed for short-term recovery and longer-term full employment;

4. building reservoirs of needed works and services (both public and private) to help meet these needs;

5. mobilizing private and public financial resources to meet these needs to the fullest extent possible, without relying exclusively on public funds from larger units of government; and

6. mobilizing whatever additional resources may be needed from state and federal government.

In all these activities, priorities should be developed for people who have suffered the most from discrimination, for areas of the worst unemployment and for distressed economic sectors. The many problems involved should be brought fully into the open at community public forums and aired through the press, radio and television.

No local area, to paraphrase John Donne, is "an island, entire of itself" but rather "a piece of the continent, a part of the main." No neighborhood's present or future can be understood without seeing it in the context of the whole city. He or she who is "street-wise" only can be system-stupid. It is also stupid to pretend that a metropolis or state can be understood apart from the national and international context. The marble cake cannot be reduced to single strands of vanilla, chocolate or anything else.

To attain broader perspectives, local governments need new kinds of help from state and federal agencies. Thus, the proposed democratic planning legislation provides for pass-through planning grants for the states. A new Council of the States would allocate these grants to foster in every participating state the kind of local planning functions we have referred to above. Each state would also try to integrate the many local plans and take part in state- and regionwide assessments of unmet needs. Through such positive actions, it might be possible to replace the beggar-thy-neighborhood schemes that are the hard core of present-day state planning.

California and a few other states have already taken the initiative in tapping the huge financial resources of public and private pensions funds. The possibilities of using these funds to finance public and private developments in the public interest are enormous,[12] but the full fruition of this powerful idea depends upon a public guaranty to protect the contributors to the pension funds. This FHA-type federal guaranty, now available only on mortgages, is beyond the scope of most state governments. Besides, it can be rationally provided only on a national basis. The assumption of such a responsibility, as provided in the Conyers planning legislation, could be handled in a manner that would foster more constructive planning initiatives by both state and local governments.

Behind all the flaming rhetoric on the scope of national government, there is substantial agreement on one theme: the need for positive federal action. The differences center around the *type* of action. Reaganoids favor the expansion of uncontrolled tax entitlements for the rich, more military spending, larger subsidies for American capital in other countries, overt and covert protection of transnational investments, monitoring of dissidents and prying into personal affairs. While going along with part of this package, neoliberals stress federal "industrial policy," by which they mean more corporatist planning of industrial growth, with government footing the bill and a few national labor leaders giving their blessing. Liberals favor the expansion of social programs and public works. A few old-time radicals, still enamored of the command economies set up in preindustrial societies, see Cuba, China or the Soviet Union as their models.

We see democratic national planning in America departing sharply from each of these formulas. First of all, the federal government should neither seek the omnipotence of command economies nor allow itself to be reduced to impotence vis-à-vis Big Business. Second, there is no need for any serious growth in the size of federal government (other than that resulting from population and productivity increases). What is needed instead is a major *shift* of resources and employment from the military-industrial complex and the agencies of domestic and foreign repression to meeting unmet needs for productive investment and improved social programs.

An immediate need is the creation of permanent policies and institutions to foster sustainable recovery from recession or depression in the United States or any of its areas. Part of this task can be carried out by measures that require no additional public spending or revenue loss. These include reduced interest rates, tax reductions for lower-

and middle-income groups, voluntary work-sharing, the elimination of compulsory overtime, and the reduction of the weekly working hours on which overtime is based. More important will be the creation of a permanent Works and Services Administration to help finance public and private works and service projects to improve the infrastructure of America's public works, human services, private industries and natural resources. The Conyers planning measure includes both of these provisions. It also provides for emergency aid "to protect both the unemployed and farmers, merchants and other small business people victimized by recession or depression against utility cutoffs, the loss of housing through eviction or mortgage foreclosures, and the loss of health insurance or unemployment compensation."

Both short- and long-term measures should be combined in a national Recovery and Full Employment Plan to bring together—and at the same time provide guidance and financial help for—the multitudinous plans of local, regional and state agencies. The national plan would provide the framework for fiscal, monetary and anti-inflation policies geared to recovery and full employment. It should be backed up by statutory guidelines to relieve a democratized Federal Reserve System of its present dependence on the monetary fads of shortsighted commercial bankers. It should be based on a statutory commitment to support an international economic order based on rising living standards, as contrasted with the shortsighted austerity policies now imposed on many countries by the International Monetary Fund and World Bank.

THE PINCER APPROACH TO BUREAUCRACY

The literature of public administration and business management brims over with constructive proposals for overcoming the stifling aspects of public and private bureaucracies. So do the filing cabinets and wastepaper baskets to which such ideas may be unceremoniously consigned. Without support from above and below, good ideas are driven out of circulation.

Viable proposals for bureaucratic reform can emerge, in our judgment, only from a social environment with enough antibodies to combat the diseases inherent in bureaucracy and nourish democratic organizational reform. This kind of environment can be created through an application of what we call the "pincer approach" to bureaucracy:

1. general guidance and careful monitoring by elected executives and legislators on behalf of people-oriented plans and policies, and

2. public-interest activism in the form of legislative initiatives and participatory bill-drafting as well as the full variety of consultative arrangements.

When these two forces are connected by common values and a popular party or coalition—*and only then*—we have a pincer. Under these conditions, bureaucrats will respond more fully to their own consciences and to popular rather than corporatist interests. The sense of public responsibility and accountability may then sprout and blossom.

Each part of the pincer, of course, needs more elasticity than a stick and more creative vigor than a wet noodle. Executives who try to democratize a subordinate bureaucracy by formal reorganization alone will soon learn the truth in the maxim that the more things change, the more they remain the same. Far better to set a shining example of dedication to efficient service in the public interest.

The United States is a country where the normal channels of public activism are more widely used than in any other large country of constitutional capitalism. These channels include voter registration, candidate selection, electioneering, and efforts to influence elected and appointed officials through lobbying, petitioning and consultation. Yet popular interests can often best be served only when activists also engage in marches, demonstrations, strikes or, in some cases, open civil disobedience. Rarely do technique-oriented planners recognize this simple truth.

But local activists need to communicate with others to produce national changes. In the United States, the nuclear freeze, jobs-with-peace, neighborhood and tenant movements provide varying examples of a bottom-sideways communication. In each, localism is overcome through some sort of national organization in which the inevitable tendencies toward oligarchy are combated. Each uses nonmedia and small media channels instead of relying on the major mass media.[13]

This is quite different from the top-top networking practiced by transnational corporations and the global banking community, and the nationwide linkages among American corporate, military and political leaders. It involves not the VIPs but rather the great majority of middle- and low-income people at the bottom of the Eiffel Tower pyramid of wealth and power. Like the top-top (or horizontal) communication of the elites and their technocratic aides, it is oriented toward developing common purposefulness. But the basic purpose itself is entirely different—namely, to democratize the structure of money and power.

If this is to be done, the immobilizing effects of most mass media must be countered by message systems that mobilize and energize. Theory, rational analysis and open debate in community forums are all necessary. But the majority of a people can never be brought together at the intellectual or verbal levels alone. For Gandhi, personal example was the message. And this was reinforced by cultural communion—music, poetry and religious ritual. What has happened to the songs of the earlier civil-rights movement? Where is the poetry of the future?

By the end of the century, might we escape the fragmented approach of those of us who, during the past two decades, have advocated in quick succession new economic, informational, communication, technological and political orders? Might we invent global planning for a *new international order in holistic terms?*

In our judgment, no visions of this type can be made real through sole reliance on top-top communication in the United Nations or other intergovernmental organizations. People-to-people communication is also essential to make the whole world truly kin. This would not only mean more tourism, more intermarriages and more educational, cultural and scientific exchanges; it would also require people-to-people forums on a regional and global scale and the transnational organization of labor in its confrontations with transnational capital.[14]

Movement away from top-top and top-down modes never meant away from dependence on charismatic leadership, too. That would be no easy task in a media-driven society.

During the 1960s and 1970s, an antileadership reaction set in against the hero-macho-charisma model. Some activists revolted against the very idea of leadership, organization or both; the world was to be saved rather by the unled, unorganized spontaneity of the masses.

But more constructive models of multiple leadership and honeycomb (rather than hierarchical) organizational structure have also come into being. In the affinity groups of the antinuke and antiwar movement at the Greenham Common in England and many places in the United States, there is no one leader, spokesperson or executive committee. When feasible, decisions are reached through consensus. In the National Coalition Against Domestic Violence, the Ethics Committee has been developing "a cooperative rather than competitive process, through which all members could join in effectively considering the organization's leadership and . . . reflect the ethic of empowering women, of empowering each group member."[15] In some neighborhood and workplace groups, people operate on the principle of leadership rotation. The superior-inferior relationship is supplanted by "reciprocal superiority." Thus many people can have alternately what John Stuart Mill called "the pleasure of leading and being led on the path of development."[16] Still more can synergistically exercise, in the words of Mary Parker Follett, "power *with*" as an alternative to "power *over*"—that is, "a jointly developed power, a coactive, not a coercive power."[17] More often than not, these new forms of leadership and organization are initiated by women seeking alternatives to patriarchy.

TOWARD A PLANNING SOCIETY

"But what would democratic planning cost?"

For the super-privileged, the cost would be a reduction in power and in the ability to subordinate the larger interests of society to their own drives for personal gratification and institutional aggrandizement. This loss to a few would be counterbalanced by enormous benefits for the many. These benefits would come in the form of more security in the world, more economic security at home and larger opportunities to take part in decisions affecting themselves and their families, workplaces, communities, country and world.

In economic terms, democratic planning would mean major shifts in the use of resources. With major cuts in the enormous wastes the country now suffers,[18] full recovery and full employment could be attained with *no increases in the absolute or relative size of the federal deficit.*

Another important shift—too often obscured by rhetoric from both Right and Left—must also be mentioned: *a general change in the structure of corporate profitability*. On the one hand, the **rates** of profit on invested capital would be reduced by higher wages, less market shortages and anti-inflation measures. Many companies would no longer be able to get excessively high rates of profit through high administered prices or other practices that milk a market dry and undermine long-term profitability.

On the other hand, total profits (as distinguished from profit rates) would be larger. With expanding market demand, more output and less recession or localized depression, even smaller companies could aspire to more stable profits (or, in technical terms, discounted cash flow) over the long run. This shift would be in tune with the historic change from enormous profit (and loss) rates in the earlier phases of industrial capitalism to the smaller rates associated with mass production. It would induce American companies to follow the current Japanese policy of competing in international markets through low profit rates as well as high quality.

But when? Isn't all this highly improbable?

Planning for the improbable is often the only way to make the highly desirable more feasible. From the viewpoint of the aeons, life on this planet was highly improbable. Since then, some of the most important of humankind's advances—from the freeing of slaves and serfs to the rights of suffrage and the many cures for contagious diseases—have been cases of the improbable being converted into the actual. Short-term feasibility is the domain of alienation, and probability the realm of entropy, oppression and nuclear devastation.

Throughout the world, fortunately, there are people and groups moving toward the many kinds of structural change that challenge patriarchal, bureaucratic and corporatist planning. Many of them directly attack well-entrenched traditions of male, white, Western or capitalist superiority. Some concentrate on neighborhood activism, workplace democracy or corporate responsibility. Some are rank-and-file trade unionists seeking a substitute for "headquarters unionism." A few are organizing the unemployed on behalf of the right to earn a living. Others are trying to extend, not merely defend, civil rights and civil liberties. A few are developing new bills of rights: economic, technological, informational. A growing number are following the example of Mohandas Gandhi and Martin Luther King, Jr., in nonviolent militant opposition to militarism. Some are trying to invent a world order in which the superpowers negotiate nonviolent adjustments of their inevitable differences.

These efforts aim at both substantive and procedural democracy. They are already contributing to the invention, slow and piecemeal though it be, of democratic planning in practice. In the words of John Dewey, the philosopher of American pragmatism, by this route might lie not the planned economy but rather "a planning society."[19]

Notes

1. Hazel Henderson, *The Politics of the Solar Age: Alternatives to Economics* (Garden City, N.Y.: Anchor, 1981); Frederick Thayer, *An End to Hierarchy and Competition,* 2d ed. (New York: Franklin Watts, 1981); and William G. Scott and David K. Hart, *Organizational America* (Boston: Houghton Mifflin, 1979).
2. Bertram Gross, "Central Guidance Clusters," *The State of the Nation* (London: Tavistock, 1966; and New York: Barnes & Noble, 1966). Also in Raymond A. Bauer, ed., *Social Indicators* (Cambridge, Mass.: M.I.T. Press, 1966).
3. "Individualism in a Planned Society," in Henry Metcalf and Lyndall Urwick, eds., *Dynamic Administration: The Collected Papers of Mary Follett* (New York: Harper, 1942).
4. Russell Ackoff, "Management Misinformation Systems," *Management Science,* Dec. 1967.
5. One of the first proposals on social accounting, as distinguished from indicators, appears in Bertram Gross, *The State of the Nation,* op. cit. For a general review of this subject (now somewhat dated), see Bertram Gross and Jeffrey Straussman, "The Social Indicators Movement," *Social Policy,* September/October 1974.
6. Jay Gould, *Input-Output Data Bases: Uses in Business and Government* (New York and London: Garland STPM Press, 1979).
7. *Beyond the Wasteland* (New York: Anchor, 1983).
8. *A New Social Contract* (New York: Harper & Row, 1983).
9. John Stuart Mill, *The Subjection of Women* (Cambridge: M.I.T. Press, 1970 edition), 7.
10. Morton Grodzins, *The American System: A New View of Government in the United States* (Chicago: Rand McNally, 1966).
11. *A New Social Contract,* 203.
12. Maurice Zeitlin, "Democratic Investment," *Democracy,* June 1982. An important critique by David Vogel appeared in a subsequent issue of *Democracy.*
13. Kusum Singh, "Mass Line Communication: Liberation Movements in China and India," in George Gerbner and Marsha Siefert, eds., *World Communications: A Handbook* (New York: Longman, 1983).
14. Kusum Singh and Bertram Gross, "The MacBride Report: The Results and

Response," in George Gerbner and Marsha Siefert, eds., *World Communications: A Handbook* (New York: Longman, 1983).

15. Linda M. Shaw, "Choosing Leaders—A Cooperative Model," *Aegis: Magazine on Ending Violence Against Women* (Box 21033, Washington, D.C. 20009), Winter 1982.

16. John Stuart Mill, *The Subjection of Women,* op. cit., 95.

17. Mary Parker Follett, "Power," in Henry Metcalf and Lyndall Urwick, eds., *Dynamic Administration: The Collected Papers of Mary Follett,* op. cit.

18. In summing up "the costs of corporate power," Samuel Bowles, David Gordon and Thomas Weisskopf estimate total waste in 1980 as $1.2 trillion (45% of total GNP), stemming from unutilized labor hours, surplus supervisory hours, wasted labor effort, productive inefficiency, and excesses in military spending, advertising, energy use and expenditures on health care and crime control. *Beyond the Wasteland,* op. cit.

19. John Dewey, "The Economic Basis of the New Society," in Joseph Ratner, ed., *Intelligence in the Modern Society: John Dewey's Philosophy* (New York: Random House, 1939), 431–432.

19

How to Expand Political Participation

Curtis B. Gans

Historians are unlikely to view Ronald Reagan as one of the great democratic spirits of the age.

Yet, it is indisputably true that one of the by-products of his administration has been a surge in voter participation—a temporary reversal of the two-decade-old trend that saw a smaller and smaller fraction of eligible Americans cast their ballots in both presidential and congressional elections since 1960.

That such a reversal has occurred is clear. In 1982, the nation experienced a 3.6-percent jump in voter participation, cutting by one-third the 10-percent decline in voting in off-year elections since 1966. After two decades in which more than 15 million Americans dropped out of the political process, 1982 saw a net increase of more than 9 million voters. Blacks, for the first time in history, voted at nearly their proportion in the population; others—Hispanics, farmers, unemployed workers, and Republicans—also showed marked increases in participation: and as of this writing, a similar, though perhaps not as marked, increase in both black voting and that of the general public is expected in 1984.

That this reversal, too, is temporary is also clear, but perhaps not as self-evident.

Almost all of the 1982 increase in voter turnout is directly attributable to the degree to which the policies of the Reagan adminsitration polarized the American body politic; angered blacks, other minorities, farmers, environmentalists and women; caused fear among the recently unemployed and incipiently unemployed; and propelled many to the polls who had either lost or had not acquired the habit of voting.

Curtis B. Gans is director of the Committee for the Study of the American Electorate.

It is because the increase in voter turnout in 1982 was inescapably attributable to anger and fear, rather than hope, that ensures that this increase will be ephemeral.

Voting is by nature a religious act. It rests on the belief that despite the evidence that an overwhelming majority of elections are not decided by one vote, the individual's vote will make a difference—that somehow the course of history, the betterment of the individual's life, the quality of the community or outcome of a particular issue or interest will be determined by the act of casting one's ballot.

It is an act of faith in the efficacy of both the political process and the adjudicating process of government.

Voting is also a lowest-common-denominator act.

Those who vote may become more deeply involved in the workings of American democracy as contributors or participants. Nonvoters seldom do. Sustained voter participation is thus the key to the involved voluntarism upon which democracy depends, not for its existence but for its health.

Thus, a surge in voting predicated on anger and fear (or, for that matter, the appearance of a black candidate or a particular issue on the ballot) is no basis for continued voter and citizen participation. Rather, the surge in voting in 1982 (with the exception of the slight increase in Republican voting in that year) represents the continuation of a trend where a varying number of citizens, usually smaller, have voted negatively since 1964—that is, they have voted to reject the person or policies of one candidate (Goldwater, McGovern) or administration (Johnson, Nixon, Carter, Reagan) after another.

It is thus likely that after the polarizing years of the Reagan presidency, voter and citizen participation will resume its decline. For none of the underlying problems that have undermined citizens' faith in the American political process have been addressed or solved.

In a sense, it is not surprising that voter participation in America is low and has been declining. On one level, the United States is one of the few democracies in the world that puts the entire burden of both registration and voting on the citizen and makes casting a ballot a two-step process. It is also one of the few countries in which the major political parties are so heterogeneous that they inadequately reflect either broad class or issue interests.

On another level, after Vietnam and Watergate; and after Johnson, Nixon, Carter and Reagan; in a society whose issues have grown increasingly complex with no concomitant clarity in addressing them; a society in which institutions have grown increasingly large and remote and in which the citizen feels increasingly impotent in coping with them; in a society whose transportation and telecommunications move with blurring speed without pause or context; and in a polity in which increasingly narrow interest groups get the majority of public attention while mediating institutions such as political parties grow increasingly weaker and incapable of separating the wheat from the chaff either in defining issues for public consumption or implementing public policy, it is little wonder that fewer and fewer people go to the polls.

Sadly, not voting is becoming a rational act.

But as the electorate grows smaller, the influence of the narrow interests—those with an ax to grind or a vested financial stake—grows proportionately greater, and the danger is that American government will become a government of, for and by the few.

In theory, reversing this trend sounds easy.

After all, if faith in the efficacy of government is at the heart of citizen involvement (and, conversely, lack of such faith at the root of citizen disenchantment), then what appears to be needed are candidates who, in their campaigns, can address the problems the public perceives and deliver on their programmatic promises once elected.

For if it is desirable that candidates address real and perceived needs, there must be a consensual public agenda. There is presently none. If the candidate, once in office, is to deliver the goods, there must be some organized force that exercises some degree of discipline to implement policy. None now exists. And if this is all to be intelligible to the voter, there must be a mechanism of both public and political communications that focuses on something broader than the opposition's warts or the most telegenic event of the moment.

It might be well to look at each of these problems separately.

THE PROBLEM OF POLICY

It is fashionable now—and has been for some years past—to lament the quality of the candidates proffered to the public in both presidential and lesser elections. We are, the critics say, offered no real choices; candidates either pander to special interests or are unable to articulate a coherent vision of what a good and just America might be.

The critics, of course, are not wrong. But the problem is not with the quality of the candidate; rather, it is with the state of the political art. To put it simply, there is no present consensual vision of what a good and just America should be.

For three decades, from the 1940s until the 1970s, there was such a consensus. Emerging from the New Deal, the nation accepted the economics of Keynes, the welfare state of Roosevelt, the belief in federal government intervention to solve specific social ills and contain foreign expansionism, a global role foisted upon the United States in World War II by fascism and accepted gladly in the World War II aftermath when the specter of global communism loomed on the horizon. What differences existed within that consensus were ones of degree, not kind. Republicans, by and large, were more isolationist than Democrats in foreign affairs, less interventionist than Democrats in domestic affairs, but no large group questioned the basic premises of the consensus.

The events of the 1960s revealed the inadequacies of the policies underlying the consensus. The war in Vietnam showed the limitations of American ability and resources to control events throughout the world. Persistent stagflation showed the limitations of Keynesian economics. An overburdened federal budget, declining productivity and the erosion of the quality of American life revealed the limitations of the welfare state. And the newly emergent problems of the environment—the atrophying American city, among others—showed that there were negative by-products of the litany of growth and of attacking each social problem piecemeal without looking at the long-term effects of each particular solution.

But if the consensus was destroyed, it has not been replaced.

What all this has to do with the quality of political leadership is that for three decades a candidate for office had a sure sense of what was right and wrong on a range of policy matters and could articulate that position clearly, seeming in the process to be exerting leadership. Because what the candidate was advocating was part of a national consensus, he did not need to stray far from the political center, something a candidate does only at his peril.

The problem of the present is that there is no similar consensus to which a candidate can repair, and the examples of Eugene McCarthy and George McGovern seem too strongly emblazoned on the politicians' consciousness for any but the brave or foolhardy to get too experimental. It is simply easier to attack an opponent's weaknesses or yield to the clamor of interest.

The deeper problem is that the old consensus was forged by Franklin Roosevelt in office as a response to the great crises of his day— the Great Depression and World War II. The public was largely willing, in a time of crisis, to suspend its skepticism and chart a new course.

While the crisis of leadership in the present may well be as serious as the crisis of events in the 1930s and 1940s, it will not be events but an act of will—of leaders getting together and forging a new consensus —that will create a new sense of national direction. And this, while essential, is a very difficult thing to do.

Yet, until there is a defined consensus that goes beyond Keynes, redefines the role of government and citizen, takes a longer view in attacking social problems and finds a creative, if more limited, role for the United States in the world, it is unlikely that people will be satisfied with their candidates for some time to come.

THE PROBLEM OF PARTIES

If there has been one consistent strain in political literature of the past few years, it has been the political scientists' loud lament at the decline of the political party. They have been quite rightly concerned about the cacophony of special pleading and the lack of mediating institutions able to sort out the important political concerns from the others. They are correct in their worry that political parties now exercise no creative role in the development of program and have no effective means of enacting and implementing legislation.

The heyday of the American political party was in the mid- to late 1800s. Since then the party has been in decline. Internal corruption and narrow oligarchic rule mandated the creation of the political primary to give the rank-and-file party member some of the power then wielded by bosses. The New Deal took employment patronage out of the hands of the local party leader and placed it in the hands of the federal bureaucrat. Civil service replaced patronage, and television permitted at least some politicians to appeal to the electorate directly without the filter of party leadership.

While it is possible that the number of primaries, at least in presidential politics, will be reduced (there are already two fewer in 1984), that some power will be restored to local leaders as a result of the inexorable trend toward federalism in the administration of some programs, and that civil service may be modified to permit more changes following elections, the party as an institution will likely never have the authority it once had.

Yet, if some order is to be created out of the present chaotic condition of American politics, and if voters are to have some belief that their votes will matter not simply in the choice of officeholder but in the course of public policy, then the party will have to be resurrected.

It is here that the majority of political scientists are, it says here, wrong. For they have focused almost all of their attention on reforming the procedures of party conduct, especially of nominating presidents, as the means of creating more viable and disciplined parties. The problem is rather the present alignment of the American political party.

In a rational world, the dialogue going on in the political marketplace would be one between the American equivalent of the British Liberal party and the equivalent of British Labor; between the middle-class concerns of greater quality in living conditions and the lower- and middle-class concerns of having an adequate livelihood. What the United States presently has is, on the one hand, right-wing fanatic populism coupled with large corporate greed (the Republican party, tempered only somewhat by the moderation of some of its leaders) and mush (the amalgam of every other interest the Democratic party attempts to represent). It is little wonder that people perceive few relevant choices in the political marketplace.

This condition has occurred for a variety of reasons—the success of the New Deal in lifting many Americans out of poverty and by so doing reducing the appeal of New Deal–type materialistic programs; the splintering of the New Deal coalition of labor, minorities, urban interests and southern conservatives by such things as the civil-rights movement and the war in Vietnam; the emergence of a new middle class of educated professional and white-collar workers who have an outlook of their own that is adequately represented by neither political party; and the labor movement and its split between those who vote their pocketbooks and those who vote their fears.

It has also occurred because of the dominance of two major families —the Rockefellers and the Kennedys—over the affairs of the liberal wings of their respective parties. While both of these families have contributed greatly to the welfare of the nation, their dominating presence has been an inhibitor of constructive change within those parties. So long as Rockefeller was the dominant force within the liberal wing of the Republican party, no other liberal had a chance for real power. And because Rockefeller believed the media could carry him to the presidency, there was no organizational effort among moderate and liberal Republicans to maintain control of the Republican party at the grass-roots level. The result was that the right-wing populism organized by Goldwater in 1964 and nurtured by Ronald Reagan in the ensuing years became the dominant force in the Republican party. Similarly, because the Kennedy family was the dominant force in the liberal wing of the Democratic party and there was always a Kennedy heir apparent to the presidency, it was next to impossible for other innovative leadership to emerge.

But whatever the historical reasons for the present condition of partisan politics, the fact remains: There will be no rational debate about relevant directions for public policy, there will be no effective way to develop or implement programs, unless and until the Republican party becomes broader and the Democratic party becomes narrower, or until a third party of the type that John Anderson promised but singularly failed to deliver appears on the American scene.

THE PROBLEM OF TECHNOLOGY

Part of the weakness of the American political party derives directly from what constitutes modern campaign techniques. It is also one reason fewer Americans cast their ballots.

On one level, political campaigning has become so sophisticated that campaign managers target only likely voters for their causes; people who haven't previously voted, or seem in any given situation unlikely to vote, are given no attention whatsoever. Thus, by inattention coupled with increased alienation of a portion of the voting community in each election, the voter poll gets smaller and smaller.

Perhaps of greater significance is the trend toward a candidate-oriented rather than party-oriented campaign. Increasingly, the concomitants for entry into the political marketplace are money, a pollster and a media adviser. The money buys television time, the pollster determines the candidate's strengths and the opponent's weaknesses, and the media adviser packages television commercials that exploit the candidate's strengths and the opponent's shortcomings. The result is a political process that by virtue of cost limits access to the few and by virtue of methodology is totally unresponsive to anything but the desire of the individual candidate to win.

The central actor in all of this is not the candidate or party but the political consultant (the media adviser), whose sole aim is to win in order to prove his or her effectiveness and gain additional clients and new revenue. The result is, on the one hand, tactics of negativism that, used right, work in the sense that they achieve victory for some candidates, but in the process denigrate all candidates and the political enterprise itself. On the other hand, this approach makes the parties impotent, robbing them of any role in the developing of candidates and policies and the disciplining of membership for the enactment of program.

The question herein raised is an offshoot of what is probably the central question of this generation. Not all technology can be seen as constituting progress, and the central problem of this age is to sort out which does and which doesn't and to bring that which doesn't under control. This is no less true in the area of politics, for unless the technology of politics and especially the technology of media are brought under control, it is likely that the centripetal forces of individual and special interests will continue to rip the American body politic apart.

THE PROBLEM OF COMMUNICATION

Much has been written about the failure of television in covering political campaigns: their nightly-news tendency to concentrate on the horse-race aspects of political races to the detriment of substance; the choosing of certain candidates above others for coverage; the creation of expectations for candidates' performance rather than the reporting of results; the tendency to announce results before the public has a chance to vote. All of these criticisms are valid to some degree, but they do not strike at the heart of the central problem of political communication—the problems of atomization of American society and the problem of context.

It is probably no coincidence that voter participation has been going down since television became the primary staple of American communications and the primary method of political campaigning. For what television has done more than anything else is to send the majority of the public home to watch the tube rather than continue to participate in community or political activities. As a result, the individual citizen has become a consumer of politics rather than an involved participant, and this in turn has tended to make American politics both more atomized and more selfish. There is no collective to which the individual repairs. His needs are not subordinated to the larger needs of a community or interest. His outlook is not shaped by participation in a collective but by what he chooses of the options which are afforded him as a spectator. In a climate of comparative disengagement, it is little wonder that fewer and fewer Americans find the motivation to vote.

The problem of the uninvolved voter is compounded by the creation of confused voters. Because of the nature of the medium, television news comes to the public in undifferentiated one-and-a-half-minute blips that tend to focus on the visually interesting. By the nature of modern political campaigning, the issues raised by campaign advertising tend to be those that pollsters and campaign consultants believe will most further their cause, whether or not they are most central to the fate of the Republic. And there is no historical context presented from which the viewer can form a judgment of what is important and what is not. Little wonder that a majority of the public often seems confused about both policies and leaders.

Remedying either of these conditions is not a simple task, for the nature of television is not likely to change and the print media (witness *People* and *US* magazines and *USA Today*) are becoming more like television in tending to enhance the visual at the expense of the substantive and to reduce serious content in favor of frills and features.

Only a concentrated effort at civic education in the schools, a rededication to reading and an enormous exercise of constructive will by the journalistic profession are likely to overcome the deleterious effects of the television age.

All of which is to suggest that the problem of low and declining voting is likely to be with us for some time.

It can be mitigated by a number of small steps: reducing the time between the close of registration and voting, or permitting Election Day registration, or, better still, by universal enrollment—eliminating registration altogether. We can and should hold fewer elections and have more polling places and shorter ballots. We can make our registration requirement and polling districts uniform.

But unless and until we address the larger questions of political program, parties, technology and media, voter participation is likely, with brief and short-lived hiatuses, to continue to decline and the question "Suppose we gave an election and no one came?" will have resonance as a real and frightening possibility.

20

Rebuilding the American Commonwealth

Harry C. Boyte

In the fall of 1980, following his nearly victorious populist campaign for the Texas Railroad Commission and before setting out on his quest for the office of Texas secretary of agriculture, Jim Hightower reflected on the reasons for his return from Washington. "Let's face it," he began with an admission in the *Washington Monthly,* "the generation of progressive activists to which I belong, considered by many the most promising in decades, has surprisingly little political power." In explanation, he pointed to the Washingtonian lure that had pulled Sixties activists prematurely onto the terrain of national politics. "We forgot to pack any political power, and too few of us have returned home to get it."

Hightower learned the lesson well. As he put it in the idiom of Texas country folk, "I 'put the chairs in the wagon' to go home." It paid off handsomely in his striking victories in the primary and general elections. Yet Jim Hightower was a rarity indeed in 1982: a leader from the liberal side of the political spectrum who dared raise issues of corporate power—and was rewarded for it. Indeed, the ironies have multiplied.[1]

Against the background of eroding support for Reaganomics, the national coalitions on the democratic left meant to address economic issues—groups like the Progressive Alliance, the Democratic Agenda and COIN—have all but disappeared. The very week of Ronald Reagan's election in 1980, Gallup polls showed public confidence in big business at a new low. As impeccable a conservative as Kevin Phillips argued in the *New York Review of Books* that Reagan's attachment

---

Harry Boyte is the author of *The Backyard Revolution: Understanding the New Citizen Movement* and *Community Is Possible: Repairing America's Roots* (forthcoming).

to "west coast millionaires, mink coats and Cadillac Fleetwoods" would prove his undoing. Yet the Senate Democratic Task Force on the Economy urged an "abandonment of the tradition that state power should be used to counterbalance corporate power" and argued instead for "making government an ally of business." In the various campaigns of leading Democratic party contenders for the presidential nomination, phrases such as "economic democracy" and "corporate power" are no longer even distant echoes.[2]

The problem is deep-rooted. What Hightower described as the "voluntary uprooting" of progressive activists from their native home bases has applied to far more than geographic separation. The dominant language on the liberal left in recent years has been criticism on the one hand: The left is "against" war; militarism; racism; sexism; big business; discrimination against gays; pollution and so forth. On the other hand, progressives are "for" a kind of economism, promising that support for their measures will mean dollars and cents off utility bills and more money for education. Yet for the enormous and volatile "middle-American" constituencies at the center of the American electorate—the family farmers and small business people, the skilled workers, the lower-middle-class Jewish neighborhoods in New York or the Polish-American enclaves in Chicago—economic dislocations are emblematic of deep, traumatic disruptions in values and in their ways of living.

In contrast to the liberal idiom, Ronald Reagan came to power in 1980 as rhetorical champion of "the people." His convention speech invoked the spirit of American rebels like Thomas Paine. Promising "a government that can do the people's work without dominating their lives," he also vowed to "renew the American compact" and rekindle American aspirations. Again and again, Ronald Reagan has decried "abstract economic theories" that ignore "concrete human pain" and slight "simple values" like religious convictions, neighborliness, hard work and family loyalty.[3]

The stark differences in political vocabulary suggest both the reasons for liberal collapse and the lingering appeal of Reaganism, despite the multiple, often dramatic failures of the Reagan program. Yet the key to regaining a momentum toward a more just and open society will involve far more than refashioned language.

Even in the circumstances of today, progressives talk as if one could assume widespread outrage at social injustice and popular confidence in a better future as givens—that people will be roused to action when their "consciousness is raised" about various problems. But it is precisely public principle and public confidence that have eroded with accelerating speed in recent decades, as the very ground of community and identity have weakened.

In such a context, only a return by progressives themselves to the sources of moral renewal and community transformation in America offers hope for a democratic future. These are the positive dimensions of community and, more broadly, the best elements in American populism that articulate communitarian values in social and political terms. Indeed, a great wealth of indigenous American, radical democratic themes still remain to be recovered and remembered, woven through the experiences of the myriad of peoples who have come to inhabit this continent. The challenge ahead is to weave from such threads an alternative vision, different from the capitalism of multinational corporations and the European-style socialism and social democracy of vast public bureaucracies, one that can move from the margins of our political culture to become the new, insurgent mainstream.

The Book of Laughter and Forgetting, the great novel by Czech writer Milan Kundera, rages against the official obliteration of history in Communist countries: "The struggle of man against power is the struggle of memory against forgetting." As Robert Darnton has pointed out, in the Solidarity movement Poles reworked the chronology of history as a central part of regaining a sense of dignity and control over their future. Yet what does it mean to be a citizen of America when our memories disappear through more subtle and less visible processes and the very ground of memory—enduring, continuous relationships nourished and renewed over time—collapses?[4]

Even as late as a generation ago, large parts of the population sustained older traditions of place, religious identity and cultural heritage relatively intact. And the powerful movements of this century—the struggles of workers, of blacks, of women—drew directly upon strong bonds of community life, voluntary organization, ethnicity and religion as the resources with which to mount challenges to concentrated power. Yet recent decades have exacerbated corrosive tendencies long at work. The growth of the mass media, the consumer culture, the mobility of the population and the consolidation of corporate and bureaucratic power on a tremendous scale atomize and marginalize serious alternatives to dominant values and institutions. A deep discouragement has spread through our country, and most Americans focus on those pressing concerns they know only too well: Their children may get into trouble; their closest relationships may end; they may be robbed or assaulted in their own neighborhoods; they may never find work that is meaningful, satisfying and dignified.

Herb Mills, an activist for many years in the fabled Longshoremen's Union in San Francisco who has doubled as historian of the docks and the San Francisco labor movement, tells a story that makes vivid in capsule form the problem facing the progressive movement as a whole. The union, whose legendary battles against the city's elite in the 1930s helped inspire the formation of the Congress of Industrial Organizations, had drawn its strength from the rich and intricate life of the waterfront areas and the work patterns that encouraged a spirit of workers' mutual self-help and cooperation, linked to pride in craft. Along the docks, a maze of storefront churches, missions, reading rooms, saloons, newsstands and other small shops catered to the waterfront workers. The nearby neighborhoods of fishermen and women added to the color and spirit of the area. Small boats, cats, dogs, parrots, bait and tackle shops, marine-supply stores, repair facilities and food-processing plants spread out from the hiring halls on Fisherman's Wharf. "You could always find a card game, dice game or bookie," wrote Mills. "You could always find a new political tract and someone ready to discuss it, a place to drop a crab pot or a place to simply watch the passing parade and the waters of the Bay in solitude."[5]

This was the setting for the union, built on "a relatively tight, self-conscious community, knit together by work, a turf, a commitment to unionism and labor solidarity and a wide range of social activity." In the 1960s, however, the simultaneous development of the waterfront area and the automation of much of the work process of loading and unloading largely shattered the bonds that existed. As the city began to attract the headquarters of such multinational corporations as Southern Pacific, Standard Oil, and Bank of America, the appetite for space proved irresistible. The city's Redevelopment Agency director put it simply: "This land is too valuable to permit poor people to park on it." Skyscrapers began to crowd the shorelines like some giant thicket, and the neighborhoods around the docks quickly disappeared. "Pier after pier on the old Embarcadero was abandoned," explained Mills. "Successive portions of our world were thereafter buried beneath concrete and glass, steel and potted redwoods." Simultaneously, the new technologies of unloading destroyed the informal work groups that had long controlled much of the process, and "deskilled" the work force at the same time. "The need for initiative, ingenuity and innovation is all but eliminated" in the new system, Mills argued. Moreover, "most of the work associated with a modern operation is performed by individuals who can only communicate by radio from the cab of their machines. It's even hard to know who's on the job with you."

Again and again across the country, one hears these sorts of stories from veterans of labor and other movements. Nellie Stone Johnson, a black leader in Minnesota who organized unions during the Great Depression, said that the movement in those years was sustained by "a vision of a communal society where people helped each other out, what we called 'the commonwealth,' which people have forgotten today." But the vision was not abstract; it emerged directly from mutual aid in the community. "During the Great Depression, everybody's house was open. Nobody had anything, but you'd share the pot of beans or whatever as far as it would go. That's where labor's spirit came from." Thus, the erosion of local community has the most far-reaching of consequences: It destroys the foundations on which any decent society must be built.[6]

Conventional progressive approaches are especially unprepared for such eventualities. Liberalism begins with the claims of individual dignity against the arbitrary power and parochialism embedded in community life, fashioning an advocacy of civil liberties and a strong demand for equality of opportunity. The New Deal and the Great Society added a more collective concern for social welfare and redistribution as well. But government programs in the welfare state *substitute* for communal relations, which are assumed to be dissolving in any event. In the dominant progressive imagination, government is overwhelmingly *for* the people, not of and by them.

In the contemporary political climate, however, candidates of the Left will never generate much positive enthusiasm or support as long as their basic message is what *they* will do when elected and what the government should be doing for the society. Appeals to compassion, tolerance and redistributive justice are not sufficient when people fear an uncertain future and believe that the government itself demobilizes and thwarts the democratic impulse. The Right's invocation of a communal past when life was simpler is full of hypocrisy and cynicism. Indeed, it forms a Madison Avenue version of community, the substitution of afterglow image for a living substance that is fading away. But in a time of drift and despair, such imagery strikes a more responsive chord than do calls for larger bureaucracies and more centralization of power.

To tap once again the latent generosity of the American people, our politics must consist of more than proposals for humane priorities, though such proposals are essential. And to build a more democratic society, we must develop instruments other than electoral races, though candidates can be an important part of the many-sided effort to galvanize constituencies for action. A rebirth of democratic politics will mean, most crucially, a transformation of the meaning of democracy itself—an understanding of democratic action as a process that is not mainly achieved by casting ballots and sending checks to lobbying groups. If we are to create a new mainstream, ordinary people throughout America must learn to become activists in their own behalf, taking leadership, challenging the experts, acquiring the skills of an authentic public life and remembering the values of neighborliness, mutual aid and cooperation. In sum, there must be a wide and deep metamorphosis at the grass roots. Repair of the very fabric of daily life forms the only ground from which serious, lasting and decent change will emerge.

On one level, such a project requires a kind of utopianism, and in truth American progressives need to learn again to imagine, as a matter of course, possibilities that now seem "unrealistic" and "impractical." Yet democratic ferment of a serious, practical and successful character has already begun to spread at the grass roots of American society, lacking a common vision but nonetheless building real foundations for change. In the first instance, a renewed politics must involve appeal to and support for those places where people rebuild responsible relationships and seek a broader voice in public affairs.

Indeed, the widespread indices of public alienation from dominant institutions have a positive side which can be tapped. The recent growth of citizen activism around the nuclear-arms race represents the culmination of trends that have been building for over a decade. Trend monitor John Naisbitt suggests that "for the first time in the nation's history, there is more decentralization than centralization taking place in America," pointing to signs of public mood. The failure of large-scale approaches to problems, disenchantment with the impersonality and corruption of big institutions, the changing economic base of society, all feed a growing impulse: "We saw that those macro, top down solutions didn't work," argues Naisbitt. "The only thing that really works is local initiative." Such initiatives have multiplied everywhere.[7]

At the local and neighborhood levels, tens of thousands of neighborhood groups, block-watch programs, women's service projects, cooperatives, environmental and consumer groups, workers' health and safety organizations, working women's projects and other variants of citizen action have formed in recent years. The number of Americans who volunteer to work in their communities seven or more hours a week increased more than 93 percent between the mid-Sixties and 1981—to 46.4 million citizens. National networks such as Citizen Action, National People's Action and the Citizen Labor Energy Coalition have given the new ferment a growing national visibility and been at the forefront of resistance to the Reagan administration's offensive. America's "poet of the tape recorder," Studs Terkel, has described the growing activism as the invisible countertrend to the "new privatism." "There is a flowing of life juices that has not been covered on the Six O'Clock News," said Terkel in *Parade*'s Sunday magazine. "The heralds are from all sorts of precincts: a family farmer, a blue collar housewife, a whistle-blowing executive—noncelebrated people who bespeak the dreams of their fellows."[8]

That *something* has begun to stir into existence once again seems unmistakable; as the Eighties progress, it has been gaining notice in major media and been charted by pollsters. For such ferment to develop a vision and vocabulary with power and depth requires not only description but also an understanding of the ways in which today's citizen action renews old traditions in America and gives them a relevance to our future. Specifically, I believe that democratic action in the present revitalizes concepts of citizen involvement as the transformative ground of democracy itself; conceptions of government as primarily of and by the people—not mainly acting *for* the people; and, finally, economic visions that subordinate concepts like growth, progress and efficiency to the actual life of communities themselves, and nourish an understanding of the common forms of wealth over which the present generation serves properly as stewards.

America has always held a contradiction at the very center of our civic life. On the one hand, ours has been the land of speculators, robber barons, developers and J. R. Ewing. Book titles like *Look Out for Number One* and *Winning Through Intimidation* line paperback shelves, glorifying wealth, power and individualism detached from any communal responsibility whatever. Indeed, despite the rhetoric, such is the philosophy of Reagan's favorite pop philosopher, George Gilder. Emphasis on such values inexorably leads to a politics of narrow 'interest grays,' destroying the common fund of values and purposes essential to any authentic public life.

Yet a very different understanding of "success" and politics has warred with these notions from the beginning. When Alexis de Tocqueville, the French nobleman and observer, toured America more than 150 years ago, he marveled at the propensity of citizens to form voluntary associations of all kinds. And he argued that only through such civic involvement could Americans counterbalance the corrosive individualism and commercialism that threatened to undermine democracy: "By dint of working for the good of one's fellow citizens, the habit and taste for serving them is at length acquired."[9]

Such a notion of success of civic involvement reaches its fullest expressions within groups and peoples not included in John Winthrop's vision of a "city on a hill." In the legacy of gift-giving among Native American Indian peoples, of mutual-aid societies and fraternal and sororal orders within black, Hispanic and other ethnic ghettos, in quilting bees and barn raisings and voluntary fire departments in small farmer's communities, the understanding of communal responsibility as the foundation of a free society has been kept alive. Moreover, the movements of the poor and dispossessed throughout American history have repeatedly asserted such principles against the dominant culture. From the small farmers, fighting for control over their lives and communities during the late nineteenth century, through the mining communities in the South and West battling giant energy cartels, or Indian reservations seeking power over their own resources and land, a populist tradition has long articulated a far different understanding of "local control" than that mouthed by the allies of corporate executives and local plantation owners. And in its dominant animus, the populist impulse in America has had a positive, not negative, meaning. In their best, most democratic variants, American populist movements have been schools for citizenship through which people acquire public skills, knowledge of the world, and values of cooperation and self-reliance, and a sense of our "commonwealth" connecting diverse communities. This was precisely the meaning of Martin Luther King, Jr., when he described the civil-rights struggle as "democracy in action," which taught the requisites of citizenship and a new sense of dignity as its most important achievements.[10]

Community organizing and other forms of citizen action build upon these traditions and at their best give them a new discipline. In recent years, the most powerful activism has developed what is sometimes called a "value-based" approach, grounded in reflection on the themes of community, justice, the dignity of the poor, participation and reconciliation.

Traditional organizing approaches gave little notice to such issues, often mirroring the world in which groups operated, using a narrow language of self-interest. Yet over time, many groups have deepened and changed. Through such a process they have broadened the conception of "self-interest," not by abandoning immediate, specific and concrete concerns—taxes, utility rates, housing conditions, jobs and so forth—but by casting such questions in terms of fundamental values as well. This is the approach of Communities Organized for Public Service in San Antonio, which now serves as a model for organizing in many cities and has had tremendous impact on economic development patterns. It is also the approach of the East Brooklyn Organizing Project, and the San Francisco Organizing Project, an alliance of black Pentacostals, Catholic parishes, synagogues, Protestant congregations, trade-union locals and community organizations. In St. Louis, the Cochran Gardens public housing project, once "handed over" to gangs and drug pushers, is now run by tenants themselves. It serves as an example of neighborhood spirit, voluntary action and community safety for community groups across the country.

In groups organized along principles of value discussion and community renewal, more conventional political tools—from voter mobilizations to mass actions at City Hall—are used. But they are used in the context of reflection about the meaning and implications of such actions, and a continuing attentiveness to the centrality of community and family relationships. Moreover, key leaders and organizers are well aware of the transformative processes that occur at the heart of such organizing. Ernesto Cortes, first organizer of the COPS group in San Antonio, calls these organizations "universities where people go to school to learn about public policy, public discourse and public life." Bertha Gilkey, the remarkable black woman who has spear-headed the revival of Cochran Gardens, speaks with simplicity, power and toughness of people once again learning to "value life, care about the community, and respect themselves."[11]

Such community-renewing, value-based organizing approaches, moreover, redefine conventional American definitions of *politics* that focus narrowly on "political personalities," on various forms of advo-cacy *for* the people, and on the activities of government rather than people themselves. COPS, for example, is widely credited with achiev-ing the Mexican-American city council majority in San Antonio, and the COPS-inspired network of community groups now spreading throughout Texas had much to do with the victories of Jim Hightower and other Democrats in 1982, as progressive publications like the *Texas Observer* have detailed. Yet for COPS, electoral activity, like voter registration, is decidedly secondary to community renewal and empowerment. "Politicians' work is to do your work," explained Sonia Hernandez, the president of the organization. "When you've got somebody working for you, you don't bow and scrape. It's not meant to show disrespect. When politicians deliver, we applaud them, but not until then." The point of COPS, she continued, is simply not "politics as usual. . . . COPS is about people, mainly poor people who have decided to do something about their lives. There isn't anyone around, not a Mayor Cisneros or a Governor White, who is going to come in and do anything for them. People are doing it for them-selves."[12]

Often less self-consciously, this kind of sensibility has spread through a range of community-based activities. It can be seen in the grass-roots religious base of the peace movement, in women's projects, neighborhood renewal efforts and multiethnic festivals. Taken to-gether, such activity embodies the wisdom that democracy—as Thomas Paine observed—is only *possible* when people learn to mutu-ally support each other.

In a similar vein, community activism revives the vision of govern-ment by the people and of the people. Ronald Reagan and the right wing more generally have spoken frequently in the abstract about "voluntary action" and "local control." Yet at the same time, they have sought to dismantle exactly those programs that communities have won to aid local initiatives. The so-called hit list of community organizations barred from using VISTA volunteers under the new administration included moderate and conservative working-class and ethnic groups like the Whitmore Neighborhood Corporation in Kansas City and the Massachusetts Association of Older Americans.

The reason is not hard to untangle. The sort of citizen activism that the Reagan administration has preferred is that which is seen and not heard—it consists of individual acts of charity. Any independent, grass-roots community initiative that empowers ordinary people is viewed with tremendous suspicion and hostility. The fact is that the Reagan administration stands in a particular tradition of American political theory, represented by figures like Alexander Hamilton, who believed that the rich and well born properly held "the permanent share of power" in government. Underneath the rhetoric, what Reagan has meant when he has spoken about transferring power to local levels is a transfer of authority to local elites—to the large economic interests, the plantation owners and ward heelers who have always used rhetoric of local control as a cover for maintaining their privilege.

Community activism incubates a vision contrary to this. It develops the conception of renewed democratic government owned and operated by the people themselves.

Through the late Sixties and early Seventies, communities first organized against traditional liberal big-government programs, from urban renewal to social services that slighted neighborhood resources and institutions. But as the community movement has developed, instead of demanding an end to government programs, it has fought for their change into a policy that "works in, for and through the neighborhoods themselves," as the National Neighborhood Commission put it in 1979.[13]

By the late 1970s, community groups had begun to have an impact on a number of federal programs, decentralizing parts of the operation and design of federal efforts like the Comprehensive Employment and Training Act, the Community Development Block Grant Program, energy-conservation efforts, Volunteers in Service to America, crime prevention and others. Moreover, community groups had won new programs and legislation, such as the Home Mortgage Disclosure Act, the Neighborhood Self-Help Program and the National Cooperative Bank that furnished direct technical assistance, information and resources to local communities to begin their own work.

On balance, such programs represented the first inroads into an unresponsive federal bureaucracy. And the community movement that won them represented a new political constituency, far different from the population of dependent clients created by many of the traditional social services. It is this sort of "trickle-up" citizen initiative that the administration could not tolerate. The Catholic bishops' social-justice funding effort, Campaign for Human Development, found that the eight programs of most use in community self-help had all been specifically targeted for elimination by the new administration.[14]

A communitarian political approach for the 1980s, however, will be based on the nurture and support of such self-help initiatives. It will see government neither as the enemy nor as itself the solution. Rather, communitarian approaches envision government as the instrument of the people themselves, of living communities joined together. Again, this is an old notion, drawing on the Iroquois confederacy and New England town meetings, embodying the vision of radical democrats throughout American history, from Frederick Douglass and Susan B. Anthony to the youthful activists in the Student Nonviolent Coordinating Committee of civil rights and the authors of the Port Huron Statement in the 1960s New Left.

Finally, communitarian vision represents what can be called a "commonwealth economics," the centerpiece of the old populist idiom renewed recently by figures as diverse as Ralph Nader and Coretta Scott King. If the liberal Left typically looks to government as the problem-solver, the Right characteristically looks to what is called "the marketplace." The marketplace has a kind of magic in dominant conservative thought—and indeed, it was in the name of a supposedly free competition in the marketplace that the Reagan administration justified all its economic policies. The rhetoric held that Reaganomics would unleash the great entrepreneurial energy of small businesses, the backbone of a free-enterprise economy.

There is a pseudopopulist appeal in this message. Candidate Reagan separated himself from the country-club set and promised to "relieve the small businessman of the burdens of excessive regulation" and to "lift the burden of taxations from the backs of the working and middle classes." President Reagan followed policies strikingly different. Under the Reagan tax plan, 80 percent of the tax breaks went to the largest corporations. The high-interest-rate policies of the administration proved devastating to mom-and-pop stores—but they left many larger businesses that raise funds internally, or from interlocking financial interests, largely untouched. The administration sharply backed off antitrust policies, resulting in a wave of take-overs by large corporations.[15]

What is systematically overlooked by the ideologues of the marketplace in ways that result in such cynical duplicity is the communal dimensions of economic life. In theory, businessmen's pursuit of profit maximizes benefits to consumers. In practice, however, it treats people as individual purchasers of goods, neglecting entirely what are called "externalities"—the efforts of corporate practices upon people joined together. Love Canals, the costs in pollution or hazardous waste, the ravaging effects if a corporation decides to pull up stakes and move elsewhere, the bitter effects of systematic discriminatory policies against blacks, women and others—all these things are rendered invisible in the logic of the marketplace. Moreover, though the ideology of individual entrepreneurship is the dominant motif in Kiwanis Club luncheons and small-business award dinners, in reality the community context is the central factor differentiating small from larger enterprises. Smaller businesses are far more directly responsive to variations of local taste and interest. They are owned locally and their customers tend to be attracted not simply or mainly through abstract marketing appeals but rather through informal networks of shoppers who establish relationships with the businesses over time. In sum, they are rooted in the life of their areas, while giant corporations are unaccountable to any particular place or tie. As the White House Conference on Small Business summarized the difference in 1980: "The U.S. has evolved into two economies, one consisting of many small local enterprises in the community and one made up of gargantuan organizations whose gains are small businesses' losses."[16]

A Left approach that attempts to counter right-wing rhetoric with proposals that center on federal programs or new, TVA-style public planning agencies will fail. The basic flaw in such proposals is that they similarly abstract economic policy from the specific and individual life of communities. And there simply is no popular conviction that public bureaucracy is better than private. As Staughton Lynd recently observed, "faced with the alternatives of investment decision making by the U.S. Steels and Lazard Fréres of the world, or investment decision making by an omnipotent deputy director for national priorities, one would be hard pressed to choose."[17]

The American populist tradition, here again, furnishes rich material for an alternative to both statist and corporatist solutions by stressing the necessary subordination of economic activity to the needs of living communities. This was the vision of the commonwealth, described by the magazine of that name in 1893: "For our virtue as well as our wealth, for our moral ideas as well as our material possessions, we are under infinite obligations. . . . We owe all that we value to the community in whose life we live and move and have our being."[18]

The most powerful challenges to corporate policies have emerged in recent years through such an approach. When Communities Organized for Public Service several years ago took on the corporate-development agency in San Antonio for its promotional activities advertising the city as a "cheap labor," nonunion town, corporate interests throughout the state of Texas reacted with ferocity. But the organization held firm. It combined its enormous strength in the Mexican-American barrios with support from labor, and it made an argument that found resonance among the city's small businesses and local officials: Any industry coming to town must be judged in terms of its impact on the whole community, not the number of jobs alone, and the whole city should be involved in the discussion about such location. With such an approach, COPS won a major victory, and neighborhoods began to gain an unprecedented voice in city development patterns.

In New Bedford, Massachusetts, in 1982, Gulf & Western sought to force concessions from a United Electrical Workers local through an implied threat to shut down the local machine-tool factory the corporation had recently acquired. But instead of acquiescing, the union local went on the offensive. Armed with research from a local group, it demonstrated how the conglomerate had bought out the machine-tool plant for the sake of "bleeding off" profits and planned eventually to shut it down in any event. With such information, the union was able to mobilize a remarkable alliance of community institutions—ranging from local government and the chamber of commerce to churches and neighborhood associations—around a vision of local self-determination. Gulf & Western was dramatically forced on the defensive, and the union won pledges from the corporation that the machine-tool factory would remain, and major gains in the contract negotiations.[19]

National economic strategies that build from the "bottom up" suggest ways of translating this kind of initiative into a powerful alternative to a corporatist future. For instance, employment programs calling for public-works jobs designed and controlled by local community-development corporations—like the program recently proposed by the International Association of Machinists—would offer major resources for small business and cooperatives; capital improvements in bridges, sewers and other decaying elements of our ageing physical infrastructure; and alternative energy production. National legislation like that contained in the Corporate Democracy Act of 1980, limiting corporate ability to relocate from an area, begins to demand ways to call giant economic enterprises back to accountability.

Beyond such measures, a commonwealth economics also looks at the ways in which the forms of wealth we already own in common can be controlled for the common good. Pension funds, for instance, own more than 25 percent of all outstanding stock, yet at present such capital is controlled almost entirely by trust departments in banks and invested in ways that completely ignore community values. Religious and educational institutions own enormous resources in the form of stock portfolios, insurance policies and other assets, which are similarly wielded without regard for local impact.[20]

A commonwealth economics says that such forms of our common wealth must be made accountable to our communities. It expresses precisely the vision of the Episcopal Urban Bishops Coalition, which issued a statement in 1982 proposing cooperative and community ownership of major industries. "We question whether inequality structured into the workplace and jobs made vulnerable to the self-interest of absentee corporate owners will not invariably cripple family and community life," read the declaration. "We know of no more sinister power and threat to the welfare of the human community than that flowing from corporate structures which remove control of resources and decision making from the people most affected."[21]

Such, then, are the elements of a communitarian populist vision: a civic life grounded in concepts of the renewal of moral community;

a politics predicated on belief in self-government; and an economics that looks at our commonwealth of resources and riches and seeks to render them accountable to our communities. Such a vision, respecting the positive resources, traditions and institutions of our communities, will have the potential to draw broad support. It will tap the goodwill of constituencies that have all too often been written off by progressives as backward and unenlightened—small farmers, small businesses, religious groups, ethnic communities. And it furnishes a yardstick for judging all proposals for reform or politicians' campaign ideas with the question: Does this plan transfer more power and resources to the whole people—does it open up new mechanisms of decision-making, new models of cooperation and new terrain on which people can act for themselves and others?

In the coming years, there will be urgent need for broader organization that can adapt to the rapidly changing terrain of American society, that is able to focus resources on specific crucial issues, that has the capacity to communicate the symbols and language of democratic ferment to many arenas. Yet a new moral vision for America in the 1980s and beyond must draw its inspiration from the grass roots, from the neighborhoods, from the repair and recovery of the finest American traditions. The unchecked, continuing erosion of our memories and our communities can only lead to growing fear and ultimate disaster, and it must be reversed as the starting point for change. In sum, we need to see our land as a nation of potentially vital communities where, as Herman Melville once put it, "all tribes and peoples of the world will form into one great federated whole." Such a vision of communal diversity and vitality, self-government and dedication to the common good represents the best of the American dream. And it holds the key to the future.[22]

Notes

1. Jim Hightower, "I Didn't Lose, I Just Ran Out of Time," *Washington Monthly,* October, 1980.
2. Figures on confidence in corporations from Gallup poll, *Minneapolis Tribune,* November 9, 1980. Kevin Phillips, "Post Conservative America," *New York Review of Books,* May 13, 1982, p. 27. Senate Democratic Task Force quoted in Maurice Zeitlin, "Democratic Investment," *Democracy,* April, 1982, p. 70.

3. See for example, "The Basic Speech; Ronald Reagan," *New York Times,* February 29, 1980; also reports on the convention.

4. Milan Kundera, *The Book of Laughter and Forgetting* (New York: Penguin, 1981); Robert Darnton, "Poland Rewrites History," *New York Review of Books,* July 16, 1981.

5. Herb Mills, "Labor, Technology and Culture: The San Francisco Waterfront" (Berkeley: Institute for the Study of Social Change, 1982), quoted from pp. 10–18; The San Francisco Redevelopment Agency Director, Justin Herman, quoted from Joe Feagin, *The Urban Real Estate Game* (Englewood Cliffs, N.J.: Prentice Hall, 1983), p. 174.

6. *Ibid.,* interview with Nellie Stone Johnson, Minneapolis, March 29, 1983.

7. Naisbitt quoted from *Advertising Age,* April 5, 1982.

8. Figures on voluntarism are available from a number of sources. See, for instance, Bruce Stokes, "Self Help in the Eighties," *Citizen Participation,* January/February, 1982, which also demonstrates the particular growth of voluntary involvement in the new community activism. Studs Terkel, "Across America There's a Flowing of Life Juices," *Parade Sunday Magazine* (Chicago Sun Times), October 12, 1980.

9. Alexis de Tocqueville, quoted in "What Does America Stand For?," pamphlet published by the Citizen Heritage Center (Minneapolis: 1982), on the anniversary of Tocqueville's travels, p. 6.

10. King's description of the civil rights movement as a "Crusade for Citizenship" was given, for instance, in William Robert Miller, "The Broadening Horizons," in C. Eric Lincoln, ed., *Martin Luther King, Jr.: A Profile* (New York: Hill & Wang, 1970), pp. 50–51.

11. Ernesto Cortes, interview, San Antonio, July 4, 1983; Bertha Gilkey, interview, St. Louis, August 20, 1983.

12. Sonia Hernandez, interview, San Antonio, July 5, 1983.

13. The "hit list" of organizations was listed in Friends of Vista mailing, June 5, 1983, by Mimi Mager, which also described the Massachusetts Association of Older Americans; in the Dallas *Morning News,* November 29, 1981, and in the Kansas City *Star,* January 3, 1982, which described the Whitmore Neighborhood Corporation. National Commission on Neighborhoods, *People, Building Neighborhoods* (Washington, D.C.: U.S. Government Printing Office, 1979), p. 62.

14. Kathy Desmond, "Preliminary Results of Survey of Impact of Budget Cuts on CHD Funded Organizations," April 3, 1981.

15. The impact of Reaganomics on small businesses and the benefits to large corporations in Mark Green, *Winning Back America* (New York: Bantam, 1982), pp. 48, 106–9; and in Neal Peirce, "Reagan Fails to Aid New Small Business," *Minneapolis Tribune,* March 29, 1981.

16. House Conference quoted in Green, *Winning,* p. 107.

17. Staughton Lynd, "View from Steel Country," *Democracy,* Summer, 1983, p. 26.

18. Joseph Wood, "Wealth Versus Commonwealth," *Commonwealth,* Jan. 7, 1893, p 14.

19. The COPS fight with development interests is described briefly in *The Backyard Revolution* (Philadelphia: Temple University Press, 1980), pp. 164–166, and in more detail in *Community Is Possible: Repairing America's Roots* (New York: Harper & Row, forthcoming, 1984); the New Bedford effort

by the U.E. local is described in Dan Swinney, "UE Local 277's Strike at Morse Cutting Tool," *Labor Research Review,* Fall, 1982.

20. The extent of pension fund investment in corporate America and strategies for exerting control over such investments are described in Martin Carnoy and Derek Shearer, *Economic Democracy* (New York: M.E. Sharpe, 1980), especially pp. 96–124.

21. Quoted from Paul Moore, Jr. and John Burt (leaders in the Urban Bishops Coalition), "It's Time to Explore Industrial Policies that Aid Communities," adapted from Bishops' Statement, *New York Times,* September 6, 1982.

22. Melville quoted in Boyte, "Democratic Visions: Progressives and the American Heritage" (Minneapolis: Citizen Heritage Center pamphlet, 1981), p. 3.

21

A Party for a Change

John Atlas, Peter Dreier
and John Stephens

In 1982, Doreen Del Bianco, a former member of the Hospital Workers' Union (District 1199), ran as the Democratic candidate for the Connecticut legislature from Waterbury and defeated the Republican incumbent. What was notable about her campaign was the strong support she received from the Legislative Electoral Action Program (LEAP), a new left-of-center coalition that includes the United Automobile Workers, the International Association of Machinists (IAM), the Connecticut Federation of Teachers and other unions, women's and environmental groups and the Connecticut Citizen Action Group, a community organization that Del Bianco cochaired. She ran an issue-oriented campaign calling for lower utility rates, property-tax reform and the cleanup of toxic wastes. Thanks to her links with labor and single-issue groups, she was able to mobilize a small army of experienced, energetic campaign workers.

Del Bianco is one of a growing number of politicians whose roots are not in traditional party politics or right-wing moral crusades, but in the burgeoning progressive citizen movements of the past decade. These organizations represent an important new force on the Left, not just for 1984, but also for creating a viable strategy for social change beyond. We call it a "party within a party" strategy.

Progressives who want to offer an alternative to both Reagan-style conservatism and Carter-style liberalism have generally considered three options. All of them, however, have serious defects.

John Atlas chairs the New Jersey Public Interest Political Action Committee and is active in the Hackensack-based New Jersey Tenants Organization and Citizen Action. *Peter Dreier* is a contributor to *Who Rules Boston?* and special assistant to Mayor Raymond L. Flynn of Boston. *John Stephens* is assistant professor at Brown University.

The easiest, but least effective, choice is the candidate-centered approach. At the presidential level, it means jumping on the band-wagon of one of the Democratic candidates. In 1984, this "anybody but Reagan" theory leads some progressives to shop around for a lesser-evil Democrat. Cranston is the "peace" candidate; Hart empha-sizes his youth and spouts trendy, neoliberal ideas; and Mondale is the front-runner, prolabor and (according to the *New Republic*) "the most experienced at governing." This crop of essentially identical Demo-cratic candidates, however, symbolizes the bankruptcy of ideas among mainstream Democrats. Their views on women, the environment and civil rights are acceptable, if not on the cutting edge. However, except perhaps for Jesse Jackson, they are all wedded to the corporate-dominated "free enterprise" system, to government welfare (tax breaks and subsidies) for big business, to pacifier programs for the poor and to a globalist foreign policy designed to maximize corporate profits. They all, to different degrees, pay lip service to the nuclear-freeze idea, without directly challenging militarism and the perma-nent war economy. None of them is as progressive as Robert Kennedy in 1968, George McGovern in 1972 or Fred Harris in 1976, candi-dates who tried to inject issues of economic and social justice into the national debate.

Progressive organizations, looking to translate their concerns into political issues, may hitch their wagons to candidates for everything from city councils and state legislatures to Congress and the presi-dency. Trade unions have been doing it for years, and more recently, groups such as the National Organization for Women (NOW), nu-clear-freeze groups, the National Abortion Rights Action League, environmental organizations, tenant and community organizations and others have taken steps to endorse and work for political candi-dates.

But candidate-centered campaigns have a piecemeal, ad hoc quality about them. Each progressive candidate has to piece together a new coalition, drawing on different grass-roots groups and their activists. In one election, a women's group and a labor union will find them-selves working side by side. In the next election, the union stays on the sidelines, but the women's group is behind a prochoice candidate, this time working alongside an environmental group or a tenant orga-nization. Grass-roots groups, in other words, are constantly reorgan-izing and reconstituting themselves, drawing on shifting reservoirs of campaign volunteers and donors, depending on which self-selected candidates present themselves in a given election.

Charismatic candidates can ignite enthusiasm and attract volunteers. But the problem with candidate-centered politics is that no long-term strategy or working relationship can develop among grassroots groups. Lacking the continuity of an ongoing coalition, momentum can't build from successes. Whether a progressive candidate wins or loses, the campaign's resources (mailing lists, staff, volunteers and research) tends to scatter until the next campaign. In between, there is no mobilization for other elections (including referenda issues), no fund-raising, no issue development, no search for progressive candidates, no training of staff or volunteers. This is something that in some other countries political parties do, but that is not how parties have developed in the United States. This leaves a huge vacuum, waiting to be filled.

Under these circumstances, a third-party strategy may seem more appealing. This is the second option for progressives. The Citizens party, for example, has articulated an anticorporate program, enlisting activists in chapters around the country, and has even elected a few local officials. But these small triumphs do not add up to a national strategy. The odds against third parties in the American political system are staggering: Witness the fates of the Progressive and States' Rights parties in 1948, the Peace and Freedom party in 1968 and the American Independence party in 1972. Their failures did not result from bad intentions or lack of organizing skill, but from the structure of American politics. America's winner-take-all electoral system (unlike proportional representation found in European democracies) encourages voters to cast their ballots for one of the two front-runners. Voters don't want to feel that they are "wasting" their votes by casting their ballots for a minority party that has no chance of winning, since that party's vote will not translate into any formal voice in government. Twenty percent of the vote doesn't get a 20-percent voice in the government.

Candidates and parties need to win the *most* votes—a majority or a plurality—in order to gain a voice. Otherwise, they get nothing. Because of proportional representation, protest parties in Europe can get a foot in the door. But there can be no "greening" of America.

Third parties, in fact, can be harmful, leading to conflict between potential allies. Progressive groups (labor, women's, minority, citizen action, peace, environmental) organize around immediate gains and are unlikely to abandon their short-term goals and victories in the hope of comprehensive change in the long term. The two-party system forces compromises, or concessions, to bring movements into the mainstream. Most pragmatic groups won't give up opportunities for immediate reforms in order to build a third party. And in some situations (particularly in New York), third parties have actually thrown victories to the more conservative candidates by taking votes away from liberal Democrats. When that happens, squabbles among progressives become open wounds, and take years to heal. A vote for the third party is a vote wasted.

The third option for progressives is to continue working in grass-roots movements and ignore electoral politics altogether. This is the Saul Alinsky/Ralph Nader theory of electoral politics. Let Tweedledee and Tweedledum fight it out, and then attack the winner—with protest demonstrations, scorecards rating their records, letter-writing, lawsuits and lobbying campaigns. According to this theory, efforts to bring grass-roots groups into the electoral battles only sap their strength and co-opt their issue focus into a cult-of-the-candidate mentality.

This approach has many adherents and, given Americans' cynicism about politicians and government, builds on people's angers and frustrations, while putting issues ahead of personalities. However, there is a weakness in an approach that, through public pressure and embarrassment, implicitly threatens public officials with defeat, but does nothing to carry out the threat. Sooner or later, politicians realize that the threats are empty and take the groups' demands less seriously.

Also, for people interested in building a coherent movement that has a chance of taking power in Washington, the ad hoc nature of those tactics is a serious drawback. Grass-roots groups have no vehicle for uniting behind a common political agenda. As in the candidate-centered approach, their power is diffused and lacks an institutional context. Politics becomes a grab bag of single issues, narrow constituencies, and rival organizations competing for turf, often working at cross-purposes. This approach also leaves the job of nominating the Democratic candidates to the traditional powerbrokers within the party. You can't win the game if you stay on the sidelines.

Is there a way to merge the strengths of these three options while avoiding their defects?

We believe there is: a "party-within-a-party" strategy. Contrary to popular assessments, the last decade has seen a tremendous amount of progressive political activity. Campaigns for rent control, regulation of toxic chemicals in the workplace and the community, tax reform, a nuclear freeze and the Equal Rights Amendment have employed a wide variety of tactics and won many victories. Groups like NOW, ACORN, Mobilization for Survival, Massachusetts Fair Share and 9 to 5 have involved millions of Americans, raising their political awareness and honing their activist skills. In recent years, some of these groups have moved into the electoral arena, providing funds, endorsements and campaign workers for issue-oriented candidates. Under the party-within-a-party strategy, they would unite in a permanent coalition within the Democratic party, supporting a program of economic democracy. The coalition would support and run candidates in party primaries, initially in local, state and congressional races. By mobilizing its supporters and launching massive voter-registration drives in these campaigns, it would work to defeat Reagan in 1984 (and his counterpart in 1988), but not waste time and effort on the presidential primaries.

Similar coalitions have been established at the state and local levels. Groups like the New Jersey Public Interest Political Action Committee (PIPAC), the Montana Committee for an Effective Legislature (MONTCEL), the Ohio Public Interest Campaign (OPIC), the Illinois Public Action Council (IPAC) and California's Campaign for Economic Democracy (CED) have coalesced women, blacks, Hispanics, environmentalists, neighborhood and tenant activists and senior citizens into effective political forces. Working with labor unions like the UAW, the IAM, AFSCME, the Steelworkers, the United Food and Commercial Workers, the Service Employees International Union, the International Union of Electrical Workers and the Communications Workers of America, the coalitions have engaged in lobbying, developed "hit lists" of conservative incumbents and backed candidates who are not tied to corporate interests. In 1982, for example, IPAC members campaigned door to door in nearly every Illinois community with more than 5,000 people. They visited some 50,000 households and helped elect a progressive candidate, Lane Evans, to Congress.

In California, the CED, founded after Tom Hayden's surprisingly effective campaign in the 1976 Democratic senatorial primary, has become a progressive caucus within the state Democratic party. It has helped elect candidates, hammered out a platform that emphasizes housing and energy issues, and drawn unions, minority organizations, tenants' committees and women's groups under its broad banner.

In New Jersey, PIPAC, founded in 1981, has brought a number of statewide single-issue groups into an umbrella organization. Spearheading efforts to form the committee was the eleven-year-old New Jersey Tenants Organization, which has more than 80,000 dues-paying members and which has won rent control in more than 100 cities and helped push through the toughest landlord-tenant statutes in the nation. NJTO endorsed many members of the state legislature, who in return supported the group's legislative agenda. But it eventually recognized the limitations of single-issue politics and turned to coalition-building, bringing together representatives of the Environmental Voters Alliance; NOW; the auto workers', communications workers' and machinists' unions; the Hispanic Political Action Committee; senior citizens' groups and SANE. The groups discovered that many of their friends and enemies in the legislature frequently overlapped, so they decided to work together to elect (or defeat) candidates. Because of its late start and lack of money, PIPAC had only limited success in the November 1981 elections. But in 1983 PIPAC supported a 25-year-old newcomer named Steve Adubato, Jr., who defeated a conservative incumbent for the state legislature.

The Rhode Island Community Labor Coalition (CLOC), formed in 1979, consists of fourteen labor unions, six community organizations, and individual members. CLOC initially worked on two legislative issues—a plant-closing bill and a tax on oil companies. But its leaders felt that if the coalition was to be effective, it had to be able to threaten defeat for those legislators who opposed its efforts. CLOC successfully ran a candidate for state legislator in 1983's Democratic primary; he later won the general election. It plans to run four or five candidates in 1984.

The first steps toward party-within-a-party coalitions are now being taken in other states as well, such as Massachusetts, New York, Pennsylvania, Oregon, Minnesota and Virginia. Citizen Action, a nationwide federation of fourteen state-level community groups (such as Massachusetts Fair Share, Ohio Public Interest Campaign and Virginia Action), has played a critical role in nurturing these alliances. Several years ago, its leaders formed the Citizen-Labor Energy Coalition (CLEC) to test the waters of working with unions on national issues such as natural-gas decontrol. Other groups—such as NOW, ACORN, Jobs with Peace, environmental, senior-citizen, civil-rights and other organizations—have shown increasing willingness to forge coalitions and work in electoral politics. Progressive groups are working together within the Democratic party while continuing to pursue their own goals outside it. The next step is the formation of a party-within-a-party at the national level, which would coordinate tactics and enter candidates in local, state and congressional Democratic primaries—and perhaps in the 1992 presidential primaries.

To be sure, many people have serious reservations about working within the Democratic party, pointing out that it includes some of the worst racists, sexists and corporate fat cats in American politics. But by the same token, it also includes almost all of the most progressive figures: Governor Toney Anaya of New Mexico, Representatives John Conyers, Ronald Dellums, Byron Dorgan, Pat Schroeder, Barbara Mikulski, George Crockett, Esteban Torres, Bruce Morrison, Barney Frank, Marcy Kaptur, Robert Torecelli and Tom Downey; Mayors Ray Flynn of Boston, Andrew Young of Atlanta, and Harold Washington of Chicago; Texas Agriculture Commissioner Jim Hightower, North Dakota Tax Commissioner Kent Conrad, Alabama Secretary of State Don Siegelman; city council members Ruth Messinger of New York, David Cohen of Philadelphia, David Orr of Chicago, Harry Britt of San Francisco, Saundra Graham and David Sullivan of Cambridge, Massachusetts; Essex County (New Jersey) Executive Peter Shapiro; and state legislators Julian Bond of Georgia, Harlan Baker of Maine, Tom Gallagher of Massachusetts, Tom Bates, Maxine Waters and Tom Hayden of California, Tom Towe of Montana and Harriot Woods of Missouri. Most of the prominent activist politicians on the Left today—those who helped establish or attended the meetings of the Conference on Alternative State and Local Policy, for example—are Democrats. Also in the Congress, the Black Caucus, the Hispanic Caucus and the Progressive Caucus are in the forefront of developing and advocating alternative agendas. Their members, too, are Democrats.

Why now? What makes us think that the Democratic party can be transformed? Why spend our time and energy reinventing a crooked wheel?

Two trends give this strategy a potential it would not have had a decade or so ago. The first is a change in the rules of electoral politics. The second is a transformation of the broader political economy.

The growing number of primaries, the notable success of recent voter-registration drives (partly due to less restrictive laws) and the decline of political bosses have opened up the party and decentralized power within it. In recent years, for example, the traditional Democratic party monopoly in the South has been challenged by right-wing Republicans. This has forced Democrats to reach out to blacks, Hispanics and labor; to loosen voter-registration laws, and to give long-disenfranchised groups a larger voice.

Also, since the mid-1970s, the uneasy alliance between "corporate liberals" and organized labor, which exerts a strong influence on the Democratic party's policies, has been severely tested. During the postwar growth years, as both Alan Wolfe and Jerry Berman remind us, the Democrats were somewhat receptive to the needs of the poor and the working-class. It was the Democrats who passed the Voting Rights Act, Medicare, Legal Services, VISTA, CAP (with its requirement of "maximum feasible participation" of the poor), low-income housing programs, the Occupational Safety and Health Act and similar post–New Deal achievements.[1] But corporate interests are no longer willing to make the concessions to the poor and the working class that they made during the era of economic expansion following World War II. Now they want give-backs and take-aways. They want to "reindustrialize" the country on the backs of those with the least to give up. Living standards for the bottom two-thirds of the population are declining. All the 1984 Democratic presidential candidates espouse some version of neoliberalism, with its call for cooperation between business and labor. But neoliberalism offers little to the electorate outside the upper middle class. It is also not sufficiently sensitive to the concerns of feminists and environmentalists, particularly when they directly challenge corporate privileges and profits.

The Democratic party is in a transition period, looking for new ideas and a new social base. An organized progressive strategy could move it to the left and turn primaries and caucuses into genuine political contests.*

---

* We recognize that many mainstream Democratic operatives may be threatened by the style, rhetoric and action of grass-roots movements. Southern Democrats may view this approach as a strategy of blacks and minorities. Ethnic working-class

An alternative to both Republican Reaganomics and Democratic neoliberalism is a program of *economic democracy*. This would close tax loopholes for the rich; dramatically reduce nuclear arms and defense spending; direct public funds toward a national health-care system, mass transit, and nonprofit housing; give employees and consumers a greater voice in corporate decision-making; reform labor laws to strengthen organizing; and reform campaign finance laws to reduce the political advantage of corporations and the rich. This program would put America on the road to full employment and improve chances for a lasting peace. It would also promote a vision of a humane society, of technological resources and human will directed toward meeting human needs, and of government as the instrument of social betterment, not of corporate greed and political corruption.

A detailed blueprint is unnecessary here. A proliferation of excellent ideas is contained in Mark Green's *Winning Back America;* Derek Shearer and Martin Carnoy's *Economic Democracy* and *The New Social Contract;* Tom Hayden's *American Future;* Bowles, Gordon and Weisskopf's *Beyond the Wasteland;* the wide range of publications of the Conference on Alternative State and Local Policy; and S. M. M. Miller and Donald Tomaskovic-Devey's *Recapitalization of Capitalism.* More concrete programs will emerge, as they did in the New Deal, out of the ideas and experiences of labor and citizens groups working at the local, state and national levels.

With an effective national organization, progressives running for office on a platform of economic democracy would be able to mobilize the millions of alienated citizens who don't bother to vote because they can find no candidate or party that represents their interests.

Voter registration is a crucial part of any progressive strategy, and it is here that the grass-roots organizations in a party-within-a-party coalition would play a particularly important role. In the 1980 election, 76.5 million people out of the 163 million who were eligible to

_____

citizens, who want to preserve neighborhoods and so-called traditional values, may interpret it as a program of liberals committed to abortion, integration and homosexuality. Environmentalists may see it as a stronghold of unions committed to preserving smokestack industries. We could note other potential divisions. We have found, however, that while the potential divisions are real and important, they are not as great as many think—witness the recent election of so many of the men and women mentioned in this article.

vote—47 percent—stayed home. They were mostly blue-collar workers, members of minority groups and the poor—those who have suffered most from the policy failures and broken promises of politicians in both parties. But experience shows that when candidates offer workable solutions to pressing problems, voters turn out in large numbers. The New Deal brought millions of people into the political process with the promise of Social Security, public-service jobs, subsidized housing and rural electrification. Harold Washington's mayoral victory in Chicago proved the effectiveness of large-scale voter-registration drives among the powerless.[2]

To make the party-within-a-party strategy work, the various state coalitions and national groups must form an umbrella organization that will plan how best to use their collective resources. Its activities might include:

1. Creating a think tank to generate ideas and policy proposals. Such a body could draw on work that is already being done by the Institute for Policy Studies, The Democracy Project, the Conference on Alternative State and Local Policy and similar groups.

2. Designating a shadow cabinet composed of individuals from the progressive Left who could fill positions in government related to their areas of expertise. Prominent figures like Barry Commoner (energy), Frances Moore Lappé (agriculture), Ralph Nader (commerce), Richard Barnet (defense), Ron Dellums (health and human services), Elizabeth Holtzman (attorney general) and William Winpisinger (labor) could provide critiques and proposals on a wide range of issues.

3. Establishing a communications network, drawing on publications like the *Nation, In These Times, Mother Jones,* the *Progressive, Dissent, Social Policy,* and *Socialist Review.* These magazines could publish discussions of ideas, strategies, values and goals. The national coalition might also start a syndicated column, a news service and a cable network in order to reach a wider public.

4. Compiling a scorecard to rate elected officials' voting records and public statements. Many progressive groups already produce such ratings, which are often published by the mainstream press. While individual groups should continue to rate politicians according to their own litmus tests, the coalition could compile a comprehensive scorecard on all the issues that are important to the Democratic Left.

5. Hiring a field staff of organizers, who would recruit candidates capable of strong leadership, help groups and candidates on the national coalition's priority list, teach campaign techniques and coordinate voter-registration drives. Both Project Vote and the State and Local Leadership Project have started this process.[3]

We are not merely asking people to pull the Democratic lever and abandon grass-roots organizing; activist groups should, of course, continue their efforts to democratize unions, build community organizations, organize the unorganized, challenge environmental devastation, fight for equal rights, reshape universities and foster worker control of corporations. The strength of the party-within-a-party strategy is that by maintaining an independent political base, it avoids the pitfalls of being absorbed into the Democratic party. The grass-roots movements continue organizing and consciousness-raising. Meanwhile, they are taking advantage of the two-party system to build on what activists are already doing.

The growing number of successful coalitions at the state level will provide the building blocks for a national strategy. It will be necessary for some sectors of organized labor to oppose the AFL-CIO's current direction, including its attachment to a cold war foreign policy, its lack of imagination in fighting the tighten-your-belts austerity mentality, and its weak efforts to organize the unorganized. Fortunately, more and more union mavericks—leaders and rank and file alike—are working to shake up old-style business unionism. A revitalized labor movement, with allies in the new progressive citizen movements, would push most of the Democratic party's business support into the Republican camp and open the field for greater numbers of progressive Democratic candidates.

This strategy also provides an opportunity for the ideological Left (intellectuals and socialists) to join forces with the pragmatic Left (grass-roots movements organized around immediate reforms). Much of the ideological Left continues to waste its time and energy debating and fine-tuning its theories of the state and of social change. There is still some suspicion that electoral politics or short-term reforms lull people into the system and co-opt protest, but a growing part of the ideological Left has taken part in the past decade's revitalization of the grass-roots politics, either as organizers or as sympathetic journalists and "think tank" policy advisers and strategists. They help to guarantee that the long-term vision of the Left is not lost in the day-to-day struggles for a better life today.

Can the party-within-a-party strategy work?

New political directions always involve some risks. That was the case in the decision of industrial unions to break from the AFL to form the CIO in the depression; the decision of black activists to employ civil disobedience as a major tactic to challenge southern racism; the decision of early suffragists to establish a movement for women's voting rights despite the cultural and political obstacles; and the recent courage of the Catholic bishops to get involved both in citizen action (through their Campaign for Human Development fund) and in the peace movement.

The resources and skills are there. Whether activists can put aside their organizational rivalries and ideological squabbles to forge a broad coalition is a matter of will, not predestination. But the trends we outline here suggest that they can.

Only one thing *is* certain: The progressive Left must step up its political and organizational attack. Otherwise, the living standards of those who are employed will continue to decline, and the plight of the unemployed will continue to worsen. Even if the Democrats win with a Carter clone in 1984, their policies will lead voters to swing back to the Republicans four years later. The Left must offer a *real* alternative, one that will shift the basic priorities of national politics. The party-within-a-party strategy offers the best hope not only for defeating worst-evil Republicans, but also for moving the nation toward peace, freedom and justice.

Notes

1. Alan Wolfe, *America's Impasse;* and Jerry J. Berman, "Mainstream Politics," *Democracy,* Summer 1983.
2. Richard Cloward and Francis Fox Piven discuss the potential of voter registration in "Toward a Class-Based Realignment of American Politics," *Social Policy,* Winter 1983.
3. Heather Booth, "Left with the Ballot Box," *Working Papers,* May/June 1981, and Sanford A. Newman, "Project Vote: Tapping the Power of the Poor," *Social Policy,* Winter 1983, both discuss these developments.

About the Editors:

Alan Gartner is executive director, Division of Special Education, New York City Board of Education. Colin Greer is vice president of the New World Foundation. Frank Riessman is director of the National Self-Help Clearinghouse, Graduate School and University Center, City University of New York.

About *Social Policy:*

Social Policy is a major vehicle for the new debate unfolding in the country about what should be done given the demise of the old liberal coalition and ideology. There is a new consciousness regarding the ways in which military expenditures distort our economy. Portions of the business community—the country's corporate elite—increasingly are disturbed by the budgetary deficits tied to military costs, signaling an opening for substantial social change. With growing awareness that supply-side, trickle-down economics doesn't work any better than Keynesian heating-up variety, *Social Policy* strives to raise consciousness about a forward-looking economic program built around public investment, decentralized national planning, economic democracy, and employment-centered growth. It may be possible to begin to spread the deep participatory themes in American life from the consumer area to the workplace with the demand for economic democracy.

Frank Riessman
Editor, *Social Policy*